Thank you for supporting

your

independent bookstore

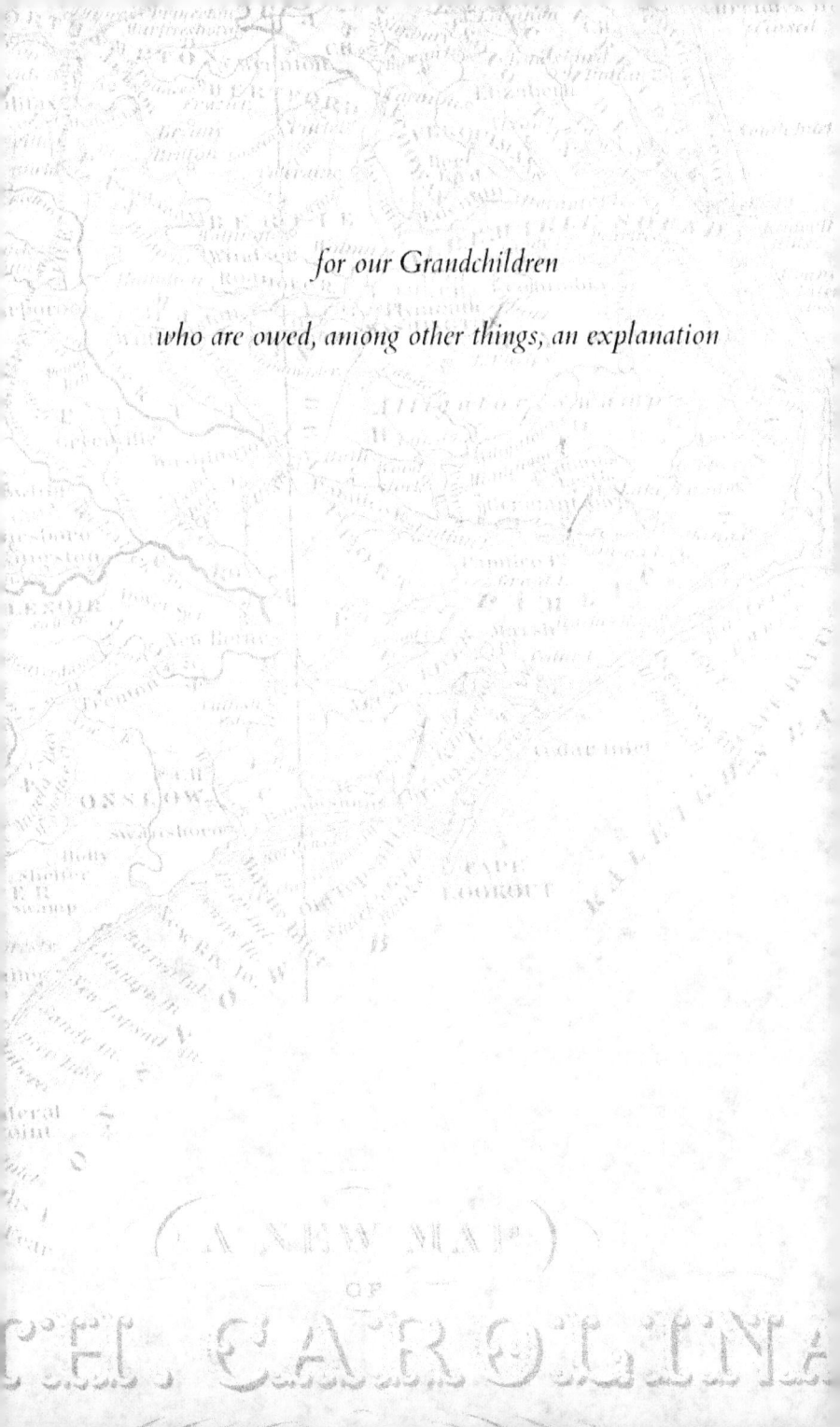

for our Grandchildren

who are owed, among other things, an explanation

WORK

HARD

FOR

YOUR

DOG

IN

THE

FIGHT

Contents

Work Hard for your Dog in the Fight

Hello

In 1995 NationsBank loaned me $87,000. As collateral they got my fiscal potential as a windsurfing instructor. I used the money to buy a home and subsequently discovered the meaning of predatory lending. I was a 25-year-old college dropout living at the beach; those white collar pirates knew I wouldn't be able to hold $528, look between the youthful image in the mirror and the bar across the street and habitually choose equity and shelter over inebriation and coitus.

OK, so even with five years of college under my belt I was never able to meet girls in a bar. I also wasn't able to figure out how the bank made money by loaning it to people whom they didn't expect to pay it back; but everybody at the bar assured me that's what was going on. It was an economic certainty in the file of corporations wanting everybody to be too poor to buy their products and Wal-Mart being greedy for saving folks money.

Well, NationsBank didn't know what they were getting themselves into when they loaned money to a windsurf bum. I had a small axe for that big tree and I'd emancipated myself from mental slavery way back when my feet were my only carriage. Unlike most victims of subprime usury I was so tired of festering in my VW Quantum that I actually wanted to sleep in a house of my own. I liked the idea of owning a cottage on a side street, near the library, even nearer to the ocean, and right next to a bar; it meant that I could step outside, grab a 'tini and a Nora Roberts, go surf fishing, and run home for potty breaks. It had been a clear but chilly evening when I filled the bank paperwork out on my steering wheel and I knew right then that I was doing the right thing. I didn't even mind that watering holes, libraries, side streets, and the ocean lured schizophrenics, potheads, drunk drivers, and tourists to my neighborhood like seagulls to a loaf of Wonder bread. Actually, since this was my peer group it had never even occurred to me.

Property ownership in such a distinguished neighborhood made me realize that there was only one way that I could pay my mortgage. And so, six months after becoming a homeowner I collected all of my most prized possessions and moved back into the Quantum. The schizophrenics, potheads, drunk drivers, and tourists became my tenants and for the next few years I spent my days in the library finishing college. Ever wonder who uses the bathroom at the library? Homeless people. It's a thing.

There wasn't a day that went by that I was not frustrated by the prospect of being too rich to hope for change but too poor to buy it.

Since I was a car-dwelling hippy and all I decided to reinforce the Hollywood stereotype of bums being deep and introspective. I did this by majoring in philosophy with a focus on Asian religions. Eventually I received my BA from the University of North Carolina at Wilmington, and in the spring of 1999 I reaped the painful reality of extramural life. With a degree in liberal arts my career choices consisted of continuing to teach windsurfing, or advising people on how to be less materialistic through deep breathing and then charging them for it.

Complicating matters was what a lousy Buddhist I'd become. I was an Olympic-quality Theravada Buddhist in terms of not-desiring-material-stuff, but when it came to the opposite sex I was hopelessly westernized. More specifically, I was doomed to remain in *Saṃsāra* because of my attachment to my girlfriend.

Her name was Kelli and she was my rock. Kelli was graduating from UNCW and I didn't want to lose her to some chach who lived in a house or had "a real job" or something. One day after a particularly engrossing meditation on the color taupe I attained complete awareness of my existence as a less than ideal suitor for a girlfriend as hot as mine. Quickly identifying the skillful means by which University life had instilled materialism in me I uttered a hearty *viva la impermanence* to my nonexistent *sangha*, shuffled off my ascetic coil and seized the certainty of employment that only a community college could offer. I also asked Kelli to marry me and she agreed with the condition that we didn't spend the honeymoon in the Volkswagen (I scored us a primo site at the Oregon Inlet campground instead). The Earth circled the sun a few more times; I became a paramedic and my bride took a management position at a fitness center.

Years of skimping and scraping crept slowly by and eventually we started making ends meet with enough profit left over to enjoy Friday lunches at our favorite Mexican restaurant. We even had 2.3 kids counting the dog. It was all very grown-up. We were in our 30's and we owed more money than ever before, but for the first time since the womb our work and sacrifice appeared to be paying off. Being $180K in the hole was oddly liberating. Life was interesting and occasionally it was even fun.

Although we were still lower-class by United States standards, we had more money than our parents during the same stage in their lives, and we had more stuff than 99% of everybody who wasn't American. There was no light at the end of the tunnel, but there was no darkness either; it just seemed that if we planned, worked and held to our commitments that we could set reasonable goals for ourselves and accomplish them. The query of our existence had undergone a subtle change from "what do we want?" to "do we really want *that?*"

Then one day as we slogged along through debt utopia we were confronted with *TARP*. The *Troubled Asset Relief Plan* was followed quickly by *Stimulus* and later by the

Affordable Care Act. It seemed that within the span of two years the United States had morphed into some weird kingdom in which our debt and sacrifice were identified as wealth and privilege by people who were far wealthier and more privileged than we were. For our transgression of choosing a dingy home over shiny toys we'd been deemed responsible for paying the way for those who apparently felt that they shouldn't have to do the same. Furthermore, it appeared that empathy had become the intellectual property solely of those who worked for the government. Politicians were labeling those of us who had set goals for ourselves and succeeded as merely being lucky and thus our opinions had no value. As evidence of this I suggest that within the last paragraph most readers have started developing one of two opinions about the author: either they are among the handful of folks who understand what I'm talking about or (more likely) readers are developing a sense of disappointment similar to that felt when one learns that a particularly catchy song on the radio is Miley Cyrus. Believe it or not, if you are of the majority predisposition then this book is for you. *Us people* aren't really as bad as we've been characterized. I mean we're as bad as anybody, but take into consideration that Miley Cyrus isn't one of us. The Tea Party sucks at number of things, the biggest of which is the management of propaganda spread by people who literally want nothing other than to be more popular than a bunch of misfits. As Malcolm X said when his opponents labeled him racist:

> "They take one little word out of what you say, ignore all the rest, and then begin to magnify it all over the

world to make you look like what you actually aren't."

Compared to the racial repression that caused Malcolm X to demand that others not tread on him, the financial repression fought by the Tea Party was merely an inconvenience. Nonetheless, in 2010 thousands of regular people tried their hands at the apparently-degenerate affair of running for public office. I was one of those people. Few Tea Party candidates knew how to be popular or even how to lie without being sarcastic; all we really knew was that the proletariat was being punished for taking responsibility for its own edification. Like the unpopular people who stood up for themselves in high school, *teabaggers* were successfully marginalized and stereotyped by the same authoritarian preppies who'd gone on to run for class president at the state and federal levels. This book is a collection of my thoughts and experiences, some humorous, some not so much, during the weeks leading up to the 2010 North Carolina Republican primary. I was competing for a chance to run against incumbent G.W. Butterfield (D) in our state's first congressional district. To truly understand what it means to be a Republican in North Carolina however, one must first know some rotten and abhorrent things about the political history of my home state.

esse quam vidiri

North Carolina had an outstanding beginning. In October of 1774 a woman from Edenton, North Carolina spearheaded what became called the Edenton Tea Party. Forty-six year old Penelope Barker and fifty other women made a point of not "hiding behind costumes as the men in Boston" and signed a petition outright against British taxation without representation. Barker sent the petition directly to the press in London.

Less than a year later in my home state, the governing figures of the area now known as Charlotte adopted the *Mecklenburg Declaration of Independence*. The declaration gave North Carolina the distinction of being the first state in the Union to give our colonial oppressors the legislative finger. Then in 1776 while the thirteen colonies were under constant British attack, residents of one eastern North Carolina area defied Cornwallis by naming their town after then-General George Washington of the Continental Army. Washington, NC was the very first town in America to be named for the future President. These first acts of Americanism on behalf of North Carolinians happened before the sovereignty of the United States was even fully secured.

Then the Revolutionary War ended and political parties happened.

It was over a century before America suffered her first and only successful domestic *coup d'etat*. The coup was staged in Wilmington, NC by a mob of political partisans. In 1898 the Democratic Party was struggling to hold onto offices, and in desperation it played the race card. The Democrats asserted that the Republicans wanted to 'put y'all in chains' and they did it by identifying their opposition as *The Party of Negro Rule*.

Wilmington voters were not intimidated, and on Wednesday November 9, 1898 several black candidates retained their positions in Wilmington public office. On Nov. 10th, Democratic Party leaders in Wilmington penned the *White Declaration of Independence*. On the 11th, Democrats stormed the town using Wilmington's own Infantry. Anyone who fought the insurrection was killed and the Democrats took by force every government position that they did not already hold. There was no response to the coup because by then the vast majority of the North

Carolina government was run by the Democratic Party. With Democrats definitively controlling North Carolina, Jim Crow laws and poll taxes were swiftly implemented, and for the following 112 years the party-of-playing-the-race-card remained in control of our otherwise respectable state.

In 2010 the Republican Party again gained a foothold in the North Carolina Legislature. Since the Democratic Party had already tranquilized the majority of black North Carolinians with government dependence it had little choice but to blame their loss of power on the economy. Within a year of the upset, Democratic Governor Bev Perdue was asked by her constituents what she could do to turn things around for the Democrats. Being among friends the Governor made the mistake of putting into words the opinion that perhaps every straight-ticket partisan has when they fear losing even more seats to their opposition:

> You have to have more ability from Congress, I think, to work together and to get over the partisan bickering and focus on fixing things. I think we ought to suspend, perhaps, elections for Congress for two years and just tell them we won't hold it against them, whatever decisions they make, to just let them help this country recover. I really hope that someone can agree with me on that. The one good thing about Raleigh is that for so many years we worked across party lines. It's a little bit more contentious now but it's not impossible to try to do what right in this state. You want people who don't worry about the next election.

By "we worked across party lines" Perdue was referring to the Democratic Party taking tobacco money, fighting desegregation, and gerrymandering the absolute crap out of our state for the previous 113 years. But the bit about "suspend, perhaps, elections for Congress" was not something that the Democrats could openly share a good chuckle over. Somebody would find out. Having let slip her true feelings about living in a republic Perdue's political days were numbered. After that the Democrats of North Carolina were stuck holding their breath and praying that nobody blabbed the real reason that the Republicans had gained a majority in the state legislature for the first time since 1898. The true reason that the Democratic Party lost its stranglehold on the North Carolina Legislature in 2010 was because a silent portion of it was punishing their Party for letting a black man become president.

The Ku Klux Klan is still around in North Carolina; and it is now, just as it has always been, a branch of the Democratic Party. Democracy after all is about doing what the majority wants. You can't argue in favor of republican enforcement of minority rights when you want the minority to shut up and do as it's told.

Having said that, one can't help but think that the KKK must have felt quite comfortable siding with the Republicans given what came next. Quickly seizing their once-in-a-century opportunity to make changes to our state, the Republican-controlled legislature placed up for public vote some anti-homosexuality wording to the state Constitution called "the Marriage Amendment". When the vote was over, 13% of the population of North Carolina

10

had empowered their government to tell 100% of its population which cultural rites of passage to follow. Just as in the days before the Revolutionary War North Carolina had again distinguished itself by being among the first in America to rise up in the face of tyranny. Unfortunately, this time North Carolina wasn't fighting tyranny but saluting it. In what we euphemistically call our republic the government of North Carolina has somehow become responsible for enforcing the cultural rites of a mere 13% of its population.

I'll say it: the only thing gayer than gay marriage is a constitutional amendment banning it. The gay marriage debate is nothing more than a slap fight between identity conformists and identity nonconformists, each of whom contribute nothing more to society than whiney attempts to influence the *status quo*. Identity politics is the mirror dance of the socially dependent, but the time and money squandered on placards and hair products are neither borrowed from Social Security nor added to my commute to work. By casting our attention to the political cool-people / uncool people we are just encouraging them to further utilize the government to implement their narrow version of justice. Politically the arrogant micromanagement of the religious Reich versus that of the Progressives may seem like separate ideologies but they aren't. The religious right is the cross; the progressive left is the fire that engulfs it; and both crowds are so desperate for social merit that they seek an official government stamp of approval on their personal versions of our cultural rites of passage.

The republican form of democracy is designed to defend the rights of the nonconformist minority from the oppression of mob-rule democracy. The republic was created for nonconformists by nonconformists. The concept that is lost on identity nonconformists however is that nonconformity in thought is the complete opposite of nonconformity in social identity; whereas the former requires thinking in a manner that is unique, the latter is accomplished by purchasing either black lipstick or hair bows, visiting a tattoo parlor or JoS. A. Bank, or developing an entire lifestyle around orgasms that either always or never yield offspring. In short, while it's just as easy to purchase a nonconformist identity as it is to join a fraternity, religion or political party; in America being an identity nonconformist is *cool*.

Anybody can be a nonconformist in identity. This truth, coupled with the fact that most people never question their own behavior, yields the statistical inevitability that with time a majority of the voters in a republic will identify themselves as members of a nonconformist minority. Once the majority of a republic's voting population identifies itself as a minority the rationality of economics, psychology, sociology, and the scientific process will give way to the rationalism of morality, cultural relativism, status quo, and political correctness. When the identity nonconformist defies the status quo he will cite the virtues of his republic, and when he condemns a minority he will tout the justice of democracy. By the ignorance of a voting population that is unified solely by its desire to ask what their country can do for them, the vocabulary of the suffragite begins to shrink. As evidence of this I propose that in 2010 the American status quo is complete and utter ignorance of not merely the name, but of the danger of a government that has an official position about your cultural rites of passage.

The state motto of North Carolina is *esse quam vidiri*. We North Carolinians like having a motto in Latin because it makes us feel more sophisticated than Latinos. Translated into our native tongue however, *esse quam vidiri* means "to be rather than to seem"; which is perhaps the true reason that we keep it encrypted in Latin: North Carolina may seem like a republic, but it be an oligarchy.

First in Flight

I live with my family in the small tourist town of Kill Devil Hills, North Carolina. Kill Devil Hills is located in what tourists have named *the Outer Banks*. Back before tourists started calling it the Outer Banks, our home was a quiet and tranquil place to live. Now the beach is being systematically transformed into every place that the tourists couldn't wait to leave. It is as if half of the people who come here are self-appointed missionaries who want to turn us into Myrtle Beach, Atlantic City, or some other seaside monstrosity.

Before the Outer Banks was subjected to such progress a normal beach yard consisted of sand and the three things that grew in it: sea oats, blanketflowers and cacti. Now every yard has a sprinkler system and you can't visit a new neighborhood without feeling like you've teleported to a cul-de-sac in Raleigh. Of course this isn't the end of the world, but those of us who like the real beach can't help but wonder why visitors and transplants want everything to be paved and fake just like the places they left. The east coast is chock full of beaches that have been ruined with commercialization, concrete and mini golf courses. Why can't people who like that kind of crap just vacation at one of those places and leave us bumpkins to fester in what's left of reality?

Such is the way of progress and I am resigned to the stupidity of the mob. Humans in groups have some primal need for politicians, politicians can't give themselves raises if they don't collect more taxes, and the easiest way to collect more taxes on the Outer Banks is to cram the beach full of people who think that sea oats and blanketflowers are *so* 1980's. Rich people need to feel important too, so we let them play dictators-in-the-sand.

I was able to ignore the aristocratic meddling of my local government until the fall of 2009. That was when I was not asked, but told by the Kill Devil Hills Planning Office that I was prohibited from making my home safer for my children.

My family, which is comprised of myself, my smokin'-hot wife, two hell-raisin' school-age boys and our chocolaty-brown dog, were eating dinner on our porch. We live in a flood zone, so our house is on pilings. We were dining eight feet above our 50' by 100' slice of sand and cacti-filled heaven. Dinner consisted of corn on the cob and pork-n-beans, both of which steamed gently from atop a wooden spool that the boys and I had liberated from a dumpster down the street. Younger son Joshua was sitting on a stool and, as kids do, he leaned back too far and fell over. Cups and forks paused in their trajectories as we watched him fall, and within an instant we figured some tears were imminent. Instead of turning into kid-shaped lump and stopping however, Joshie just kept on rolling. Our son was clinging so hard to his corn-on-the-cob that he'd turned into a rigid kid-log and was rolling straight for the eight foot drop off the edge of our porch! My wife and I leapt into ridiculous stances of reaching that would've never done any good, but at the last second Josh flattened out, stopped rolling, and lost his corn and one of his Crocs over the edge of the deck.

One cannot overstate the importance that getting safer deck railing had immediately become to us. Our house was 900 square feet in size, the yard was full of sand spurs and cacti, and ever since we kicked the schizophrenics, potheads, drunk drivers, and tourists out of our house they'd returned to the street. The porch was the only place for our kids to play.

On my next day off I set to work replacing the two horizontal slats that had served as deck railing on our house for the thirty years since it had been built. After working for about an hour I'd removed all of the old railing when suddenly a pickup truck pulled into our driveway. Within moments I was accosted by one of the minions of the Kill Devil Hills Planning Office and informed that to continue working on my railing I would need an engineer's blessing for the new railing ($900), a building permit ($100), a blueprint called a "footprint" of our house as it was "before construction" ($500), and for everything to not simply be better than it had been for the past 30 years, but *up to code*. I was also informed that I was not allowed to put the old railing back up while I magically obtained the money to pay for all of these things.

Naturally I practiced civil disobedience. I casually sipped my coffee as Cortez cruised away in search of additional instances of liberty to crush, and as soon as the white pickup was out of sight I dropped my cup and frantically worked all night to put up the new railing. Twelve hours later the sun was coming up and my porch was back together; only now my kids wouldn't roll off of it as they tried to decide between corn-on-the-cob and flaccid paralysis.

Breaking the law was not completely unfamiliar territory for me. I've driven like a maniac on numerous occasions. I babysat pot plants over spring break in college. I once stole a street sign that said *Ashley's Way* for a girl I liked. I've even had premarital sex in a red state. Twice. But these were all clandestine efforts against the establishment. Having blatantly violated the government's wishes with the exterior of my house was a caliber of misbehavior with which I was not completely comfortable. Not only was I breaking the law overtly and in broad daylight, but I was trying to make the world a better place for those around me. This was a far cry from hanging around on a street corner at one AM with an adjustable wrench and a flask of Southern Comfort. It was unnerving. I only had one thing going for me: history. If challenged I would tell my oppressors in the planning office that I was grandfathered in because my house was built before the implants had turned Kill Devil Hills into a Fascist douchebaggery.

Back before progress was such a lucrative oppression, people took steps to insure that their property actually survived harsh weather. Perhaps this ethos was no better exemplified than in the architecture of old Outer Banks houses. The original Nags Head beach houses were all constructed with thick wooden shutters that hung down from the tops of the windows. The shutters were hung from the top rather than from the sides because there was no air conditioning, and when the shutters were propped open to let in the breeze they still blocked out the blazing North Carolina sun.

The top-hung shutters of old Outer Banks houses only permitted the sun to shine directly into the house in the early morning and late afternoon. Inside the house the day would progress by colors. The mornings were bright yellow like the smile at breakfast of that chain-smoking loved one that you hadn't seen in a year. As the sun crept up the sky the glare on the ocean would give way to vibrant blue which seemed to energize the children as they noisily gathered their things and ran out to the beach. Midday inside the house was kind of how you hoped death would be. When you first came in from the beach it would be so dark that you couldn't see a thing and the only sound was the white noise of a large metal fan. Somewhere in the dark there was always an aunt or grandmother sitting and waiting just for you; waiting to listen sympathetically about how your brother had thrown sand in your eye or stomped on

18

your sand castle. She would put down her glass of tea, pat her lap, and hold you until the darkness of the interior of the house gave way to the soft tones of knotted pine walls and floors-- and to the fact that somebody had been to Cahoon's or Seamark and brought home groceries while you were out playing.

Afternoons were a hazy yellow. Men would come home from fishing smelling of beer and sweat. The younger men would jump in the ocean with the kids, the older ones showered and took a nap. As the sun lowered itself toward the Roanoke Sound it would again peek around the edges of the top-hung shutters and send the pinks and reds of the hazy sunset through the windows on the west side of the house. As the sun set, the aroma of Old Bay would creep down the halls, and those who sought it were given iced tea and put to work shucking corn or snapping beans.

Nighttime was intimate. The windows became black rectangles stippled with the dingy white of moths hanging on the metal screens. Incandescent bulbs behind ancient lampshades illuminated knots in the pinewood walls. Some of the knots made grotesque faces that would leer at you at the beginning of the week, but by the end they were familiar and endearing. The relatives would spread throughout the house and form clusters. Some played games, others read, and girls did whatever they did up in their rooms. There was usually a baby that slept in somebody's arms for hours.

In addition to the top-hung shutters on the exterior of the houses, every old Nags Head house had at least one trap door. The trap door opened to the underside of the house, and it served as a portal for sweeping out the sand and water that came in during floods.

Sometimes the flooding was due to hurricanes, but more often it was due to nor'easters. In the early 50's my grandparents were raising my mom, her three brothers, and her baby sister in a two bedroom cottage on the beach in Kitty Hawk. The 158 by-pass was only in the planning stages, and the beach road was made of concrete slabs that were tarred together end to end. The beach road was literally a road made of beach, and in the pavement you could see the same shells and small stones that churned endlessly in the shorebreak. My grandparents had one neighbor next to them to the north. To the south there was not another house in sight. Across the beach road from their cottage was Virginia Dare Hardware and the foundation was being laid for a grocery store called Winks.

My mother shared lots of memories of living in Kitty Hawk in the early 50's. For example, although their house was oceanfront, it took the kids about five minutes to walk from the porch to the shorebreak. Next to the door that faced the ocean was a metal can of kerosene and a rag for wiping the tar off of your feet before you came in the house. Sea oats, now federally protected, were allegedly fun to pick, light on fire, and run around with whilst making tribal hoots and hollers. Hot water for the house was provided by a black hose coiled around a reservoir on the roof and heated by the sun. And floods were scary because no matter what was placed on top of the trap door, the waves would still push it up and whitewater would spill through the cracks and into the house.

My grandparents moved away from Kitty Hawk in 1952, and they sold their house to one of my grandfather's cousins. The next year the entire house was washed out to sea by one wave during the Ash Wednesday Storm. The cousin who'd bought the house had never moved in, and the house was sparsely furnished with my grandparents' unmoved belongings. A few days after the Ash Wednesday Storm subsided, a single coffee cup and matching saucer washed up. They had belonged to my grandparents and were all that was left of the house. The neighbor who had watched my grandparents' house float out to sea found the cup and saucer and saved them for my grandparents. My grandmother still keeps them by the sink in her kitchen.

After the Ash Wednesday Storm the Army Corps of Engineers brought in heavy equipment and pushed the sand along the beach into one large, continuous dune that stood between the ocean and the beach road. With time, sea oats sent roots down deep into the sand, making the dunes a bit more sturdy. The yard where my mother played is now the beach access at Eckner St.

In 1953 the Town of Kill Devil Hills incorporated itself. Within the town lines of Kill Devil Hills lies Kill Devil *Hill*, which is the site where the Wright Brothers flew their airplane. Prior to the incorporation of Kill Devil Hills the area was called Kitty Hawk, which is why the history books say that the Wright Brothers flew there instead of where the Wright Monument is located, which is in Kill Devil Hills.

Today it is illegal get hot water from a reservoir on your roof, to build a house with a trap door in the floor, and even to rebuild your house on the oceanfront in Kitty Hawk after a storm washes it away. We've also been liberated from our architectural tradition of using top-hung shutters due to legislation written by construction lobbyists which requires us to put expensive, impact resistant windows in our houses. In Kill Devil Hills it is illegal to use a sling shot or ride a bike without both hands on the handlebars. It is illegal to sleep in your car. Only elitist snobs consider these restrictions to be progress. Today it's illegal to be hardy and resilient. It's illegal to do what you want with your own property. Today it is illegal to not be dependent upon, and subservient to, the government.

The American government's chronic treatment of citizens as helpless sissies who are incapable of taking responsibility for their actions has resulted in an abuse of resources that has literally left our nation bankrupt. Insurance, although it is not yet entirely controlled by the Federal Government, is a perfect example. In the old days people placed shutters on their houses because they wanted to do everything that they could to prevent their house from being damaged. They cut trap doors in their floors because when something did happen to their house, it was their responsibility (not the insurance company's) to get things back to normal. If your house was destroyed you were stuck paying for it, so you built with both ingenuity and modesty.

Nowadays, insurance will pay for your broken windows, stripped shingles, water damage and shredded siding. People don't care whether or not their house is damaged in a storm because they figure that making a claim will justify paying for insurance in the first place. Since the vast majority of houses on the Outer Banks are now rentals, the price of insurance premiums-- as well as the higher taxes-- are conveyed to those who rent the houses. Furthermore, since it is now possible to build a house on the beach and insure it, the price of oceanfront property has increased exponentially. Where in the old days rugged living on "the back of the beach" was reserved for those who had more resilience than money it is now the exclusive domain of those who are rich enough to afford the insurance premiums. Through legislation and insurance, our government has pushed all of the independent individuals of our nation out to the far edges of the swamps and jam-packed the oceanfronts with *Snookie* & *Pauly D* wannabees who only ever leave the air conditioning to lounge in the sun.

So back to me staying up all night to put a new railing on our porch. A couple of days after my civil disobedience I went into the planning office to see what I could do to make protecting my children a more lawful act. When it became my turn to bow before Saruman and confess the benevolence that lurked in my heart, the civil server behind the counter recognized me by my address. I was informed that the building inspector, or his minion, or whomever'd come to my house and told me knock off the safety dance had been "very upset at me" for putting my porch railing back up.

Very upset at me.

I waited silently for the charges that were going to be levied against me for disobeying the powers that be, but after a few minutes of uninterrupted castigation I realized that in spite of my deplorable behavior, no actual laws were being cited as broken. It was slowly becoming apparent to me that the town was very limited in the paths it could take to punish me for improving a house that I owned and lived in. While the planning office has no reservations about condemning a residence over appearance or other stuff that is absolutely none of their business, the Fourth Amendment prevented a good portion of the town code from actually being enforced beyond placing liens on a person's residence. I didn't know why I hadn't recognized it before, but suddenly it occurred to me that the triflin' micromanagers of the planning office were nothing but a bunch of bullies armed with paperwork instead of brass knuckles. They rationalized their thuggery by pointing at building codes written by construction lobbyists, never once giving any thought as to whether or not what they were doing was of any tangible benefit to anybody. The people who enforced the building codes were literally no different than the supercilious pokeys who man the registers at the Kill Devil Hills K-mart.

From the desk of the planning office I looked out the window and saw the giant form of the Wright Brothers Monument pressing sluggishly into the top if Kill Devil Hill. I imagined the setbacks and disappointments that the Wright Brothers must have had as they attempted to get as far off the ground as my porch without falling. It was mind boggling to me that the code enforcement dude was "upset with me" for fixing *my own house*. I stood there at the counter of the planning office, staring out the window at the Wright Monument, feeling myself getting more and more pissed off. Satan's minion was upset with *me*? Methinks these unctuous bluebloods have no idea what 'upset' is. While basking in the protection of the Fourth Amendment I quickly recalled the other Amendments and decided that from that moment on I would not hesitate to test them whenever and wherever the Town of Kill Devil Hills was concerned. I decided to start with number One.

I cleared my throat and directed my voice toward the top of the stormtrooper's head. "You know what's ironic".

The guy didn't answer; he was busy pretending to be wrapped up in thought as he searched the file cabinet for additional forms for me to fill out.

"If Kill Devil Hills was just 50 years older the Wright Brothers would have never flown because the building inspector would have never approved the plans for the Wright Flier."

The shuffle of manila folders became more intense.

"I mean, look at the wings of that thing" I said.

For some reason I motioned toward the wall of the planning office. Across the street in that direction was a life-sized, all-weather model of the Wright Flier. It was complete with brass renderings of members of the Lifesaving Service who helped the Wrights on that cold day in 1903.

"Those wings are well over eight feet long, and they don't need 36 linear board feet of pressure treated two-by-twelves to strengthen the gap and withstand high wind."

The kid remained in his crouched position so I looked at the guy behind me in line. This poor sap was on his third trip to the planning office just trying to get permission to install a new spigot at his house. He shot me a silent but tremendous brown grin of missing teeth which suddenly disappeared in a look of solemnity. I turned around to see that the counter creature was glaring at us both. He had a stack of papers for me to fill out: my apparent penance for protecting my kids.

I filled out the paperwork and my plans were denied, of course; but again, the paper tigers couldn't do much about it other than be "upset". For the next year, every time I walked out of my house with the sagging siding, crumbling shingles, fog-filled windows and decrepit steps, I smiled at my nice, safe, straight, porch railing. To the passing drunk driver, schizophrenic, pothead, or tourist my deck railing may have looked like a simple collection of treated lumber and deck screws, but to me it was a gigantic sign that said "bite me you Progressive micromanaging Fascist elitists of the Kill Devil Hills Planning Office". And it was good.

The Dictator Game

Not-falling-off-my-porch isn't the only thing that I don't like the government helping me with. I don't know why anybody would want unsolicited advice on how to manage their finances, plan for the future or live their life-- particularly from an institution that knows absolutely nothing about them. Having the government tell you what to do with your house would be like having me tell you what to do with your house, only I would never place a lien on your property if you didn't listen to me. In spite of my aversion to unsolicited government supervision I am nonetheless a materialistic American and am content to rationalize liberty as an acceptable thing to trade for more toys.

Prior to *TARP* I had not given much thought to the possibility that one political party was pushing an agenda of giving the Federal Government the power to control American citizens. I always figured that an insatiable hunger for power was the flaw of individual politicians. I figured that political parties were the institutions of ideology that differed on how to best implement American liberty. Democrats wanted democracy tempered by the Constitution and Republicans wanted a republic fueled by capitalism, but neither was interested in ruling the nation *per se*. I thought they disagreed on how to implement liberty. The actions of the Democratic Party under President Obama were a cornucopia of evidence that I was wrong.

Rather than pulling a Limbaugh and attempting to use common sense to describe the myopic culture of the contemporary Democratic Party, I think it might be time to try a more academic approach to broadening the views of people who vote Democrat out of a nescient need to be cool. Let's have us an allegory about American political liberalism.

Within the semi-reality of academia there exists a psychological experiment called *The Dictator Game*. The Dictator Game involves the cultivation of a clever lie. That's OK though, because lying is the *modus operandi* of most psychological experiments.

If you are a psychological test subject, chances are good that you are going to be lied to, you are going to consider lying to yourself, you are going to be subtly encouraged to lie to the people around you, or some combination thereof. When it comes to psychology the term *experiment* pretty much just means *lie*: the scenarios are fabricated and both the test administrators and subjects are participating in a pursuit of personal gain. A psychological experiment is an acceptable series of lies for which the participants receive compensation and sometimes alcohol. It's easy money and it's more fun than being on the OJ Simpson jury.

If a psychological experiment involves human beings, the experiment will designate to those involved either the role of test subject or of test administrator. Humans who volunteer to be test subjects do so for one or more of three reasons: for the money, for course credit, or because a psychology professor is requiring it. Note that two thirds of the reasons for participating in a psychological experiment involve appeasing a college professor. And what is the caveat of a psychological experiment? In exchange for a modicum of credit, pay, or academic merit the human beings pretend to be themselves while their behavior is recorded.

The Dictator Game is a psychological experiment which takes test subjects and tells them that they have been given ten "points". Each point can be exchanged for a dollar after the experiment is over. Each point that is exchanged for a dollar is in addition to the compensation that has already been agreed upon by the subjects and the test administrators. The test subject is then informed that there is a person sitting in a nearby room. The test subject is assured that they do not know the person in the nearby room. No other information about the person is given to the test subject. The test subject is then informed that they can give any amount of their points to the anonymous stranger in the nearby room simply by informing the test administrator of the amount that they would like to donate.

GO!

Gee Brain, what kind of jerk do you have to be to volunteer for a psychological experiment and then get guilt tripped into lowering the amount that you get paid so that the test administrators and/or your professor will think nice things about you? Let's see if we understand the test subject's role in the Dictator Game correctly: they're supposed to give money to an alleged anonymous, faceless, description-less person. They don't know if this stranger is a homeless person in need of lithium or some doctoral candidate embezzling funds. For that matter, how do they even know that there *is* an anonymous person sitting in another room? It's a psychological experiment: they're being paid in exchange for letting lies run their course. Obviously the administrators of the Dictator Game know who the anonymous person is and *they* don't think he's worth treating like everybody else.

But the fallacy of the Dictator Game is not in how it is conducted. The experiment yields data that provides powerful insight into the minds of the participants. Unfortunately the academic world is looking at the wrong participants.

The only outstanding data that the Dictator Game yields lie in the conclusions which the test administrators assert about the test subjects. Test subjects who donate more of their "points" to the anonymous person in another room are labeled by the test administrators as being more "generous", "prosocial", and "altruistic". The test subjects who hold on to their points are regarded as being less generous: as if redistributing wealth is somehow noble if it is done on a person who only exists in one's imagination. But let's try to understand why the administrators of the Dictator Game label the students who gave their points away as being "prosocial". What kind of person gives money to an anonymous, nondescript person whom they only know to exist out of hearsay . . . in an experiment? An altruistic person? An empathetic person? A compassionate person?

An *altruistic* person gets nothing in return for their effort. This is not to be confused with a person who puts forth effort in pursuit of social merit. For the relative price of a couple of bucks that they never even had, the test subjects of the Dictator Game get to enjoy an elevation in social status by the test administrators. Recall the two types of people who participate in psychological experiments: those who actually need the money, and those who are doing it for their professor. The accolades for those who put up an identity of being altruistic are published in the test administrators' academic papers. Let me identify this phenomenon as a hypothesis:

Paid Test Subjects in a Psychological Experiment Will Forfeit a Portion of Their Payment in an Attempt to be Viewed Favorably by the Administrators of the Experiment.

An *empathetic* person gives money to an anonymous stranger because by the definition of empathy, they themselves would like to receive money from an anonymous stranger. Giving money away because you would like to get money is either a nod to karma or is some kind of schizoid financial Munchhausen's by proxy.

It is also possible that the "empathetic" test subject in the Dictator Game is assuming that the anonymous stranger is more in need of money than they are. Given that the empathetic person knows absolutely nothing about the anonymous stranger, yet they assume that the anonymous stranger is socioeconomically inferior to them suggests that the empathetic person is more of a sympathetic-yet-egotistical person. Since the sympathetic aristocrat suddenly has disposable wealth in hand and is being observed by the dictators of the Dictator Game, the test subject undergoes an elevation in social class and desires to reiterate that status by throwing their wealth around, even if it is to an anonymous stranger. Even more confusing is how the "empathetic" test subject who, for giving points to a hypothetical, nondescript stranger in a psychological experiment gets labeled "generous" in the world outside of the experiment. For all the test administrators know the test subjects whom they label "less prosocial, less altruistic, less generous" are saving their psychological-experiment cash to give to an actual, real-life human being who needs it rather than some imaginary, nondescript stranger in a psychological experiment. The most the test subject can know about the hypothetical, nondescript stranger in the other room is that he or she is a test subject just like one's self. I don't know what the condition is for a person who assumes that a stranger in the exact same psychological experiment is more in need of a couple of bucks, but the

Dictator Game is a good way of diagnosing it.

Finally, a *compassionate* person is one who understands intimately the goings-on in an Other's life and strives to understand how and why an Other feels the way that they do from moment to moment. Compassion can never, *ever* be accomplished by thinking about a nondescript, anonymous stranger that may or may not exist in another room. Frankly it can't even be accomplished if some things are known about a stranger in another room. Even if a stranger is characterized as being "poor", in what manner are we to assume compassion for them? Do we know just how someone feels if they only "make" a couple of taxable dollars a year like John Kerry? Are we totally down with the anonymous stranger that allegedly exists in the next room because he or she makes lots of money but spends it all on drugs and thus has nothing to show for it? Perhaps we can completely relate to the fact the anonymous stranger *had* millions of dollars but they voluntarily gave up material things because they found inner peace and happiness.

So to answer the question of what kind of person gives money to an anonymous, nondescript person whom they only know to exist out of hearsay? The answer is unquestionably a *politician*. And what kind of person authoritatively labels that politician as "altruistic" for throwing money at imaginary strangers? That would be a *liberal*.

I would like to take this opportunity to insist that being a liberal is a good thing. I define civilization as the existence of compassion, and liberals are attempting to engineer a more compassionate world. The problem is that compassion can be neither transferred nor governed; it can only be voluntarily given directly from one person to another.

Only in post-Me Generation America would anybody characterize not-giving-money-to-a-total-stranger-whom-you-know-absolutely-nothing-about-- in a great experiment no less-- as an exhibition of a relative lack of altruism. The Dictator Game is a perfect example of contemporary politics all the way down to the funding. Almost all psychological experiments are funded with grants, which in turn come from taxes taken from the citizens under the threat of imprisonment. The dictators (the administrators of the Dictator Game) are the American voters who assume that because their opinions will be documented and tallied that they are actually facts. The test subjects are the politicians who strive to gain noble status in the eyes of the dictators by giving money that isn't theirs to anonymous strangers. In return for giving money that isn't theirs in the form of entitlements to people that they don't know, the test subjects gain favor from the dictators who grant them the label of being "prosocial", and they submit their assessment to favorable media outlets. There are three methods for studying the behavior of the administrators of the Dictator Game: the *subjective* method, the *reputational* method, and the *objective* method.

The subjective method of studying the behavior of the academicians who administer the Dictator Game reveals that these academicians are actual dictators. They

34

are above scrutiny and their conclusions about the test subjects are absolute. The dictators have no clothes. In fact they don't even question the validity of either the experiment or the conclusions that they glean from it. The administrators grant themselves higher social standing simply for performing the experiment and their subjects are obliged to blindly accept their conclusions. This is consistent with the Democratic Party's view of both themselves and their assessment of social status in America: they are the self-proclaimed authorities on social status and morality, they identify themselves as intellectuals because of their assertions on these topics, and they answer to no one. This is also how the Republican Party is about religion.

The reputational method of studying the behavior of the people who administer the Dictator Game is fairly easy to do. The Dictator Game is regarded by the "authorities" of social science as being entirely about the behavior of the test subjects and not about the judgment of the test administrators, and the publications regarding the findings of the Dictator Game reflect as much. The acquisition of higher social standing and power is the purpose of both political parties, but the (contemporary) Democratic Party is more representative of the administrators of the Dictator Game because the Party prides itself upon being the distributor of tax revenues which, if spent on a faceless demographic that may or may not exist in another area of the nation, is stamped (by themselves) with the moral judgment of generosity, altruism, and prosocial behavior.

Finally, the objective method of studying the people

who administer the Dictator Game is, unfortunately, not something that can be accomplished by those who are of lower social class than the academicians who hold a monopoly on state-sponsored research. By applying B.F. Skinner's tenet that a scientist can never be sure what a person actually thinks, but can only extrapolate thoughts from behavior that is observed, the administrators of the Dictator Game enjoy carte blanche to assume that test subjects do not suspect that there is *not* actually an anonymous stranger in another room. Ironically, liberal thinker Herbert Marcuse touches on this very phenomenon at the political level:

> *Discrimination would also be applied to movements opposing the extension of social legislation to the poor, weak, disabled. As against the virulent denunciations that such a policy would do away with the sacred liberalistic principle of equality for 'the other side', I maintain that there are issues where either there is no 'other side' in any more than a formalistic sense, or where 'the other side' is demonstrably 'regressive' and impedes possible improvement of the human condition.*

This passage, penned in 1968, is a staple argument of Americans who in 2009 are suppressed and labeled "conservatives" by the dictators of the Democratic Party and the vast majority of the print and TV media.

The dictators of the Dictator Game also get to assume that the test subjects are too stupid to realize that if there were an anonymous stranger in another room and that person was, in fact, in need of a couple of dollars, then it is the dictators-- the people who actually know the anonymous person in the other room-- who are the ones who are screwing that person by leaving their welfare up to the financial prowess of people who value being (mistakenly) viewed as altruistic over cash and consequently use the latter to purchase the former. But just when you thought B.F. Skinner was ruining psychology for everybody, we get to apply his tenet to the test administrators. The academicians who execute the Dictator Game divulge their judgments in compositions that they call research and present them for publication within benevolent circles. Although we have no idea what is going on in the minds of the test subjects of the Dictator Game, we know exactly what moral judgments the test administrators make about them. In this light it makes one wonder if the Dictator Game was actually engineered to make a mockery of those who use it for research. Clearly the true dictators of the Dictator Game are the test administrators who allocate all the funds, make all the rules, are above scrutiny, who lie to the test subjects for their own personal gain, and hold absolute authority on moral judgment of the test subjects' behavior. If you are a citizen whose interaction with society is based upon experience, compassion and empathy instead of stereotyping, social merit and sympathy, then you are capable of recognizing that the Dictator Game is a flawless analogy for Socialism in practice all the way down to the administrators' denial that they are the flaw in the experiment.

A Year that will Live in Infamy

Hopefully 2009 will go down in history as the year that the American Government most closely mimicked the National Socialist German Worker's Party. For the first time in over a decade the Democratic Party owned the president, had a majority in the House, and was one lawyer away from having a filibuster-proof majority in the Senate. It was as if the country had been taken over by a TV ministry which had substituted prayer with hope, switched the congregation with Congress, appointed the choir to czar positions, multiplied tithing times four and made it your legal obligation, and then borrowed trillions of dollars against your tithe and blown it all on ways to make people come back for seconds on communion. Even in the face of the total failure of the *Stimulus Package*, *Cash for Clunkers*, and the voluntary continuation of the Bush Administration's

Troubled Asset Relief Plan there was no sudden nationwide grasp of economics. There was no awareness that all we had to show for our debt was overdue spring cleaning of the infrastructure of other people's towns, more indentured voters for the Democratic Party, and research on energy sources that we had become too broke to afford. It was like President Gatsby was amassing history's largest debt as he stood with his arms outstretched, pleadingly grasping at the green light at the end of Robert Mugabe's dock.

Rounded off to the nearest $100 billion, President Obama increased the federal deficit from $10 trillion to $13.5 trillion during the first two years of his presidency. The next greatest two-year increase in the deficit was less than half that much at $1.5 trillion borrowed during the only two years of the Bush Administration when there was a Democratic majority in both the House and the Senate. Deficit spending during the Obama Administration was literally like the worst years of the Bush Administration without the hindrance of George W. Bush. It was as if suddenly it became OK to print money to pay off debt because there was a Marxist in the White House. If there is one positive thing about Obamanomics it is that it begs the mind-expanding question: if you can print money to pay off debt, why borrow it to begin with? Is paying off the interest on a loan with make-believe money somehow beneficial to Americans? Does this keep China from invading us? Prithee dear Obama Administration spendthrifts, if there is an unseen perk to inflicting inflation on retirement neighborhoods, please utilize some of this 'transparency' we've been hearing so much about and share your superior knowledge of this topic with the rest of us.

With its borrowed dollars the Obama Administration commissioned the purchase of 33% of the stock of General Motors, which was once again bankrupt from overpaying the United Auto Workers. The exorbitant salaries of the UAW have translated into crippling inflation and widespread unemployment for the citizens of Detroit who do not tighten bolts and push buttons for a living; and the Democratic Party's influence in Detroit has culminated with crime and poverty that is so bad that even white kids rap about it. As if turning Detroit into Port-au-Prince was not enough, Obama wanted the UAW to branch out and start destroying the lives of working people all over the nation. Since the UAW is nothing more than a bunch of straight-ticket Democrats it was not surprising that the Obama Administration used taxpayer dollars to bail them out. What was unexpected was that the Administration would go so far as to kill off *Saturn*, which was the sole American car that was not manufactured with UAW labor. As if to warn people to look the other way as the nation turned to Fascism, our 'transparent and unifying' Administration began shutting down Chrysler dealerships based not on the dealership's financial solvency, but on some top-secret criteria which had no apparent depth beyond whether or not the dealership owners donated to the Republican Party.

And of course there was *The Stimulus Package*. *Stimulus* was intended to decrease the unemployment rate and instead the unemployment rate went up. The Obama Administration even went so far as to say that the reason that unemployment went up instead of down after *Stimulus* was because we still hadn't borrowed enough money and poured more concrete. Watching Democrats defend *Stimulus* was like watching a bunch of Creationists rationalize how carbon dating is nothing more than a mathematical trick. The figures for the complete and utter failure of *Stimulus* continue to be readily available and irrefutable, but if the government deems its failure to be success then apparently the peons will believe it. *Stimulus* worsened rather than shortened the recession, and our grandchildren will pay for Obama, Pelosi & Reid's astigmatic financial dogma with every facet of their standards of living from their health to homeland security.

No political party will ever admit that one of their policies does not work. It is up to the voters to realize which government programs work and which do not, and they need to do it by looking out into America rather than into mass media. How many people do you know who have stopped living off of the government and have learned to take care of themselves? How many people do you know who are being denied health care? How many of the people who were defaulted on their loans were living in houses that they could afford? Maybe as a segue into getting the voting population to think for itself we need a Joe Bob Briggs style "Legislation Total" that can tell us what a law is like before Congress votes on it:

The *Healthy and Ethical Americans Act*-- half a million constituents thrown under the bus, seven naked kowtows to the poultry lobby, a title that has nothing to do with the Bill itself, forty billion in decapitated funds, eleven dismembered job markets, thirty-seven secret tax exemptions that no Earthly human being can reach, one anecdote about a disemboweled hog, one possible case of trichinosis, one Constitution used as presidential TP, and even though there are only half as many corpses as a Rob Zombie flick every last member of Congress has exhumed themselves from their own putrefied legislation. The *Healthy and Ethical Americans Act* gets half a star, and that's only because the *Patient Protection and Affordable Care Act* has lowered the bar to the realm of horse-face.

Unfortunately it doesn't matter how bad a piece of legislation is, if it is gets a testimonial from a celebrity then most Americans are going to believe it's good anyway.

Arguably the best illustration of Obama's agape for faux-Keynesian economics is not one of his multi-million dollar wastes, but rather a meager $89K one in the state where the red fern grows.

If you exit the front of the University of North Carolina at Wilmington, hang a right onto I-40, drive about 1100 miles and then take another right on Oklahoma exit 264-B and squint toward the northwest, you'll see the town of Boynton, Oklahoma. According to the 2000 census about one-fourth of the population of Boynton lives in poverty. While this may sound like a large number it is merely a large statistic. Boynton only had about 300 residents at the time of the census, making the actual number of people who lived in poverty to be about 75. Any

Keynesian would think that $89K would go a long way on 75 people. It doesn't. The "shovel ready" job that Boynton received from the *Stimulus Package* consisted of digging up a sidewalk that Boynton residents described as being in good shape and replacing it with . . . *an identical sidewalk*. The digging was not completed by residents of Boynton but by a construction company based out of the town of Muscogee located some 20 miles away. The only wealth that came to the 75 impoverished people of Boynton from the $89K that *Stimulus* graced them with was whatever change that the construction company dropped on its way out of town. As a tangential bit of juicy gossip, the construction company that dug up and replaced the perfectly good sidewalk in Boynton managed to operate their shovels while dealing with indictments from an Oklahoma grand jury including Conspiracy Against the State (specifically the DOT), Intimidation of a State Witness, and Conspiracy to Defraud. Perhaps the sidewalk was in disrepair because it had been built with inferior products, which was what the Muscogee-based construction company was under indictment for by the Oklahoma DOT. At any rate, as a result of the *Stimulus Package* the Federal Government essentially underwrote the legal fees that permitted a construction company to continue performing shovel-ready jobs that the construction company had been disbarred from doing and which benefited absolutely nobody in the town where the shovels touched dirt. The only things that Gordon Gekko economics changed in a town of 300 people, 25% of whom lived in poverty, was a sidewalk being changed to a slightly different shade of gray and small businesses that had to raise prices and lay people off in order to compensate for the price of *Stimulus*. As Keynesian ventures go, *Stimulus* was the WPA without ingenuity, foresight, or even an incidence of post-card-worthy craftsmanship.

The epitome of *Stimulus* benevolence consists of nothing more than a handful of infrastructure projects that were only important because they had been neglected for decades. There was some green research as well. I am as much of a fan as anybody of science for the sake of science, but green research is the hobby of a wealthy nation, which is something we no longer are. What are we going to do with green energy research-- borrow money from Social Security so that we can afford to use it? Solar, nuclear, and geothermal energy are the future of civilization and I wish with all my heart that people appreciated that, but you cannot create a market for something that people don't want, particularly after you put them into debt. If *Stimulus* had provided us with a nuclear power plant, a cheaper method of manufacturing cancer treatment medications, or a more comprehensive screening process for the TSA, then we would have something to show our grandchildren for the chunk that will be taken out of their paychecks to pay for replacing sidewalks that should have been paid for by the people who actually "wore them out". But pavement isn't all that our grandchildren owe money for. In order to insure that citizens who wanted to vote themselves gifts from the public treasury knew who their sugar daddies were, the *Stimulus Package* provided funds for the posting of roadside signs that carried the names of our president and his like-minded Democrat governors and lieutenant governors. In true propaganda style, the signs were posted in construction areas where traffic could be merged and redirected to slowly pass by the names, right at eye-level, of the president and his cronies.

With *Stimulus*, unnecessary small projects such as the resurfacing of still-passable roads were subcontracted to the same corporations that already did everything else. The *Stimulus Package* made the one percent richer and spanked the daylights out of every portion of the working class that didn't do construction or research. Keeping people employed during a recession only keeps the unemployment rate the same. Sending the bill for it to the employers just makes employment cost twice as much as it should; and that is why after *Stimulus* was instituted unemployment surpassed 8% and hasn't gone below it since[*].

These were the sorts of things that were on the minds of the people who, not having any other outlet, formed the Tea Party. The fact that every one of the Tea Party's concerns were easily sold to MSNBC as being racist just made us feel even more like the United States had been taken over by the Nazi Party. For our simple transgressions of understanding economics and recognizing the downfall of individual liberty, the governors and their media labeled us as stupid, inferior, dirty, greedy hoarders of the nation's wealth. And racists. Somehow they threw racist in there as well. Every Nazi quote on the books seemed to apply to the

---

[*] This is an unfair assertion; see the discussion on unemployment figures on p. 228.

Obama Administration in 2009:

Regarding the economics of the *Stimulus Package* and *TARP*:

Every educated person is a future enemy.

About the failure of *Stimulus*:

Make the lie big, make it simple, keep saying it, and eventually they will believe it.

It also gives us a very special, secret pleasure to see how unaware the people around us are of what is really happening to them.

For mitigating the political discomfort delivered by the Tea Party:

It is the absolute right of the State to supervise the formation of public opinion.

The lie can be maintained only for such time as the State can shield the people from the political, economic and/or military consequences of the lie. It thus becomes vitally important for the State to use all its powers to repress dissent, for the truth is the mortal enemy of the lie, and thus by extension, the truth becomes the greatest enemy of the State.

And as for the *Patient Protection and Affordable Care Act*:

The most brilliant propagandist technique will yield no success unless one fundamental principle is borne in mind constantly: it must confine itself to a few points and repeat them over and over.

The greatness of every mighty organization embodying an idea in this world lies in the religious fanaticism and intolerance with which, fanatically convinced of its own right, it intolerantly imposes its will against all others.

It seemed like the only thing that the Obama Administration did that was unlike the Nazis was give the militias we were fighting the timeline for extrication of U.S. troops from battle. War for the Obama Administration was run like a basketball game-- the Commander in Chief figured he was winning because we'd killed more people and now all he had to do was run out the clock. If public opinion dipped all the Commander in Chief had to do was draw a foul from Fox News and take some free throws on MSNBC.

When it came to Obamacare, Obama supporters had turned into a mob that was content to simply regurgitate the words *Patient Protection and Affordable Care* and believe that 'blessed is he who has not seen and still believes'. In my lifetime no larger or more-intrusive piece of faith-based legislation has been passed than Obamacare. The *Patient Protection and Affordable Care Act* has no more to do with curing the sick than televangelism has to do with curing the sick. Obamacare reminds me of something I learned when I was studying religion in college.

Religion majors who study the Abrahamic religions get to hear a lot about the study of what is called "The Historical Jesus". When you hear "Historical Jesus" think *alternative, reasonable literary explanations for Christ's miracles*. Take it from me, if you sign up for a Historical Jesus class in college there are going to be students who, just like the self-proclaimed 'open-minded' people who picked up this book, get really bummed when they don't receive a reiteration of everything that they already believe. Personally I find Jesus a lot more endearing when His stories are sans-miracles. If you leave out all the miracles in the Bible it seems like it was written by intelligent people who respected the Son of God rather than by sheep who worshipped Him. Call me rational, boring, and bound for hell, but it's just hard for me to believe a story if it is marketed like a stunt by P.T. Barnum.

One of the most likable of the historical Jesus scholars is John Dominic Crossan. Of the many heretical postulations for which Crossan is going to hell, one that sticks out in my mind addresses the story of two disciples who saw the risen Jesus on the road to Emmaus. Crossan postulates that the Road to Emmaus story is the kind that never happened-- and that happens every day. What Crossan means is that a Christian should not look for their faith in a story, but manifest their faith every day as they interact with society. At my church we call this a *glory sighting*. I know that a lot of people have faith that after I'm dead I'll regret not joining them in their dogma, but I prefer to think of the gospels of Matthew, Mark, Luke, John, and *Q* as being more cerebral than the narratives of five 'squatch hunters who believed the Earth was only 5,000 year old.

Another of Crossan's postulations regards the fishes and loaves miracle. Crossan suggests that rather than feeding 5,000 people with three Happy Meals and a can of

V-8, Jesus appealed to the crowd that was following Him to give up what food they had stowed in their garments so that the foodstuffs could be pooled and those who had nothing could be sated as well. This makes a lot more sense to me, but not because I'm looking for an excuse not to believe in the miracles of Christ. I would just like to believe that if Jesus was going to miracle-up breakfast in bed for 400,000 that it would be for a cause greater than giving his constituents something to nosh on while he performed grand rounds; you know-- like for the people who were actually sick. But hey, maybe the healing-of-the-sick wasn't quite as flashy that day. Seriously, nobody acts like ECU just beat Miami when somebody gets a cardiac stent or receives tissue plasminogen activator within the three hour window. And imagine the view from the back of a hot, sweaty crowd of 5,000:

Follower #4841 - What's He doing now?

Follower #3630 - He just fixed somebody's abdominal aortic aneurism without surgery.

Follower #4804 - Is that good?

Follower #3630 - I guess so. Say, haveth ye any gum?

Follower #4968 - Dude, my mom just made baba ghanouj. Want some?

It's your choice-- do you like to think of Jesus as the guy who miracled up lutefisk and lefse *hors d'ouvres* for a party of several thousand or as the person who convinced a horde of hungry followers to be generous with what they had? If you're a Southern Baptist try to look at it this way:

which is more of a miracle: feeding several thousand people with a small amount of food or getting a couple thousand Jews to share?

Dr. Crossan's idea of the fishes and loaves story is what I think of whenever I hear about Obamacare; primarily that it's a trick which-- no matter how it is pulled off-- will only work one epic time. As an allegory Obamacare is far more similar to the moment during the 1995 Million Man March when keynote speaker Louis Farrakhan instructed everybody in the crowd to hold up a dollar bill and then pass it forward to the stage. While a million dollars is a lot of money for one person (which was perhaps the point of Farrakhan's exercise) it is by no means enough money to do anything of consequence for a million people. Of the 75 poor people in Boynton, OK, not one of them transcended poverty even after $89,000 of *Stimulus* money was spent on them. The same is true with health care. Even if you have every man, woman and child in America pitch in $7,000 a year to Obamacare it isn't going to be enough to cover everybody even if you cut out the expense of redistribution. And Obamacare isn't just offering $7K worth of medical care to each and every person in America, legal or non; Obamacare is supposed to be unlimited and for everybody (right?). History has invariably shown that there are only two possible results of any Socialist entitlement program-- rationing or bankruptcy. Short and sweet, the reason that it costs three times as much to get an MRI in the United States as it does in France is because in the United States you don't have to wait three months to get one.

Living in a Material World

In High School we had a chemistry teacher named Mr. Fonville. He was the master of my homeroom and one of my favorite mentors. Mr. Fonville called himself *Fonz*. He had curly black hair that he managed to slick back on top but there was always a rash of independent curls flaring up at the nape. As the day progressed the curls would take over the Fonz's head, but his demeanor remained as firm as the bond between a pair of oxygens. Fonz moved deliberately but never quickly. His voice never strained. Although his speech was a little high it was never comically so; and when he wore his lab coat we knew he meant business.

There were always things going on in the Fonz's class. One day we made aspirin and got to display our product in a window, complete with names we'd bequeathed upon our products such as *Kiminol* and *Ididmylabwrongandol*. If somebody wasn't paying attention in lecture the Fonz would call their name, say "catch", and toss a chicken egg at them. It wasn't a real egg but it did the trick. One day after rummaging through the supply room the Fonz had to call the bomb squad to come and remove the explosive picric acid that he'd discovered.

Some days with the Fonz we'd do nothing but math. We would spend what seemed like hours calculating moles and molarity and converting grams to moles or determining what percentage of a compound was carbon by weight and other awful stuff. But when we weren't doing the stuff that made chemistry science, the Fonz taught class by setting us up with a bit of new information, guiding us through it 'til we got the feel of it, and then he would challenge us with questions about what we'd learned. Questions from the Fonz include:

o Why does air pressure drop if you add water molecules to it?

o How do you single-bond six carbons together with each carbon touching two (and only two) other carbons?

o (Showing us his bottle of prescription nitroglycerine) Why doesn't this explode if I drop it?

And one day he threw us this two-parter:

1.) "If I push as hard as I can against this wall am I doing work?" As the Fonz awaited our response he turned and began pushing against the cinder-block wall. The class mumbled together. It seemed like a trick question but only a fool would tell their chemistry teacher that what he was doing wasn't work. The Fonz lowered his head and put his back into it. Beads of sweat began to form on his brow. His curls began to flatten back out. With the safety of answering in unison we finally said "yes".

2.) The Fonz straightened up and turned around to face us. We could see his eyebrows raised in surprise above the thick, square rims of his old-man glasses. "Oh yeah" he said, taking a breath. "Who's gonna pay me?"

This Fonz's last question illustrated the scientific definition of work. In science, work is not work unless the speed or direction of something is changed. The Fonz could push against the wall all day long, but as long as the wall didn't move he would not have performed any mechanical work. Mr. Fonville's question stuck with me not just through chemistry class in High School, but into my college physics, economics, business, and philosophy classes as well. To me, the scientific definition of work parallels the Marxian idea of labor. Marx asserted that the value of a commodity is equal to the amount of human labor required to produce it. Marx argued that the tremendous value of gold came from the tremendous amount of labor required to produce it. Of course Marx was wrong: gold is valuable first and foremost because humans are primates and they like shiny objects.

The idea that labor is what gives something its value is the sort of drollery that can only survive in philosophy and other liberal arts departments. Even Marx knew that just because a person expended a great deal of effort producing something, that the effort alone did not necessarily make it valuable. Case in point: I've labored a great deal on this book, but even with my generous dispensation of five cent words *Work Hard for your Dog* is worthless to anybody who believes that Socialism works.

The idea that the value of anything comes from the wages spent to produce it ignores the phenomenon of demand, which determines whether the wealth expended on labor was wasted or not; and of laziness, which is what kills every socialist / communist / Marxist venture attempted. In short, you can pay somebody $15/hr. to make Big Macs or deliver the mail, but when people don't want to pay $10 for a Big Mac or to mail a bag of weed, then somebody is going to lose money.

I suspect that the liberal arts folks of the world will assert that in spite of my sesquipedalianism my labor is worthless because I'm not writing anything that they actually demand to read. But if by some miracle I end up recouping the opportunity cost of scratching out this compendium of mumbo jumbo (and I don't mean by receiving a government grant so that my unique perspective can be preserved-- *ha-ha*) then liberal artisans will have to concede that in spite of my labor having no value that it does in fact have a price because you, foolish reader, have created a market for it. And this is the thing that Marx and his followers tend to ignore: that the value of everything from Federal Reserve notes to personal security arises not from the labor that is required to produce these things, but from the market for them. There is a market for every human experience-- not just for the warm fuzzy we get from looking at shiny yellow metal or reading stuff that we already believe.

It is unfortunate that Marxism does not work, for it is truly a lovely fantasy. It ranks right up there with the perpetual motion machine and Yoko Ono being born a lesbian. It would make a great TV show. Both Marxism and capitalism hinge upon the desire to get a little bit more profit. No Progressive envisions a brave new world full of people who live worse than they do now. Progressives want some people to have more stuff and other people to have less stuff, and they want to accomplish this by hiring Robin Hood to collect taxes for the Sheriff of Nottingham. Capitalism too, is about the acquisition of more stuff; but it incorporates individual liberty into the pursuit of that stuff. Marxist ventures by contrast, place the individual's financial well-being in the hands of the same people who won't give you back your own tax return unless you can prove they've got it.

Material wealth, not spiritual growth, is the center of contemporary socialism. There is no such thing as a person who wants to convert to socialism for a reduction in pay. In practice here are only two types of socialists who live in capitalist countries: those who want to wield the power of government over others, and those who want the government to take somebody else's money and give it to them. To look at it another way, there are only socialists who are greedy for power and those who are greedy for wealth. Capitalism on the other hand, revolves around trade. Even if a capitalist is greedy, at the very least he must obtain wealth in voluntary exchange for a product or service. Capitalists each want what the other is offering more than they want what they are willing to trade. Socialists believe they have a right to your wealth simply because they weren't aborted.

A good portion of the health care debate focuses on the fact that the United States has the highest per capita rate of individuals paying for their own health care, and that we spend more of our GDP on health care than any other nation. These facts are spun as being a bad thing by those who rely on their popularity with the gullible for their livelihood. In reality we have more people spending their own money on their own health because a.) they can afford it, and b.) they do not want to wait around for the lousy health care that the government allocates to them. In 2009 one has to look no further than to the health care plans of our senior citizens to witness the efficacy of government health care. Without exception, seniors who have both Medicare and a private health care policy use Medicare for whatever it may cover, and then they use their private health insurance if they need something done correctly or in a timely manner. In other words, nobody who has a choice goes to the VA or the Health Department for health care, and they only depend upon Medicare if they are too poor to afford real (read *private*) insurance. Unfortunately having a choice in physicians costs money, and that is what Obamacare aims to ameliorate. Even more unfortunately, the Obama Administration has implemented legislation that forces every private portion of our health care system to become less like the Mayo Clinic, Duke University, Blue Cross/Blue Shield and more like the VA, the Health Department, Medicare and Medicaid. However, I concede that it is possible that those who passed Obamacare are not actually evil, but are simply too immersed in their 1% lifestyle to recognize how much they're screwing the rest of us.

For the time being it is difficult to imagine a shortage of necessities such as health care and SUVs in America. Impoverished Americans come to blows not over the scraps thrown out at a restaurant but over disposable toys while Christmas shopping. The definition of a poor American is not one who does not have the same redundancy in necessities as others, but rather who does not have the TV, shiny rims, and fashion clothing that others have. For most poor people in America, being poor is like being an unsupervised teenager living at home while the parents vacation in Washington DC. Most impoverished Americans have everything they need, none of an obscenely long list of things they want, and they sit around all day smoking cigarettes, eating fast food and watching TV with their friends. Those who are poor are neither superior nor inferior to any other American. Of the poor, those who are sane and poor are simply more comfortable with the security and certainty of a life of dependence upon the government over the uncertainty of seeking an education or the discomfort of summoning from within themselves the empathy and effort required to provide goods or services that others want.

My opinion of my opinion about why sane people remain poor in America is one of frustration. I don't really want to believe what I believe about poverty in America; but it's the same as the crappy reality that most decent Christians are only acting nice out of fear of going to hell. I can refute what the TV tells me, but I can't deny those who have presented themselves to me in flesh and blood on a daily basis for years on end.

Furthermore, American poverty is a conundrum because there is no inherent hierarchy under our form of government. American aristocracy is the hallucination of those who are materialistic. We are not born into one of the classes of noble peerage, non-peerage, gentleman and the-rest-of-us; and yet because of this I feel like there is somehow a Taoist-type hint of nobility in those who, in other times and places, were "poor" because they were born into the wrong echelon of some noble hierarchy. America has no nobility to justify the label of 'lower class'; and the impoverished in America do not define the other classes. Just as a person is not a criminal until they find truth in the label which flitters around their head like a moth, a person is not poor in America until they place their hope for economic change into somebody else's hands. Poverty in America is a choice, but it is such an absurdly difficult choice to those who are born into government dependency that it doesn't even seem like a choice. To tell a person who grew up in government housing to 'get a job' or 'get an education' makes about as much sense to them as telling them to flap their arms and fly. When you are born poor and raised by people who live off of government programs, you are not taught the certainty that you have something to offer society other than selling recreational drugs and providing job security for those behind the counter in the welfare office.

*   *   *

Before registering as a political candidate I daydreamed about being a representative of my district 1 people. I imagined spending every Saturday and Sunday standing outside the Wal-Marts of the Albemarle area asking people how they wanted to pay off the deficit and handing out business cards. If I were engaged in conversation I imagined that I would offer opinions on people's thoughts that were either rational and clear, or I would simply say that I didn't know. Sometimes people would disagree with me, sometimes they wouldn't, but I would make a solid case for my point of view and that was the important thing. There would be none of this nonsense of such-and-such legislation being good "because it helps folks out" or bad [because-it-doesn't-help-my-constituents]. I would give actual reasons for my stances, and I would use real-world examples and utilize as many disciplines as possible to back them up. I would cite both the social and economic costs and benefits of all legislation with primary importance being on the inalienable rights of Americans and economic sustainability of the bill, then on the ecosystems of America, then on our Allies, then on nice islands to visit, then on nations with exports that we want, then on nations with benevolent governments that have asked us for help, and on and on *ad nauseam* but without ever once considering the wants or needs of Cuba, North Korea, Iran, Syria, Sudan, Venezuela, Zimbabwe, Myanmar or any quasi dictatorship. I would provide statistical and historical evidence to support my moral judgment of a Bill being either "good" or "bad". I fantasized that I would change Congress by justifying my votes with actual reason instead of the traditional political turducken of emotions, anecdotes, and hypothetical horror stories. It's a radical idea, I know. But the challenge of a capitalist constitutional republic is that although everybody has an opinion, not everybody bothers backing it up with both knowledge and reality. There are few things that I enjoy as much as attempting to mesh my inflatable pink baby pool of knowledge with my Lake Mattamuskeet-sized corpus of opinions; and I get the impression that most reasonable people would rather hear a good argument than come up with one on their own. To that end I thought I would make a good representative of the people who made me who I am today.

By living in a capitalist society we can go our entire lives without knowing anything about how the world around us actually works. As long as we are physically capable of flipping a burger at the correct time, any one of us can live 75 years without ever knowing anything, including what makes the surface beneath the pattie hot, how our spatula came to exist, or why our hand moves and stops moving when we want it to. In a capitalist society we don't need to know anything except how to do our one little job because the rest of society does every other little job for us. In that way, capitalism is kind of like communism with the exceptions of capitalism actually working, and that it permits people to select (or not select) their own career paths. In capitalist America we don't need to know how to hunt, fish, or grow food. We also don't know that economics is about human wants, needs and abilities.

In a capitalist society one can survive while living a profoundly ignorant existence, so long as they have a specialty that they can perform for their fellow human beings. The problem is that there are a growing number of people who are either unable or unwilling to differentiate between capitalism and the stupidity that it permits to exist. These people, in the name of intelligence and progress, want to eliminate stupidity from society by eliminating capitalism. As if to emphasize the efficacy of capitalism at permitting stupid people to thrive, the opponents of capitalism always fail to grasp the irony of their only having an audience because capitalism, and the sloth that it enables, creates the largest market for entertainment of any social system in the world. In essence, the only reason that we have socialists is because capitalism provides them with enough economic security and leisure time to waste their lives whining about how we aren't living in utopia. Thus, in addition to permitting stupid people to overcome natural selection, capitalism periodically spits out people whose lives are so carefree and devoid of the need to understand human nature that they spend their lives in pious devotion to delivering their stereotype of humanity into their stereotype of socialist heaven.

As a representative to those of us who are so greedy

as to appreciate the profit that is left over at the end of our paychecks, EBT cards, or withdrawals from the husbank, I wanted to help people make the political distinctions that the economically spoiled among us have never had to make and consequently assert do not exist. Our nation is too big to ever be completely unified, but if good arguments are made we can deconstruct the fallacies that divide the individuals who make up the Republican and Democratic Parties. For starters, Americans are in absolutely desperate need of learning the difference between tax *rates* and tax *revenues*.

Tax rates and tax revenues are two completely different things. If placed right next to one another on a ledger, one can observe that tax rates and tax revenues do not share a 1:1 relationship. Please, *please* try to understand this very basic fact of government.

The easiest tax for everybody to observe is sales tax. Many voters believe that if you raised the sales tax rate from one cent per dollar to two cents per dollar that it would double sales tax revenues. It won't. It is an economic impossibility.

If you only have $2 to spend on lunch and you want to buy a burger and fries off the 99 cent menu at Wendy's, you will have enough money as long as the sales tax isn't over 1%. At a rate of 1% you can get your Jr. Bacon Chee and Biggie fries, and not have to deal with any cumbersome change rolling around in your pockets. The government gets its two cents, plus the percentage that it takes out of the Wendy's employees' paychecks that your meal helped pay for, plus the taxes that Wendy's paid for everything that it took to make your Jr. Bacon and Biggie fry possible.

If the sales tax doubles to 2%, and you still only have $2 to spend on lunch, it's no biggie. Literally, you don't get the Biggie fries and you walk out still kinda hungry with 99 cents clunking around in your pocket and a decreased risk of developing insulin resistance and hypertension. The government still collects its two cents from you, plus whatever contribution your 99 cent burger contributed toward the payroll tax and everything else, and you've been socially engineered into being a healthier, hungrier, crankier person.

Wendy's on the other hand is selling 50% less of its product. The corporation is only getting half as much of the money that you actually wanted to spend. If there are enough people in your situation who only have $2 to spend on lunch (as in during a recession), then Wendy's may end up losing so much money that they have to lay off an employee or two. Wendy's will also be paying less income tax due to decreased sales revenues. From here you can extrapolate the consequences of the laid-off person no longer paying into income tax either, and the laid off employee may even begin collecting unemployment benefits. Thus, by doubling sales tax *rates* the government has by no means doubled its tax *revenues*, and it increased its fiscal liabilities in the process. *Tax rates and tax revenues are not the same thing.* The question that politicians should ask-- emphasis on should-- is whether the additional revenues collected from those who are wealthy enough to not notice the increase in sales tax, are greater than the loss in income tax revenues from businesses and laid off employees, as well as the increase in entitlement spending that the government may incur from the laid off employees.

You're thinking that things would not happen like this, and you're right. I'm giving the worst-case scenario of a 1% sales tax increase for illustrative purposes, not as an economic theorem on the actual rates. Sometimes the consequences of raising tax rates are minimal. Sometimes the only people affected by a tax increase are poor people who have to watch every penny; but that is the consequence of all tax increases. *All tax increases diminish the buying power of the poor*, even those tax increases that are supposed to be levied against "the rich". Sales tax and payroll tax are intended to be specifically against the evil corporate 1%, but *every* corporate tax is paid for *by the customers*. Sales tax-- which is the epitome of a tax against a corporation because it taxes every single thing a corporation sells-- is paid for *by the customers*. Every corporate tax is paid for by the customers, but sales tax fits neatly onto a receipt. If corporate taxes were not paid for by consumers through the price of goods and services that they purchase, where else would the money that a corporation pays to Uncle Sam come from? The employees? The management? The infrastructure?

Any tax increase against a corporation will yield one of two results: it will either make the cost of the goods and services go up, or it will make the proletariat's paychecks smaller. The only way to keep a corporation from getting your money is to refrain from casting your pearls before capitalist swine. Thus, the government's favorite way of

64

punishing a corporation that does not make adequate (tax-deductible) campaign contributions is by making that corporation's products and services cost too much for people to purchase them.

*   *   *

From the time I was big enough to take out the trash I've been told the story of the first time my parents ever gave somebody a raise. We lived in 600 square foot bungalow on Garden St. in Elizabeth City. Our house had asbestos shingles and an oil heater that we could only afford to run a couple of times a year. Dad owned one rear-loader garbage truck which he drove himself, repaired himself, and paid for himself. Mom did the bills; as young as I was I dreaded bill day because I would have to lick the envelopes while my sister would lick the stamps. My parents had one employee, and he was even poorer than we were. His name was Richard Vincent. Richard couldn't read or write. He didn't even know his birthday, which made hiring him legally a real pain in the ass. Richard lived out in a rural area called Weeksville in a 400 square foot shack in the woods. It had a dirt floor and the roof leaked. Richard worked as hard as my dad. Neither of them ever got sick, they never complained, and they shared the load. My dad would drive the trash truck while Richard rode on the back bumper and picked up trash cans. When Richard got tired he and my dad would switch places and my dad would ride on the bumper while Richard drove.

After Richard had worked with my dad for a couple of years it became obvious that they were going to stay in business. My parents trimmed every bit of fat they could so that they could give Richard a raise. They wanted to surprise him with the raise so they didn't tell him about it, they just gave him his check from the accountant.

Richard did not have a car or a phone, so the next time my dad saw him was when he picked him up for work on Monday. Richard came to the truck but didn't get in. He wanted to know what he had done wrong. My dad didn't understand. Richard said that his check was smaller this week and he didn't understand why. Richard was illiterate but he knew how to count, and he was right: his paycheck *was* smaller. My dad explained that there must have been a mistake because he had been given a raise. As he climbed into the garbage truck, Richard was very animated in his insistence that my dad *never* give him another raise.

Checking with the accountant my parents found that by giving Richard a raise it had put him in a higher tax bracket, and the government had started taking more out of Richard's pay than he had received in his raise. The accountant explained that Richard would continue to take home less money unless he either worked more hours or got another raise. My dad took a pay cut to make sure Richard took home more money.

Small businesses employ the vast majority of America's workforce. Most small business owners are like my dad and want to take care of their good employees. But it is unethical for any business owner to take a pay cut when a politician is the one who is raising the expense of operation. To take a pay cut due to higher taxes is to condone the fiscal irresponsibility of the United States government which borrows money in somebody else's name, does not earn a single dollar that it takes in, and is unable to make ends meet with the most exorbitant budget in the history of the known universe.

To be Yourself or Not to be Yourself

I would like to confirm your suspicion that I don't write books for a living. I'm an ambulance driver. It's not Hemmingwayesque either.

At the time that I was running for Congress I was working as a paramedic for a hospital in New Bern, NC. The commute from Kill Devil Hills to New Bern was two hours and forty five minutes one way. I made the drive because the hospital was an outstanding place to do EMS, and the educational opportunity for our kids was better in Dare County than anything else available to us. Fortunately my scheduling goddess at the hospital always put me on for three or four days in a row so that I could spend half the week at work and the other half at home with my family. My off hours from the hospital were spent either staying with my mom in Washington, NC or drinking microbrews by a campfire at my friend Jason's house. Usually I did the latter. That's right, I'm neither a politician nor a writer; I'm an EMT who lives part time with his mum and thinks fire is fun.

After I registered as a candidate for the 2010 election, people started behaving differently around me. Suddenly when I entered a room I could command everyone's attention by saying "I'm running for Congress". Granted, half of the people in the room would scoff, but that was more attention than I used to get. Before signing up to be a politician the only time anybody took interest in me was when I showed up with an ambulance full of narcotics.

Being the self-conscious person I am I was skeptical of my newfound popularity/unpopularity. The part of me shaped by having the crap beaten out of me by my parents pushed me to seek approval, whereas the experience of getting my ass beaten on the bus every day screamed for me to tell everybody to fuck off. Of course the only thing worse than having your ass beaten is being threatened with jail, poverty, and/or hell by politicians, pastors, and anybody with access to a lawyer. At least ass beatings eventually end, whereas the only escape from a society that looks down on you for being white trash is to become self-sufficient. Self-sufficiency (and being white trash) is at odds with being a politician. To be a politician is to promise to make people's lives better. To be a politician is to make people dependent upon you for a better life. But like all white trash I already had a dog. I didn't want a bunch of people following me around waiting for me to toss them some cheese too.

So within me arose the age-old question of should a politician always vote at his party's call or should he do what he, personally, thinks is right? Should I be a whore or a general? You can trust a whore to do what you want, which is why all successful politicians are essentially practicing the white-collar version of the world's oldest profession. Politicians who are actual leaders are few and far between. I guess in a perfect republic there would be no difference between the will of the mob and the will of the mob's representative; but what I think and what the people around me think are a myriad of different things. Right now for example, you might be thinking that the proper way to use that word is "are myriad different things". I wish our political differences were so intellectual.

Here's the greatest problem in American society as I see it: most voters use mass media as a gauge of the quality of their lives. Too many voters do not understand that mass media is not reality. Mass media is a product that is packaged and marketed for mass consumption.

All mass media has a sponsor. If a media endeavor is sponsored by capitalist endeavors then it will tell the consumer what it wants to hear and suggest that the solutions to the problems that it depicts lie in the purchase of goods and services. If the media is sponsored by the government, solutions will be implied to be political in nature. Nowhere in mass media will you find a suggestion to go out and make your own life better or to go out and make somebody else's life better, because that would decrease the amount of time you spend sitting on the couch "learning" who should take care of the problems you just learned about.

While the American voters' favorite medium for the consumption of ideology is unquestionably television, one does not have to own a major appliance to suck from the teat of American falseness. The entirety of American society is one big series of lies; and while the incredible falseness of TV may not be obvious to the average person who has watched it from infancy, almost anybody can recognize the falseness of the nightmare known as middle school.

Middle school is tough. In addition to the daily ass beatings one has to deal with hormones causing every organ in the body to behave weirdly as one attempts to find their niche in society. As hominids we have hundreds of thousands of years of natural selection pushing pubescent females toward mate selection, staring at shiny objects and rearing young; and pubescent males toward ejaculating, staring at shiny objects and burning things. Modern society has molded these predispositions into unnatural social roles and, of course, the fragrance industry.

While teenage hormones scream for the body to engage in reproduction, modern society presents a stern disapproval of teen sex and condemns teen pregnancy. The first big personal choice that we have to make as young adults is whether or not to be true to ourselves and pursue the direction that our hormones point us, or conform to society by projecting an image of chastity. Many of us chose a middle path as a solution to this dilemma: we decided that when we were around our friends we would pretend that we were sexually aware by behaving with the coolness that we believed a sexually active person would exhibit. Then, when we were around our parents or other authority figures, we turned off the image of sexual awareness and substituted it with pretending that we didn't think about sex at all. Basically, puberty is a lie-lie situation that only becomes comfortable when we accept the fact that lying about sex isn't just normal, it's central to American society.

Depicting any act involving the epithelia proximal the reproductive organs is considered vulgar in America. In case you're a middle class dolt and don't know any better, the word *vulgar* means "unrefined" or "characterized by a lack of good breeding. In other words, being candid about sex, *i.e.* being vulgar, is what lower-class, *sincere* people do. In America, lying about the existence of sexuality is what separates society people from the hicks and Latinos. But an asexual society is an extinct society, and thus the powers that be have found ways of legitimizing sexual congress by forcing people to engage in the rite of marriage. Conceding to the act of marriage exemplifies one's desire to be accepted by society, or (in my case), a complete lack of awareness that any change which arises from a ceremonial rite of passage is completely within one's mind and does not change your relationship with the person who endures the ceremony with you. Men who refuse to concede to marriage are left to struggle with the taboo of masturbation, which is only looked down upon by society because it exemplifies the power of the individual to do something for themselves without the input of the community.

Another social lie that our pubescent citizens must select is what to be when they grow up. For women the role of mother and homemaker, changed though it is, is not a terribly tremendous stretch from its roots in human history. However, American society regards the role of 'stay at home mom' to be anything from novel to oppressive. When contemplating their futures teenage girls are confronted with the dilemma of deciding not what they want to be, but whom they want to please. Should they please their parents or their teachers? Should they please their church, their friends, or the lesbians down the street? Should they follow in the footsteps of the two dimensional images that they see on TV and in the movies? As negative as this depiction is, we know that the worst path that any young person can take is to pursue happiness in its purest form by doing absolutely nothing-- not planning anything-- and thereby leaving their future to be determined entirely by other events.

In industrialized nations the traditional role of men as familial providers of food and protection is gone. The difficult and life-threatening labor of forging barriers against the elements and procuring sustenance for one's family has been replaced by paychecks and the metaphor "breadwinner". Masculinity is no longer measured by one's ability to be the master of their environment, for "the environment" is now nothing more than a couple of channels on TV and a website to which you make tax-deductible donations. Masculinity in industrialized nations is measured by how much money you make. It is no longer called "masculinity" either, it is called "success". Industrialized success is quantified in the asexual units of capital; but since wealth only purchases pleasures that are evanescent, one who pursues success for the approval of society finds that their endeavors put them at odds with their pursuit of happiness. I am not going to pretend to know enough about genetics to assert that there isn't a gene that makes people want to hurry up and get to work, but I can surmise that since the late 18th century when the industrial revolution began, *H. sapiens* has not sustained enough genetic drift to substitute the selective advantage of finding gratification in scavenging, agriculture and child-rearing with the warm fuzzy of making your boss happy in exchange for a paycheck. As evidence of this, I submit that while stay at home moms and dads are relatively happy, most professional women and men are neck in neck in the race to see who can be the first to retire comfortably.

Perhaps the innocence of childhood ends when a person learns that of all the words in the English language the one that crashes farthest from the Platonic ideal is *family*. The very heart of an individual's identity is that of blood; a prospect which the sages know to be the most widely embraced lie there is. Extrapolate this unfortunate fact to reveal that the familial ideal is the greatest influence on one's social perspective, and we can see the dark swaths that outline the common motivation of both the Progressives and Christian conservatives. Those who cannot find fault in themselves beyond their guilt by association with the flawed familial ideal cannot improve society by improving themselves, and thus they must satiate their desire to live purposefully by improving everyone else through the social engineering of Progressivism or of conservative Christianity.

The falseness of society is further enforced by fashion. Fashion only serves two functions: to distort the reality of normal bodily imperfection and to reinforce social hierarchy via pricing. Fashion makes muscles look firm, outlines look smooth, liberal arts majors look tough, slackers look professional, the religious look respectable, and bodily proportions look unrealistic to the point of absurdity. It makes boring people look interesting and nonconformists look unique. Fashion is nothing but a fun lie to yourself and everyone around you. And while it may be fun to reaffirm the status quo by pretending to be more of what society considers to be attractive, educated, important or independent, there is nothing funny about the pricing of fashion. Fashion is priced for no other reason than to reinforce industrialized society's status quo of wealth equating to worth. A prime example of this is the importance that is placed upon the authenticity of fashion items which, to the consumer, are identical except for price. Indeed, those who feel that their social status should never be in question would never settle for anything bearing the label *Prada*, regardless of quality and appearance, unless its authenticity as an upper-class item is exemplified by its costing hundreds of times more than it's worth. Society has even attempted to redefine value by labeling the act of copying designer fashion items to be "counterfeiting", as if the people who buy knock-offs of Gucci sunglasses for pennies on the dollar would in some parallel universe be dumb enough to pay full price for them if they had no choice.

The falseness of society extends into grooming, for grooming is performed in order to gain consideration from society. Whether you curl your hair to be acceptable at cotillion or grow dreadlocks to distinguish yourself from the debutantes, you are doing it for yourself in relation to society. Those who are most affected by the status quo may adopt the identity of non-conformist. Non-conformists are so dedicated to their belief in the status quo as being something concrete, permanent, and beyond their control that they genuinely believe that by grooming themselves into one of the nonconformist fashions that they are doing it for themselves as individuals, when they are clearly doing it in response to-- and therefore for the edification of-- society. It is the self-discipline-- the masochism if you will-- of adherence to the art of being a nonconformist which illustrates how being a nonconformist is no different than being a conformist. Both conformists and nonconformists are dedicated, vigilant, and hyper-social individuals who seek out group identities. It doesn't matter whether you poke studs through your face or your tie, you are voluntarily taking on discomfort, sacrifice, and discipline in response to your belief that social class is a living, breathing thing that exists outside of your mind. If what you are doing involves your appearance, you are doing it not only out of empathy for those who have to look at you, but you are also engaging in projection of your thoughts about what you see in the mirror onto what you stereotype as society in general.

As educated people it is important to make the distinction between doing something as a member of society and doing something as an individual. Our double identities as individuals vs. members of society starts at puberty and goes downhill from there. Most people give no thought to the practice of nobly flattering their superiors with fashion and grooming one moment and flattering themselves the next, scoffing 'thank Ford I'm not an Alpha'. But even though we may not be actively aware of the schizoid mentality of the individuals who make up society, there are indications that we possess what Hegel called *ethical consciousness*. White America may not realize that it has a "home face" and a "work face", but it does know right and wrong. To personify its ethics Americans adopt heroes such as *Harry Potter*, the *X-men* and Jesus. These heroes struggle to reconcile their lower-class human halves with the sides of themselves that possess the "upper class" qualities of physical, spiritual and intellectual superiority, and they are pitted against all manner of evil entities. Even reality TV has tapped into the lucrative premise of the bifurcated hero (or *Idol*) by promising to elevate regular people to the status of celebrity in exchange for rights to the fruits of their otherwise unrealized talents.

As always, pop culture has not discovered anything new. In the 1880's Robert Louis Stevenson depicted the duality of man in his classic *Strange Case of Dr. Jekyll and Mr. Hyde*. As our generation is more likely to know from the Looney Tunes film *Hyde and Hare*, a good doctor transforms himself into a monster by drinking a potion. The part of the story that we don't glean from Bugs Bunny is that in the original text Dr. Jekyll's face does not change when it becomes Hyde. Somehow, as if by a trick by the observer's eyes, the face of Dr. Jekyll becomes inexplicably hideous as he transforms into Mr. Hyde. Other characteristics of Hyde that one would not like to find in the mirror include his being substantially shorter than Jekyll, Hyde has no manners, he does exactly as he wishes and in fact he is the personification of all of the vulgar and evil impulses that Dr. Jekyll suppresses in order to maintain his place in society. Hyde lies or tells the truth as it serves him best, but perhaps the most obvious literary indication of his transformation to lower status is the change from *Dr.* to *Mr.*

Although Dr. Jekyll is of high social standing and is regarded as a benefit to his countrymen, he struggles with his desire to pursue human pleasures. Jekyll intended his potion to separate the impulsive, pleasure-seeking, lower-class portion of himself from the upper-class, studious, hard-working man of culture and breeding that he was known to be. Ultimately his concoction delivered the untoward effect of causing Hyde to emerge long after the potion was presumed to have worn off. With the feeling of liberation that accompanied his transformation into a low-class, sincere human animal, Jekyll found himself drawn toward the potion, with his only reservations being for the intolerably violent acts that Hyde committed. For a time Jekyll is able to quell Hyde by performing acts that are deemed meritorious by society, but as soon as he becomes vain about his behavior he transforms back into Hyde.

Jekyll and Hyde was written when the British Empire

was making every effort to insure that the sun never set on it. British parliament was meddling with economic forces that it did not understand and was financially crushing anybody who was not of noble stature. At the same time the entirety of the West was exchanging its fig leaves for bank notes as it ate from the tree of industrialization, and watched impotently as the industries it built tamed the world far more effectively than colonization. Our government, envious of the efficacy of business at conquering foreign powers with goods and services, divided itself into Democrats and Republicans and has ever since spent their terms quarrelling over who gets to wield power over the shareholders of America.

Today journalists gauge a leader's executive ability by his accent and the crease in the leg of his pants, and nobody can seem to come up with a solid figure on how much unemployment has to rise before anti-unemployment legislation is considered a failure. Furthermore, unemployment in America no longer means that there are no jobs available; it means there are no jobs available that you like. The pursuit of happiness has been politically interpreted to mean the pursuit of wealth, and wealth is primarily used to purchase technology that is not only misunderstood by those who purchase it, but is impossible to construct or repair with human hands. Westerners are living the epitome of civilization and it is disempowering and frightening, but the thing that is most troubling to the masses is that civilization just doesn't seem to be worth the effort. Armed forces are regarded as a drain on the federal budget. Police officers are the enemy of society. The goal of education is homogeny rather than diversity, one's health is no longer worth the money, effort, or knowledge, and liberty is quantified by how dependent one is upon the government.

The desire to hide the ugly human characteristics of ignorance, violence, impulsiveness and sloth is possibly even greater today than it was during Stevenson's time, and thus Jekyll's potion is the perfect metaphor for contemporary Progressive ideology. Every Progressive tincture of legislation that is intended to sequester the dark hearts of society produces the same results: exacerbation of the problem, the allocation of money to quell the victims, philanthropic efforts to add legitimacy to chronic failure, and the eventual deterioration of everything into a state that is worse than before.

The preceding dissertation was, of course, complete and utter carp. Only a sheltered, privileged academician would consider literature to be a useful medium for critiquing public policy. If you truly want to understand how ignorant the Obama Administration is about human nature, take business and economics classes and then attempt provide your countrymen with goods and services that they value enough to actually pay for. If that much reality doesn't cure your fiscal progressiveness, take the leap and try to hire somebody to help you do it.

The beliefs that jobs are as rewarding as child-rearing, that society is asexual, and that fashion and grooming are indicative of an individual's intrinsic worth are all socially acceptable prevarications. But the lie that is the most detrimental to American society is the identification of political parties as anything other than social fraternities. The Democratic and Republican Parties, in spite of their origins, exist merely as parasites on our universal suffrage. The majority of political issues are not issues at all; but are rather the contrived, emotional obsessions of the fringes of society. The so-called talking points that saturate mass media are repeated until the consumer of mass knowledge believes that things such as skin shape, color, and the friction thereof are somehow of national importance. The assault continues until the bored and lissome do-nothings of America choose to assume the identities of social engineers by brandishing credit cards in the name of whichever political party makes them feel more important. But it isn't the American political partisans who are the inexcusable liars of our society, for they are merely lying to themselves. Chanting *Yes-We-Can, Yes-We-Can, Yes-We-Can* genuinely makes Democrats feel as good about themselves as Republicans when they sing *Our God is an Awesome God*. The truly selfish and malevolent scumbags of the political parties are those who sell false faith to the gullible in return for capital in the form of tax revenues, tax deductions, and tax credits. The road to hell is paved with taxes, and those who clothe themselves in tax revenues are the lobbyists, political strategists, and the politicians themselves.

The Problems with Universal Suffrage

The only thing that I am sure that I have in common with the rest of humanity is that I'm a primate. As primates we are genetically predisposed to viewing our environment and the creatures within it as being here for our exploitation. Sometimes I wonder why I even bother trying to fight this predisposition when everybody else seems to be embracing their inner selfishness.

Homo sapiens is genetically programmed with communal instincts similar to *Pan troglodytes*, guinea pigs and dogs. When our species hunted and gathered, lived in caves, and died at age 35 we shared stuff with one another because it was advantageous to the survival of our species. In essence, the Stone Age was the heyday of communism because there were no rich people to envy and because the lazy people could be kicked out into the rain to fend for themselves. It was not until humans began to grow crops and trade their harvests with one another that we evolved out of communism and toward civilization. Trade forces the parasitic urges of humanity into a symbiotic relationship in which both parties either benefit from their exchange or are free to walk away from it.

It was the mutual benefit of free trade that led to the expansion of wealth and the development of cities. Cities are the centers of civilization and culture for a nation, and it follows that since free trade built great cities that it would also build great nations. But there is a tremendous difference between a great city and a fair city, just as there is a difference between a city and a kingdom; and the founding fathers believed that the difference lay not in the faith of the wisdom and fairness of a good king, but in suffrage. With suffrage arises the dangers of mob-rule democracy and political greed, and thus was developed the republican form of democracy. Between the wealth-building of free trade and the fairness of republican suffrage it was the hope of the founding fathers that if Americans were guaranteed certain inalienable rights in their pursuit of happiness that they . . . *we* would choose to utilize those rights to help ourselves walk away from our primitive predispositions toward opportunistic exploitation, selfishness, and stealing, and instead choose to pursue lives of self-determination, cooperation and trade.

As it turns out there is an inherent danger in universal suffrage. Universal suffrage dictates that in order for a politician to get elected he cannot appeal to the individual voter's sense of fairness. Fairness as it is defined by the artificial life in the marketplace is vastly different from fairness as it is programmed into the hunting, scavenging, exploitative primate DNA of *H. sapiens*. To the human primate, fairness does not mean exchanging something you want less for something you want more, it means never having to choose between the two in the first place. To the inherently exploitative human animal, fairness means being given that which you envy another for having, like a fish, or a potato, or a mortgage. To the human parasite fairness does not mean equal rights, it means equal toys. The social engineers of the west capitalize on the understanding that human parasites look upon suffrage as being free in a financial rather than a libertarian sense, and thus the voters can easily be persuaded to exchange their free vote for the promise that once in charge of legislation and the treasury 'their man' will use his power to implement fairness in the ultimate primate sense: by taking wealth from the minority that is hated by the greatest common denominator and calling it democracy. The resilience of Marxist ideology in politics is proof that we have not evolved beyond being a bunch of monkeys trapped with our fists clenched furiously inside coconuts filled with other people's rice.

The peculiarities of government became too much for me to tolerate when President Bush (with *TARP*) and then President Obama (*Stimulus*, *Obamacare* & the continuation of *TARP*) both dictated that I was going to have to start paying the way for those who had chosen to remain ignorant about how to survive on more money than 99.999% of the rest of the people in the world ever see. For my entire life I'd regarded parables about the downtrodden rising to become the masters of their own destiny as something positive, triumphant, glorious. There are no parables about what happens when free people choose to sacrifice liberty for insurance, use republican democracy to enslave the 47% who were minding their own business, and who justify their actions by calling their ideology a moral absolute that is 'for the good of society'. Maybe in 1000 years there will be a new shining city on a hill, only this one will harbor within its common values a parable that outlines the stupidity of a population that uses universal suffrage to make themselves dependent upon, and inferior to, the government. Maybe this parable will be called *The Gift of the Me Generation.*

I registered as a candidate in February 2010. I've always been a slow learner, but this time it felt like I'd waited until our nation was entering stage-four cancer before I even realized that something wasn't right.

As soon as I registered as a candidate for Congress I also realized that I had a problem. I'd been an introvert ever since my dad died. I suspect that being a kid with a dead father is kind of like being black in that suddenly every person who wants to be compassionate shows up to help you deal with whatever problems they stereotype you as having, and every person who isn't compassionate arrives to push you around and take advantage of you. Of the variety of ways that an eleven year old might address this phenomenon, I ended up making friends with the small number of people who didn't treat me like I was some sort of walking, public-access self-esteem booster. Making friends slowly became a habit, and now years later the fact that I only had a handful of close friends had turned around to bite me in the ass. Stupid *quality* friends. I knew I should have gone for *quantity!* Furthermore, of that handful a good portion of my friends were liberals. I knew my liberal friends loved me, but I also knew that there was no way in hell that they would ever vote for a Republican. The good news was that they probably wouldn't vote against me either, but it wasn't like I was going to undermine Butterfield's campaign with a half a dozen friends omitting the "Representative, Congressional District 1" line on their straight-ticket Democrat ballot. I needed to do some serious networking. But the problem remained: I am still an introvert.

One would think that a decade of college would yield an extensive social network. Most people only get to buy alcohol for the lower classmen for one year; whereas I had seven years of experience helping people fight the system. One could also assume that since I hadn't actually achieved good grades that I must have been a rather fun person to be around in college. Maybe I was, I don't know. I was depressed through most of my 20's but I was vigilant about not taking it out on anybody else. On the occasions that I drank enough to laugh I don't really know if everybody was laughing with me, at me, or at all. I played rugby at UNCW before I started drinking, so I was not very much fun then. I pledged and entered Kappa Sigma fraternity in my eighth year of college, but my short time with the fraternity was marked by my being a less than outstanding brother. There was however, one organization that I truly loved and considered my own: UNC-Wilmington. I cherish my days at UNCW. I met Kelli there. It's beautiful. Although my grades didn't reflect it I actually learned a lot. And during the decade that I attended UNCW it was small enough that the professors were all friendly, accessible, and willing to help you take your education as far as you wanted it to go.

UNCW has a semi-annual publication for alumni called *UNCW Magazine*. In it can be found all of the things that make you miss your youth and take pride in your *alma mater*. Near the back of *UNCW Magazine* is a section called *Alumnotes. Alumnotes* is a venue for Seahawk grads to write in and toot their own horns about their social and professional accomplishments. Kelli and I had just received the fall 2009 edition of *UNCW Magazine* at our home. In addition to finding that our fellow Seahawks were coupling up like hydrogens in a vacuum and reproducing like MRSA in a nursing home, we were pleased to hear that a young woman with whom I took Aikido had been accepted into an environmental journalism program in Colorado. We also learned that my old roommate had joined a dot-com association of drunk driving defense attorneys. And, some dude we'd never heard of was pursuing a master's degree in liberal studies at UNCW. This last alumnote was particularly good news because it indicated that the editors of *UNCW Magazine* would publish pretty much anything. Running for Congress had to be worthy of print. I emailed a formal announcement of my candidacy to both the alumni association and to *UNCW Magazine*.

I received no response.

I tried a second time with *UNCW Magazine*. I never even got a notification that my email had been received. Maybe I should have mentioned that in addition to my running for Congress that Kelli had recently won a free hash browns playing McDonalds Monopoly. Eventually the alumni association did send me a survey and a request for money, but I never received even one "good luck", "no thank you", or "piss off Republican" about my running for office. Well actually I guess I did kind of get the last one. When I sat down and thought about it, the only thing that a drunk driving defense attorney, an environmental journalist, and liberal arts master's student have in common is that they would never vote for a Republican.

But no matter. I knew that UNCW was full of Republican haters, but that didn't mean that they hated *me* me. Truth be told I wasn't all that sure that I liked Republican-me yet either. The important thing was that I still loved them. Furthermore, I was technically still a Kappa Sigma. Kappa Sig had a quarterly publication called *The Caduceus* and the winter 2009 issue had none other than brother Bob Dole on the cover. I'm pretty sure I wasn't as Republican as Bob Dole; honestly I probably wasn't even as Republican as John McCain. But if there was one thing I knew about fraternities it was that they celebrate people in positions of power, and running for Congress was like entering the Powerball lottery. I paged through *The Caduceus* to see what accomplishments my chapter had pulled off. During my single academic year in Kappa Sigma my chapter produced an academic scholarship for a sorority, auctioned off brothers for charity, cleaned our adopted highway, did fundraising for *Relay for Life*, and all sorts of other admittedly corny but nonetheless philanthropic stuff. Eleven years later my Mu Zetas had the distinction of being recognized in *The Caduceus* for having three brothers participate in a local surfing contest and placing first, third and fourth. I had to hand it to the brothers of the new millennium: whereas surfing at UNCW had landed me on academic suspension it had granted them national recognition. Still, I figured that fourth place was the absolute worst that I could do in the primary election, and the stakes for fixing the federal budget were a lot higher than anybody's ability to annihilate a steep, glassy bowl. I figured I was a shoe-in for mention in *The Caduceus*.

Apparently I should have gone to a few more keggers because I received the same treatment from the brothers in Charlottesville as I did from *UNCW Magazine*.

My setbacks were not confined to my lack of college networking. I also screwed up on my candidacy registration by giving my home phone number rather than my cell number. Our home phone line serves the single purpose of . . . actually it doesn't serve a purpose. We only got it because it came with the package for wireless Internet. There's not even a phone attached to it. But, being a somewhat paranoid person I figured that there needed to be continuity between my phone number and my home address on the candidate registration form. As it turns out, when you register as a candidate for public office you can put down whatever address and phone number you want because this is the information will be used by the stalkers of politicians. I gave an address that was a whole sixty miles outside of the district in which I was running and a number to a phone that never rang. I discovered my mistake by reading the newspaper.

Before we moved to Kill Devil Hills we lived in Washington, NC. My mother moved into our house in Washington after we left, and we kept most of the things-- such as the newspaper-- continuing in our name. The newspaper to which we had a subscription was called the *Washington Daily News* (*WDN*); it is the most commonly read paper in Washington. During the fourth week of February I received my copy of the *WDN* and it carried an article entitled *Four Running in District 1 GOP Primary*. Here are the Cliffs Notes, starting with the first sentence of the article and ending with the last:

> *Washington Republican Ashley Woolard will have to defeat three GOP challengers in the May 4 primary election if he wants to take on incumbent U.S. Rep. G.K. Butterfield, D-N.C.*

> *Woolard apparently has one distinct advantage in this competition: his camp has raised $36,084.20, well outstripping his GOP challengers, who haven't raised enough money to file reports with the Federal Election Commission.*

> *Woolard said he doesn't know the other three candidates in the district.*

> *In a recent interview, Butterfield said he hasn't met any of his potential rivals for the District 1 seat. He said he has done some research on Woolard.*

"He seems to be a very intelligent, well-respected citizen of Beaufort County", Butterfield told the Daily News. "Helps run a family business and, apparently, he is well-respected in his community. And I look forward to meeting him one day. I think (Woolard) is very capable of debating the issues with me."

Regarding yours truly the article read: "Miller could not be reached for comment." I was beginning to feel like I was all three stooges up in this election thingey. I quickly typed a letter to the editor of the *WDN*:

Hello,

I just read your article *Four Running in District 1 GOP Primary*. Thank you for attempting to reach me and I apologize for being so difficult to find. I would like to provide you with my contact information and give you a brief summary of myself.

I live in Kill Devil Hills, NC but work as a Paramedic in New Bern. I stay at my mother's house in Washington at least once a week for work. My wife and I only lived in Washington for eight years, but it is the longest that either of us have ever lived in one place. Washington is where our children learned to walk and swim. They went to Emmanuel Christian School. My wife and I purchased a house together on East Main St. and my mother moved to Washington to be around the grandchildren as they grew up. My mother still lives in Washington.

I became interested in public service after taking a class in Writing Public Policy in graduate school at ECU. I became frustrated that all of the other students just assumed that they would raise taxes to pay for the policies that they penned. More and more I find that no politician knows what it is like to run a small business or even to function within a budget. I don't know why politicians are not held accountable for their inability to function with the world's largest budget, but it has to stop. Like many taxpayers, I put up with things until I can no longer put up with them, and then I act. This time I am acting by running for Congress so that maybe in 2011 there will be at least one regular person writing legislation for the rest of the regular people.

Feel free to contact me if you have any questions. I would be glad to come meet with you on one of my days off and answer whatever questions you may have.

One further point-- I do not intend to put much effort into fundraising for the primary election. I am a Paramedic with a Paramedic's salary, and if I am going to win this election it will to have to be with intellect and ideas. I just need help getting the word out; so again, if there are any questions that I can answer for you, please let me know.

Sincerely,
Jim Miller

I received no response. I was beginning to wonder

if my email was actually hooked up to the Interweb. I sent a follow-up email:

Hello,

Two days ago I responded to an article which was written about Ashley Woolard's campaign: http://www.wdnweb.com/articles/2010/02/24/news/doc4b846ee9e8c57330395789.txt

I am a Paramedic and I do not make a lot of money. I am depending heavily upon the media to report my views and my faith in people to educate themselves before they make a decision. I know that I am going to lose to Ashley, but the important thing is that people at least have an opportunity to vote for a candidate who, like themselves, is middle class and not socially connected. If you are not going to print what I send to you, will you please take a moment to tell me so?

I'm so upbeat and positive. Why was I trying to be a politician? This time I got a response from *WDN* person-of-importance Mike Voss:

Dear Mr. Miller,

The Washington Daily News does not publish articles and/or press releases submitted by candidates. If the newspaper did so, we would have to allow each candidate the opportunity to do so. The newspaper does not have the space to let that occur. The newspaper will cover the races in its area as it has done in the past. Candidates tend to be biased about themselves and are not always objective when it comes their campaigns.

The newspaper also has a policy of not publishing letters to the editor from candidates or their supporters during the campaign season because candidates and their supporters tend to flood the newspaper with "form letters" that repeat the same information over and over.

As the newspaper begins to do stories about the different races and candidates, it will be in contact with the candidates to get their views on specific issues.

In other words, the Daily News *determines how it will cover the races, not the candidates or their supporters.*

It is not the newspaper's duty to help promote your campaign.

Tangent alert!

When my sister was little she was a horse nut. It was the 70's and in rural America boys were supposed to like cars and girls were supposed to like horses. I was a year older than my sister and I wasn't interested in cars. For as long as I could remember my dad had been covered in brown and black car-grease. Judging by the number of swear words that my dad grumbled beneath his breath as he fixed everything from street sweepers to school busses to Volkswagens, I had difficulty looking at cars as being anything more than a tool that required other tools. However, my lack of normal male enchantment with motorized vehicles was more than compensated for by my sister's affinity for horses.

My sister's love for all-things-horse was common

knowledge throughout both sides of our family, and every birthday she would acquire more plastic horses (model horses? horse *dolls*?). By the time my sister was eight years old she had amassed a herd of polypropylene steeds with representatives of every major paint job, as well as accessories and fencing which with to pacify them. She had the Alabaster Rearing Stallion. She had the Old Timer with Hat. She had a Buckskin and a Palomino and a Paint. Each horse not only had a name but a gender and personality as well. And when all the horses were sleeping in their stables under her bed, my sister had a stack of *Horse and Rider* magazines to study and reference.

On Saturday mornings my little blond sister would pop up bright and early and break out all of her horses for a horse fiesta. Sometimes the fiesta was a horse show, sometimes it was a rodeo, and sometimes it would be a long and exhausting drama. The crisis of the Saturday morning horse drama usually involved one horse kicking another; followed by the remaining horses trying to figure out what to do about it, complicated by the occasional revelation that members of the horse-jury were sneaking out and cantering with the "bad" horse and so on. An interesting element to my sister's horse play was that size did not matter. I would come into her room to see what was up and be surprised to learn that the little, two-inch farm horse had somehow taken first in the barrel race, beating out both the substantially larger Quarter Horse as well as the spirited Arabian; or that the entire herd was being effectively confined by a fence that only came up to most of the horses' ankles. I confess that we lived in a small house and I would, occasionally, get sucked into these ridiculous rituals.

One Saturday my little sister's new issue of *Horse and Rider* arrived. The horse show was put on hold while she pored over the glossy pages full of tack and critters and whatnot. After a relatively long period of silence as my sister examined the latest in bedazzled halters or whatever, there was suddenly the sound of little feet running through the house. Then I heard my sister ask my mother for a stamp. This was followed by some discussion that I unsuccessfully attempted to listen in on, followed by more industriousness from my sister that did not seem to involve any of the usual horse-related activities. That day passed and I forgot about it for a couple of weeks.

About a month after she'd asked for a stamp, my sister received a letter from none other than the estate of Kenny Rogers. My baby sister, whom I secretly loved to see excited even though I would never admit it, was ecstatic. She ran into her room with the letter and I heard the sound of an envelope tearing. There was a deep silence, followed momentarily by the most horrible crying you can imagine. My mother came running. I listened intently by my door. In the last issue of *Horse and Rider* there had been an entry form for a drawing to win a horse that belonged to none other than Kenny Rogers. My sister filled out the entry form all by herself, addressed the envelope and mailed it. She wanted to win a horse so badly that in the envelope containing the entry form my little sister had enclosed her life savings (which was around 62 cents) and a note addressed to Mr. Rogers stating something to the effect of

96

"Please don't lose my entry form because I really want to win a horse. Your Friend, Mary." I don't know what the letter from Kenny Rogers said exactly (I tried to find out but it had been immediately torn into a million, tear-stained pieces), but what I gathered from Mom was that Kenny's posse had very rudely informed my eight-year-old sister that they did not accept bribes, that she was disqualified from the drawing for being a briber, that she was a criminal, that Mr. Rogers blows .45 caliber holes in criminals, that she should go to prison, that her horse collection was stupid, that English riding was for sissies, that she was a sissy, that blondes do not, in fact, have more fun, and that she was never allowed to listen to any Kenny Rogers songs again. I do not know the degree to which my eight-year old sister's reprimand at the hands of the Rogers' gang was exaggerated, but I can say with certainty that my sister has adhered tightly to the not-listening to Kenny Rogers part. To this day Kenny Rogers is not even mentioned jokingly to my sister unless you want to have the Skoal slapped out of your mouth.

How my sister felt about being disqualified from the Kenny Rogers horse drawing in 1979 was exactly how I felt about Mike Voss and his excuse for the *Washington Daily News* being obtuse. It was as if Mr. Voss, who had co-authored a series of Pulitzer Prize winning articles about the danger of drinking the water in Washington (yes, seriously), was blind to the obvious bias of the article. But what was the *WDN* to do, exactly? Post an amendment to their article stating 'as it turns out, Jim Miller can be found seven blocks from our office-- he's one of our customers.'

There was no way that a Pulitzer Prize winning publication would simultaneously look like they don't know their own customers *and* undermine their campaign for the local favorite. Just like my little sister and the Kenny Rogers horse drawing, I was screwed. I decided to do what any rational, nonconformist, semi-carpetbagger would do and made my ostracision from the *WDN* official. I zapped back a final email:

Thank you for your reply.

In the future I expect that you will not be portraying Ashley Woolard as the protagonist of any more news articles as you did in this one: [http://www.wdnweb.com/2010/02/24/four-running-in-district-1-gop-primary/]

Unfortunately this was only the beginning of the setbacks that lay in store for me. It was apparent that I was not going to get anywhere with the media in Beaufort County, but it also looked as if everybody who actually cared about the primary had already selected a candidate. Being on a very small budget what I needed was some guerilla advertising in order to get the word out. I decided that I would personally email people around the district and attempt to pollute their stream of consciousness with the dioxin of my political presence. I also decided to have decals printed up and to plaster them everywhere throughout the surrounding counties. The third tine of my trident in the side of obscurity consisted of writing a blurb about myself on Wikipedia and including a link to my free Google website; that way if somebody performed a Google search for 'Jim Miller the politician' there was a better chance of them finding something other than information about Jim Miller the quarterback, the pitcher, the punter, the MMA fighter, the [successful] author, the botanist, the film editor, or the old-west assassin.

Of course as a registered candidate you will have no end of opportunities to get your name out to the people who create the environment that turns politicians into such heinous liars. As soon as you register with the election office, every special interest group in the world sends surveys and other junk to your house. The thing that makes these surveys worthless isn't so much that they are minorities trying to use the government to mold the masses into their mindless followers, it's because they come at you from all over the place. Let me explain:

Let's say that you've registered as a candidate for Arizona's 86th congressional district. Within a week you will receive surveys from *Americans for Prosperity*, the *National Right to Life*, and the *US Chamber of Commerce*. What's wrong with this picture? The problem is that a true congressional representative cannot represent both the will of the people in their district *and* the will of a *national* special interest group. This is the same reason that belonging to one of the two political parties is anti-republican. Towing the national party line of either the Republicans or Democrats is a lousy enough thing to do to the locals whom you are supposed to represent, but unfortunately it's a necessary evil that comes with having a realistic chance of getting elected. But why compound your conflict of interest by catering to the wants of a non-essential national special interest group? As a representative of a congressional district you should unashamedly represent the will of your neighbors about how they want to name the post offices and federal courthouses in your district. What you should not do is bow to the wants of a bunch of self-serving yayhoos who live 1000 miles away. There is absolutely no reason to listen to anything that Nancy Pelosi has to say, and bowing to the wants of the 400,000 San Franciscans who voted for her makes even less sense when you have 620,000 of your own constituents with their own problems right here. It doesn't matter if Americans for Prosperity has 2 million voters nationwide, the only members of it that you should be concerned with are the handful who live in your district.

In addition to invitations to conform or be shunned by national special interest groups, candidates also receive stuff that is just plain peculiar. Take this email for example:

Dear Jim,

You've heard more than your share of promises this and every campaign season. Might have made a few yourself.

In reality there is only one promise that a candidate can actually make and keep. That promise is if elected, to limit your term in office and then secure that promise with your personal assets. THIS is a promise voters will listen to and respect!

The Alliance for Bonded Term Limits (ABTL) http://www.bondedtermlimits.org is a grassroots, non-profit, non-partisan 501 (c) (3) organization. ABTL will be contacting your campaign – and your opponents' campaign – in the coming days.

The Alliance seeks to recruit candidates who will sign a promissory note pledging a maximum number of consecutive years in office, specifying a 'credible' portion of their net worth to be only paid to a pre-designated charity of the candidate's choice, at that point in future when the office holder breaks their term limiting pledge.

Eleven of your contemporaries have already taken and signed a pledge. Many more are in the process of doing so. Their promise becomes the central plank in their campaign platform, and one that voters can fully understand and embrace. A single promise that provides credibility to the rest of your platform, since your candidacy is no longer about you but rather your belief in what's right for America. For decades as well as today, 70% to 84% of America's voters support term limits for Congressional office holders.

The letter continued on for another page. As a voter I liked the idea of the Alliance for Bonded Term Limits. As a candidate however, one would have to be kinda stupid to believe that announcing the duration of your time in office is a good idea. If you don't run for re-election then the only politician that you are implementing term limits on is yourself. I will grant that the ABTL founder's heart seems like it is in the right place; after all bonding your term limit-- like offering sub-prime mortgages to those who are not economically viable-- seems like the right thing to do. But it's not.

The solution to the problem of career politicians is to implement legislation that makes term limits the law. How would anybody with a 'bonded term limit' expect to pass such legislation if all their opposition has to do is wait for their term to end? But perhaps the biggest question that the ABTL raises in the mind of a nobody candidate like myself is why is it the incumbent's responsibility to help the voters vote responsibly? If we are really to believe that "for decades as well as today, 70% to 84% of America's voters support term limits for congressional office holders" then why don't these people simply vote for somebody other than the incumbent? Are American voters really this dense? If you are one of the 70-84% who wants term limits, then stop voting for the incumbent.

*   *   *

In order to truly progress as an individual you have to make an accurate assessment of yourself, which means you must make an honest assessment of yourself. To thine own self you must be true, dawg. In this endeavor I have a slight advantage over Rousseau in that I can throw honesty in the face of the masses via the next political challenge that presented itself to me: Facebook.

Before running for office I had never been on Facebook. I had seen a few people get fired over it, but they were gossips who kinda had it coming. I'd received a bunch of threatening emails from work saying that I would get fired too if I went on Facebook while on the clock. But the thing about Facebook that struck me the most was that the people who used it shared all kinds of completely useless information with everybody they had ever met, 24-7-365. No time of day was sacred. No topic was off limits. It was like we had gone back to the 1970's, crammed every hair salon and barbershop gossip into one newsstand and provided them all with Polaroid cameras and unlimited film. I was also aware that Facebook offered something called "friending", which, if used correctly, guilt tripped people whom you hardly knew into calling themselves your friend. Obviously the political applications of these absurdities are endless.

Before I could even act on the Facebook opportunity somebody made a Facebook page for my inchoate alter ego "Candidate Jim Miller". This was an odd and unexpected development. I felt politically loved, which was kind of like being sent flowers by somebody who didn't actually know me. It made me nervous in a very politician-ey way that made me further uncomfortable about who Candidate Jim Miller might turn out to be. I feared that by having a Facebook page I would have to constantly input the minutia of the day. More specifically I worried that I would fail to leave certain minutia out. Rousseau may have originality and intelligence on me, but with Facebook I could post my sordid confessions at the speed of light.

Since I had been endowed with a Facebook page by my constituents, what I needed to do next was find some unsuspecting voters to befriend. It probably does not require reiteration, but being social is my weak area. As I fumbled around Facebook I learned that I could type in the name of my high school and receive links to fellow Eagles who were networking socially. There were bound to be people from high school who would feel obligated to befriend me. And then it happened. I typed in Northeastern

103

High School, Elizabeth City, NC and at the very top of the list was the name of the girl on whom I'd had a crush from say, the dawn of puberty until I lost my virginity, which, in case my kids are reading this, was on my wedding night.

Her name was not Doris Day, but that is what I'm going to call this woman. Even with my sample group of one I must surmise that mine was no ordinary crush. My infatuation with Doris was one of white-hot phosphorous grenade type emotional combustion. It was like standing on stage at a Van Halen concert while Eddie and the gang played straight from my hypothalamus with the amps turned to 11. If one were to somehow remove all of the bullying from my high school days, the only things left would be the continuous dread of every class except technical drawing, and an attempt to suppress what felt like living out an eternity of the penultimate strokes leading up to an orgasm that never arrived. I thought that I would literally die if I didn't end up with Doris.

On Facebook Doris looked just like she had in high school. She was still was thin & pretty, but somehow, inexplicably, she was not the Venus de Milo I had made her out to be when I went to Northeastern. Doris had been a cheerleader. Her hair was kind of coarse and brownish, not unlike the real Doris Day's. She wasn't Italian or Asian as I am instinctively attracted to. She wasn't particularly tall or tiny or athletic or slutty or blessed with the dimpled cheeks of Jennifer Esposito or any of the usual things that cause teenage boys to become fixated on a young lady. For the life of me I can't explain my obsession with Doris; she just had nice skin and . . . pheromones or something. But whatever it was didn't merely have an effect on me. She dated quarterbacks and the like. They probably even DID IT! Oh God! The mind boggles! I just wanted to cup my hands on her soft waist and stare at her forever. If infatuation with a certain cheerleader was somehow my special adolescent aptitude, then Doris was unquestionably my muse. My crush on Doris was intensely, cripplingly, incessantly, *pathetic*. And now, twenty-some years later Doris was my contact with my long (deliberately) lost days of Northeastern High School. I immediately felt like the same skinny, pimply, trench-coat mafia, picking his nose in Mrs. Pritchard's class geek that I had been in High School. I couldn't just talk to Doris after two decades as if things were still cool between us-- there was no us and I had never been cool. There was just me and my ideal of Doris as goddess of all things worth living for. To this day I cannot imagine that she ever looked at me and saw anything other than a bubbling mess of rupturing hormones. Nonetheless I cowboyed up and sent her a friend request with some generic propaganda about my candidacy. For the first time since I had registered as a candidate I felt like a tremendous fake, which again made me feel strangely politician-like, which went on to make me uncomfortable, which, since it involved Doris, was disappointingly familiar.

Within a couple of days Doris accepted my friend request. She didn't write anything back, but she did offer for me to "like" the Facebook campaign of another Republican candidate by the name of Ann Marie Calabria. Ann Marie Calabria was a Judge running for re-election to the North Carolina Court of Appeals. Nicely played Doris

Day; nicely played.

Once the Facebook stuff was up and running I needed to broaden my Internet presence. Naturally I have a few opinions about the Internet. Mostly I am astonished at what an infallible mirror the Internet is for society, although I am a little bummed out about the reflection. I understand the popularity of porn, but are we really this infatuated with sports and entertainment? Because of the Internet we have an opportunity to observe the lines that define the individual as distinct from society as they are actively being blurred. Social networking websites and the Internet in general have granted individuals the freedom to share with the general public-- without the threat of direct social condemnation-- things that would normally be kept behind closed doors. In its infancy the Internet was imagined to be the setting for an information revolution that far exceeded Denis Diderot's wildest dreams. Publicly we dreamed about how the World Wide Web would tear down the intellectual barriers which reinforced the social hierarchy that divided one class from another. Twenty years later and the Internet appears to have ceased development at puberty. We have transformed our information superhighway into what screenwriter Steven Moffat may characterize as an "enormous international database of naked bottoms". Rather than lowering the intellectual elite by making their knowledge common, the vulgarity of the lower classes has become the unofficial mainstream by using *WebMD* to interpret seasonal allergies as cancer, find our lives lacking because we don't share the lifestyle of the Kardashians, and streaming live porn to more people than voted in the presidential election. Rather than having to invade the privacy of another's home to find out that all of us are more like the Addams Family than the Huxtable Family, citizens of every class can access the muddy underbelly of society simply by summoning it to their laptops. And while the Republican mouthpieces whine about how society is being destroyed simply because the Internet makes it impossible to continue pretending that the majority is in agreement about the lack of immorality of most of our taboos, Democrats view the Internet as yet another thing to tax and regulate in their favor.

And so it came to pass in the spring of 2010 that I was to either purchase a campaign URL that promoted whoever candidate Jim Miller was, or attempt to use my URL to promote something else. I sat down in contemplative mood and attempted to identify the greatest obstacle that was hindering my campaign. Was it a lack of funds? No, being middle class was who I was, being broke is what America is, and being resourceful was what I wanted to be. I would not buy votes with tax deductions and propaganda in the primary. Yea, in the general election I'd hand out syringes with my name on them and offer massages with happy endings as fundraisers; but if Republicans were stupid enough to want slogans and buttons and cook-outs in the primary then I wasn't interested in representing them anyway. This revelation indicated that my biggest hindrance was perhaps my ideology. Well I'm not giving *that* up. Our entire nation is nothing but an idea. Most of our mind's interface with reality is based upon ideology. There aren't any real lines that divide the US from Mexico and Canada. The speed limit isn't really a limit. The police officer who pulls you over is not ordained by God to tell you what to do. The money that you bribe him with has no real value. The sparrows that nest in your car when it is impounded do not have microscopic trademarks on them that say *P. domesticus.* There is nothing about my skin color that makes me enjoy the irony of being locked in a jail cell when no man can cage my imagination; and the only hell that I'll ever experience is the one that will exist exclusively within my own mind if I compromise my ethics. Nope. The ideology stays.

Another problem with my candidacy was that most of the people who were like me had no interest in the election. Most of the people whom I talked to did not even know that a primary election was coming up. Being in the Jim Crow/revenge-for-Jim Crow South, those who were interested in the election were usually Democrats who thought that I wanted to relieve them of not just their current government entitlements, but any future ones that may come along as well. What could I say, they were essentially correct.

Of the people who understood what a primary election was *and* who were kind enough to at least say they liked what I had to say, a disheartening portion of them didn't actually live in district 1. North Carolina's first congressional district is one of the most extensively gerrymandered hunks of real estate on the planet. The district line literally went down the middle of the street in front of the hospital where I worked. When I walked across
108

Neuse Blvd. from the EMS shack to the Reagan Day Dinner I left the congressional district 1 and entered district 3. I could talk to people at work about the possibility of their voting for me, but if they turned left out of the parking lot to go home they probably weren't able to vote for me anyway. The congressional district lines in Craven County, NC are very deliberate. All the predominantly white townships that are filled with Long Islanders, such as River Bend, are carefully excised from district 1 and designated as being in district 3. Marine Corps Air Station Cherry Point was about the only portion of eastern Craven County that was in district 1, while most of the people who actually worked on the base lived in the surrounding town of Havelock, which was in district 3. This silliness was the inspiration for the URL of my campaign website.

I decided that my name was generic enough to be relatively easily remembered. I was also in love with the area that I wanted to represent. I decided that a good URL would be NCdistrict1.com. It wasn't too long, it contained information that was pertinent to the victims of our uber-gerrymandered district, and it was a fair representation of my character in that I am a person who is hopelessly *from* somewhere. Being from somewhere is a distinction most easily observed when one is positioned next to somebody who grew up in the same place you did and yet has something to prove because they are from *nowhere*. I thought that my fellow eastern North Carolinians would appreciate this. But if this is truly a book about my screw-ups as a candidate then I must emphasize that one of my biggest flaws is my having absolutely no desire to be the center of attention. To be a politician you have to want to have everybody looking at you. You must have something to prove. You cannot be a candidate for your country, your party, your district, or any other group of people; you have to be in it for yourself. You have to be a candidate for your identity. You cannot run for office as a philosopher, physician, accountant, economist, or parent. You have to be somebody who wants to lead followers, because people who vote are voting for somebody to follow. You cannot be as I was and expect people who want to be left alone to be bothered to go as far as to seek out a politician who stands for . . . *being left alone*. Seriously, which of the following would you spend your tiny little free vote on: hope, change, transparency, equal rights, world peace, affordable health care, or . . . *being left alone*? Nobody casts a penny into the fountain and wishes for autonomy. Only a moron would vote for being left alone. It's too personal. And what if you actually got what you voted for? Isn't there an adage about getting what you wish for? People will always vote for daydreams, glittering ideology, and free stuff, but nobody in their left mind would ever vote in favor of forcing the world's most powerful government to let you take more responsibility for yourself.

The Dilemma of Judging People Not by the Color of Their Skin

My wife and I were raised to not think of ourselves as belonging to a race. Our parents (and ironically our public schools) taught us that race was invented by Imperialists to categorize portions of humanity that they believed to be inferior to them. Race, like the belief that the Earth sits on top of a stack of giant turtles, is a fairy tale invented by the same people who tell us what to think about every other social issue. The scientific morphology of race is equal to that of phrenology and is as useful as believing that a face-down penny is bad luck. Unfortunately, living in the 21st century puts my wife and I at a disadvantage when we attempt to communicate with racists who label us white. This is a disadvantage that we want our kids to struggle with as well. You cannot end a war if you don't quit identifying others by borders, race, religion, or any of the other divisive things that only exist in the mind, and we have unilaterally put down our rocks.

North Carolina's first district is not particularly diverse. There are a bunch of us whom the government labels as either white or black, and the remaining handful of us get labeled something else. Thanks to the Federal Government's insistence upon dividing the population up into different shades of epithelium, our nation is now hardwired to remain as Toni Morrison said: "American means white. Everybody else has to hyphenate". But when big brother isn't watching, what North Carolina's first congressional district calls diversity consists of a handful of Native Americans who actually do know what it is like to get screwed by the American government, and a small but growing population of Spanish-speaking coworkers who remind us of our grandparents with their frugality and dedication to their families. The vast majority of people in my district work together, play together and ride the bus to school together. We sit in classes and traffic together and stand in line together at Wal-Mart and McDonalds. We endure the same climate, power company, mosquitoes, furniture stores, floods, billboards, topography, whiny coworkers, incompetent managers, commercials, supermarkets, tap water, potholes, cable channels, Internet service, hurricanes, blue laws, deer, nutria, politicians, football games, DMV employees, teachers who can't do anything but talk, and cell phone companies who screw us over. We all want our children to grow up to be happy and healthy. All of our teenagers hear the same spooky story about the couple that was making out in their car when they hear a mysterious noise; one of the lovers gets out of the car to investigate and he winds up murdered. We all look with bewildered amazement when poor people tell us how to do our jobs and when rich people act surprised when things like parking tickets and wind conspire to treat them like everybody else. We are Christians who eat too much pork, too much sugar and too much fried food. We use tobacco and have family members who go hunting on Thanksgiving. We all have a mixed-race family member who is lied to about their biological father. We purchase almost 100% of our culture. We are regarded as hayseeds by the rest of the state and as ignoramuses by the rest of the country. We are held back culturally by people who resent Yankees for burning "their" houses to the ground in 1864, and by other people who believe that the Yankee establishment owes them reparations for "their" being enslaved for the 300 years prior to 1864. In spite of all the things that we have in common, the majority of the people in district 1 still manage to hate one another due to television programming and our common lack of content in character.

The TV tells us that we are different. In North Carolina many people are raised being told that black people and white people are not only supposed to be separated from one another, but that society prefers one and the government prefers the other. One would think that our institutes of higher learning would be eager to test the hypothesis of white people enjoying more of the quantifiable entities of power, privilege and prestige. Surely there must be academic papers on this topic. The reverends of victimization have made millions off of the hypothesis of white power, privilege and prestige; they shut down businesses and raise unemployment with mere words, they give commencement speeches at the most prestigious colleges, they fly first class, they run for president, they get invited to sit on myriad boards and panels. Why not catalog their oppression with the objectivity of a scientific study?

Actually there was a study of this phenomenon. And a book. It was called *The Bell Curve*. The findings of *The Bell Curve* were a reiteration of every last one of the staple accusations that the reverends of victimization have used to procure a fortune for themselves from those whom they sold hope. Further, *The Bell Curve* actually backed up these clichés with data. Lisa Delpit, an accomplished author and distinguished professor at Southern University, is applauded for citing the same findings as *The Bell Curve* almost twenty years after its publication. In her book *Multiplication is for White People. Raising Expectations for Other People's Children*, Delpit addresses the achievement gap between African American children and other Americans because it is "The conversation that is never held". And Delpit is correct-- American society is afraid to have the conversation about why African American children fall behind other American children. And why shouldn't we be? The last time two white people tried to join the conversation, Charles Murray and Richard Herrnstein were pegged as racists simply for providing empirical data which indicated that the problem existed.

The Bell Curve laid out statistical evidence that an

American who is born black is very likely not going to enjoy the same level of either intellectual or materialistic prosperity in America as an American who is born white. Rather than utilizing the scientific data of *The Bell Curve* as the *coup de grace* against those who assert that we have attained racial equality in America, critics instead nullified the research by labeling authors Murray and Herrnstein racist. The rationalization for calling *The Bell Curve* racist is based upon the rumor that the study is actually about genetics instead of socioeconomics. So what did Murray and Herrnstein do to make people believe that their research was secretly about genetics? Did they use Punnett squares to cross the 'employed' and 'unemployed' phenotypes? Did they suggest that the allele for skin color is attached to the gene that causes one person to get paid more than another for the same amount of work? Unfortunately not. To this day the criticism of *The Bell Curve* as racist is based upon the fact that Murray and Herrnstein collected data regarding the social status of American citizens starting *from birth*. As if to prove beyond a reasonable doubt that liberals are completely helpless when it comes to anything involving math or the scientific process, critics literally accused Murray and Herrnstein of characterizing blacks as being deficient of a gene which increases an offspring's taxable income.

The flaw of *The Bell Curve* is that it is a scientific work reviewed by one or two connoisseurs of the liberal arts and judged most harshly and loudly by those who have not read it. And while *The Bell Curve* illustrates the inequality between the average black American and the average white

American, it contains no anecdotal evidence on which to pen a legislative policy, no emotional dissertations about injustice that can be preached to the masses before the collection plate is passed, and no identification of an intrinsic American evil on which the unidentified victims of the study can blame their individual predicaments. Alas, Murray and Herrnstein were merely in the business of scientifically observing and cataloguing American life. The integrity that Murray and Herrnstein exhibited by using science to chart the goings-on of our society is threatening to those whose careers are dependent upon the glittering generality of an abstract, philosophical injustice for people to fear and be angry about. For legislators, reverends, and liberal arts professors, fear and anger pay the bills. The clarity and definity of *The Bell Curve* was a threat to the murky generalizations that were so lucrative to those who made their livings off of "fixing" racism. The facts about racial inequality that *The Bell Curve* contained were effectively dispatched by their being labeled racist by the new American nobility. But unlike the racism of Conrad's *Heart of Darkness*, *The Bell Curve* will never receive lengthy academic scrutiny because that would require liberal arts academicians to actually read it.

I am a product of public education, and I truly believe that before I was born, black people were oppressed far worse than any classroom can depict. But I don't blindly follow what my educators want me to believe about the world that surrounds me today. Specifically, I have never once witnessed a black person being subjected to the level of racism that I endured in North Carolina public schools every single fucking day. Not from a white person anyway--black bullies are even harder on black pacifists than they are on white pacifists. The NAACP reports that their lawyers continue to practice social engineering from the bully pulpit of trickle-up "advancement", but to white trash it seems more like the NAACP's pendulum of social justice has swung past equality in the eyes of government and now seeks to reinstitute Jim Crow with the colors reversed. The behavior of black bullies when I went to school was rationalized by school officials as being typical of oppressed minority 'culture' and thus it was either ignored or it was rewarded with an effort to understand how the system had failed the bully. My generation never witnessed the sit-ins and riots of the Civil Rights Movement. As far as my generation knows McDonalds only hires a white kid if he is either handicapped or if nobody else turns in an application. We have always celebrated Black History Month because it is apparently a chic way to break up the monotony of the other 'successful people who aren't related to you' months. When black people get speeding tickets they're victims of social injustice but when white people get them it's because they're breaking the law. When black people get beaten by the cops it's racism but when it happens to white people they deserve it. Professional sports have been dominated by black people for as long as we can remember. Oprah has always been the richest person on TV and Michael Jackson was always the richest entertainer on the radio. In movies the black actors always get killed first because it's as a better portrayal of injustice and in reality the only person who speaks for poor white kids is

Bill Cosby and he isn't even doing it intentionally.

My generation and those who come after us are saddled with the charge of maintaining an archetype of darker-skinned citizens being oppressed as a whole, even though it is only the generations of American people of color prior to Generation X who have actually experienced what it is like to have opportunities and inclusion withheld from them by entire portions of society. If Generation X has a common faith it is that the racial unrest that handicaps our nation is merely part of the healing process that we must endure before we move on to being a nation that pursues happiness without codependency issues. But while Jim Crow-type oppression only pops up intermittently in the private sector of modern America, the shackles of low self-esteem and enabled irresponsibility are prevalent and well entrenched in American society. It is as if the black community has, by gaining equal rights, lost an identity which, although it was hated, was at least familiar. The black community has been in a perpetual state of denial and anger ever since the end of the Civil Rights Movement; and with the assistance of the reverends of victimization the black community is bargaining for a return of the food, work, and housing that slavery provided. I fear that if we do not reconcile the difference between the real oppression of darker-skinned people which led to the Civil Rights Movement with the contemporary discontent of black youths who fall into the vulgar mistake of dreaming that they are persecuted whenever they are contradicted, then we are destined to stagnate as a nation and ultimately be taken over by the first maniac with the will to exchange lives for the untapped potential that North America holds. If the government has a role in the equality of skin colors, that role must start with the treatment of all skin colors equally, not end with it.

On Sept. 15, 2008 my Paramedic partner and I drove our ambulance to a dusty gravel parking lot near the Wal-Mart in New Bern. We were to pick up the body of a 19 year old Hispanic man and deliver him to the morgue. The man was a Marine, and NCIS was wrapping up their investigation. From behind the yellow tape we could see the back of a young man lying on the gravel in the fetal position. His hips were resting in a dry pothole and his head was smashed in. About 18 hours earlier the man had been sitting in his car when he was suddenly pulled out into the parking lot by two men and ordered to get into the trunk of their car. When he refused, his assailants beat him to the ground with a stereo speaker. The dead man had a friend with him, and he too was ordered to get into the trunk of the car. The second man did as he was told and the lid was shut over him. About a half mile down the road the kidnapped man escaped the trunk and dove out of the moving car. He rolled to the side of the road and spent most of the rest of the night hiding underneath a parked car. One man had been kidnapped and the other murdered because apparently they did not heed the moral of our oral tradition regarding the couple who were making out in a car. This reminded me of an incident that happened a thousand miles west of New Bern in Laramie, Wyoming.

In October of 1998, two men kidnapped and tortured a University of Wyoming student because their hatred outweighed their knowledge of what it means to live in a constitutional republic. The young man died from his injuries within hours. My mother was living in Laramie at the time and she was an acquaintance of Matthew Shepard. I don't think that Matthew Shepard wanted to be immortalized for being gay, and he certainly didn't want it for being murdered, so it is with hesitation that I reinforce that legacy by mentioning his name on these pages. If there is one positive by-product of the lucrative ratings that accompany the media blab about hate crime, it is that at it at least reminds people that the law does not bend under the weight of strong emotions. When Matthew Shepard was murdered it was the first time that I had ever seen a familiar town capitalized upon for the worldwide sale of commercials. So when two men in New Bern let their hatred overwhelm them to the tune of committing twice the crime that happened in Laramie, I thought that maybe New Bern was in for a refresher on what it meant to live in a republic instead of a democracy. Surprisingly however, there was no media blitz about the hate crime.

A couple of weeks after the murder/kidnapping of the two young Marines in New Bern I was on scene at a fender bender with one of the officers who had responded to the crime. I had heard that the perps had been nabbed, but nothing else. I'd been expecting a media feeding frenzy. For weeks I'd been keeping one ear to the sky for the telltale thwopping of news helicopters. I had visions of Rachel Maddow and Glen Beck sitting in a local pool hall called Mickey Milligan's and selling commercials with a debate over whether murder was bad because the government said so or because it was one of the Ten Commandments. I'd looked forward to passing a CNN news camera in the ambulance and pretending that I didn't care if I was on national TV for a fraction of a second.

I asked the officer what was happening with the murderers and his face turned sour. Apparently the police department wanted to throw the book at the kidnappers/murderers and charge them with hate crimes. Unfortunately, since the men who had murdered one person and kidnapped another were labeled by the Federal Government as black, it was not politically expedient for the district attorney to prosecute the murder/kidnapping of two gay men as a hate crime due to the large number of citizens in New Bern who bore the same government label as the perps. Apparently politics prevented the charging of those who commit hate crimes with hate crimes for one of two reasons: either blacks were superior to homosexuals or it was assumed that the black community was unable to distinguish itself from black criminals.

Conservatives are often frustrated with the black community because black individuals seem to possess the awareness of the falseness of American popular culture, but the black community suppresses that awareness. Black America is on the cusp of realizing that it is living out lives of obedience and inner reverence for a group of people who do nothing more than flatter the black community while using it as a Keynesian money laundering service. Black America is like an elephant that the Democratic Party has had chained to a stake ever since it was a calf, and now that it has grown strong enough to pull up the stake it still

121

believes that it is the little elephant that was captured, chained, and broken so many years ago. Democratic politicians bloviate about leadership and giving power to the people, but a true leader makes himself obsolete as soon as possible. I wish with all my heart that I could exchange the black community's tolerance of me for their standing up, brushing off the shackles of government dependence and without even saying "anything you can do I can do better" they just went out and did it.

I was raised not to think of myself or of anyone else as belonging to a race because identifying people by race is racism, and racism is bad. I was also raised to be a pacifist. Of these philosophies the former has resulted in my being hated by liberals everywhere, and the latter resulted in my getting my ass beaten by every pet project of the Democratic Party. The irony of this is that no liberal ever questions the rationality of the person who slaps the bumper sticker "I'm already against the next war" on their car, but they think that anybody who is against designating their race on an application is an ignoramus. The reality is that both foreign occupation and racism are ideologies of bad people; but while Colonialism can only be prevented by a strong defense, racism is perpetuated by any institution that requires you to write down your skin color so that you can be stereotyped by people you've never met.

There is at least one cultural variation of the idea of race that was taught to us by European imperialists. I learned from W.E.B. DuBois that racism is defined differently by black people than it was by my parents. I define racism as the incorrect belief that race is something

122

greater and more meaningful than the method of categorizing the so-called savages that the European explorers "discovered". To believe in race is to believe that the European explorers and colonists were onto something profound when they decided to label people based upon the physical characteristics with which they were born. To me this literally makes less sense than developing a social hierarchy based upon dick size. The fact is however, that black Americans believe in the imperialist's definition of race with the amendment that it is only racist if you *dislike* another race. Indeed the scars of slavery are deep and continue to this day, for those whose ancestors were oppressed by the edicts of white supremacy are the ones who cling most tightly to the belief that they are genetically different and cannot survive in the New World without charity.

If there is a unifying ethos of the Americans who identify themselves as black it is the religion of race. As Americans we are compelled by the Constitution to respect one-another's right to practice our religions as we see fit; but the government has no more right to implement legislation based upon the religious belief of race than it does to dictate the time when a fetus obtains a soul or to regulate the people's rite of marriage as if it is a right of law.

Race-belief is a learned behavior that needs to be unlearned rather than capitalized upon and reinforced as the Democratic Party has done. As long as the topic of how black children should be treated differently from everybody else continues to be a central topic of political discourse and media ratings, black children are going to continue to believe that America is a white person's country in which they are regarded as second-class, and white children are going to believe that they are discriminated against by the government on the basis of race. I can say from experience that white kids resented the special treatment that black kids received from our government not because we believed that blacks were inferior, but because we believed we were all equal. No mature individual complains when person with Down syndrome gets special treatment, and only a slave would accept as fact that otherwise normal people are owed something by society. It is as if white kids and black kids each struggle with the belief that the other is America's favorite, and rather than growing up, some Americans spend their entire lives attempting to get as much attention as possible from their nation. The United States Government didn't build the bigotry that undermines our nation, but it certainly perpetuates and exacerbates it with the infrastructure of legislated race. As always, DuBois says it better:

> it is not a whit stronger that the argument of thinking Negroes: granted, they reply, that the condition of our masses is bad; there is certainly on the one hand historical cause for this, and unmistakable evidence that no small number have, in spite of tremendous disadvantages, risen to the level of American civilization. And when, by proscription and prejudice, these same negroes are classed with and treated like the lowest of their people, simply because they are Negroes, such a policy not only discourages thrift and intelligence among black men, but puts a direct premium on the very things you complain of,- inefficiency and crime. Draw lines of

crime, of incompetency, of vice, as tightly and uncompromisingly as you will, for these things must be proscribed; but a color-line not only does not accomplish this purpose, but thwarts it.

Perhaps when black Americans finally take responsibility for something horrible, such as the black-on-black genocide that plagues our nation, then they will recognize the fallacy of linking the color of one's skin with atrocities at which one's skin was not actually present. It is as if black America has heeded the teaching of Malcolm X to the extent that when a white person speaks of the genocide of black Americans and says "*we* have a problem", the black community is only too quick to reply "yes *you* do". Until the black community abandons the political party which subjugates it via financial dependence, the only characteristic that will remain firmly tied to the identity of 'black American' is that of being a victim who is too puerile, ignorant, and innocent to create anything greater than acts of crime without the help of white America and its white government. Frederick Douglass said "make a man a slave and you rob him of moral responsibility". If Douglass is correct, then we should not be surprised to find that the areas of America that have the most crime are the same ones in which the citizens live off the government in exactly the same manner that slaves lived on the plantation. Why would we expect an entire race of victims to do anything other than kill and steal from one another if every positive accomplishment that a black person makes is attributed by Charlie Rangel and his ilk to taxes collected from the Tea Party? The entirety of black culture is contaminated by politicians with the label of "made possible by white America".

Fred Hampton said that you don't fight racism with racism, you fight racism with solidarity. The problem with this is that it is more lucrative for politicians to divide us up by race than it is to treat us equally. Compounding the problem is that Americans are only too eager to be segregated by political figures. It is as Frank McCourt said: "It's not enough to be American. You always have to be something else, Irish-American, German-American, and you'd wonder how they'd get along if someone hadn't invented the hyphen." It is time for the individuals who constitute America to emancipate ourselves from political parties and unite against a government which has become independent of its people by pitting us against one another. The Republican and Democratic Parties don't get their stances from us, they give press releases, interviews, and commercials to tell us how to think. Rather than accepting as fact that legislation is penned to reward those who support the politician who introduces certain legislation to Congress, we should become intolerant of any citizen of sound mind and body who seeks preferential treatment by the hand of our collective wrath.

As far as my generation knows McDonalds preferentially hires blacks because they're too poor to sue when they get fired. We have always celebrated Black History Month with the desperate hope that maybe just one student will find the strength to get their self-worth from humanity rather than from society. When black people get speeding tickets and someone wonders if the police officer

126

pulled them over because he was hoping to write more than just one ticket, it is only racist on behalf *of the person who wonders it.* When black people get beaten by the cops, well, they probably deserved it but that doesn't make it right. Professional sports has been dominated by black people for as long as my generation can remember because even after 150 years of emancipation, too many black Americans are more comfortable sweating than studying. The white person who owns the station that broadcasts the Oprah Winfrey Show is the richest person on TV and the white person who distributed Michael Jackson's records was always the richest person in the entertainment industry, and the richer Jackson got the whiter he got. In movies the black actors always get killed first because you can't kill off the lead or the movie will be over.

Burning Bridges

I'm sure that those open-minded readers whom I've irritated with my attack on their stereotype of open-mindedness are ready for something a little more supportive of their faith. If you wanted to be talked down for an entire day you'd hang out with a straight-ticket Republican Christian conservative, right? Well, this is about the best I can do: the ignorance of the Democratic Party is more sophisticated than the ignorance of the Republican Party. If you are an American voter you have two choices: you can be ignorant but seem smart, or you can seem ignorant but appear to have ethics. It's lose-lose, which is why I've switched my political affiliation to -*un*. Join me and we can be not-missed together! To solidify my exile from two-party propaganda I would like to point out a few things that those who purchased the open-minded bumper stickers are right about.

Illegal Immigrants

To be an illegal immigrant in the United States is to labor like a real conservative, to cherish your family like a real Christian, to pay a libertarian's ideal level of taxes, to be part of the only group of people in the Unites States that uses social services as a hand up instead of a hand out, and to be so ignorant of American culture as to believe that political parties care about anything beyond your money or your vote. Being an illegal immigrant who works to pay his own bills is as detrimental to American society as owning an unregistered firearm. If illegal immigrants would just give up their belief in American politics they would be far better manifestations of the Americans for whom the founding fathers wrote the Constitution than any of the fat, sloppy, ignorant, lazy, X-box playing sissies who whine about losing their jobs to people who are happy to work harder for less pay like some filthy picket-line-crossing scab. The vast majority of illegal immigrants in the US are more American in the conservative [read *classical liberalist*] sense of the term than most American citizens. Where government is concerned, every single person who signed the Declaration of Independence was a far bigger criminal than any undocumented alien who has risked everything simply to earn a living. Some say that we are a nation of immigrants. I say we are a nation of outlaws. It is our heritage to work hard and fight furiously to keep the fruits of our labor from being stolen by the government. We are a nation with origins in slavery, and it is because of our sins that we know intimately that no man or mechanism has the

129

right to own another man's labor. Illegal immigrants are not immoral for taking jobs that pay $3.50 an hour-- they are to be commended for choosing to contribute to society rather than resigning themselves to being a victim and living off of welfare. If anything, it is small businesses and illegal immigrants who are the victims of American government. It is not the illegal immigrant's fault that the government keeps raising minimum wage so that it can collect more social security and payroll tax while the value of unskilled labor remains the same.

There is a lot of chatter out there in Republicanville about how poor people don't pay taxes. As somebody who grew up poor I would like to know where the line is to tell these people to go play in the street. When I was working at Domino's Pizza and making $100 a week there were five lines of deductions on my pay stub before I was left with what I got to take home. I concede that statistically my contribution to the tax kitty was zero, but it sure would have been nice if I had been allowed to keep that "nothing" instead of giving it to the people who bought pizza with their welfare checks. Republicans complain incessantly about how illegal immigrants who get paid under the table are not contributing to the tax base, and yet in the same breath they whine that people who make minimum wage are overpaid. Then they complain that people who make minimum wage "don't pay taxes" even though they take home just as much as the illegal immigrants who are getting paid $3.50 an hour under the table.

The lines of ink that divide nations on a map do not exist in reality. It is quaintly parochial to characterize the

130

borders that delineate a nation as existing outside the individual minds of the human race. At least when an ornithologist discovers a new species of bird there is an actual collection of molecules that begins and ends for that thing's own purpose; and while that thing neither recognizes itself as being new, nor a species, or even a bird, at least it continues to exist outside the mind of the being that presumes to call it these things. Compare this with the thing we call a nation and it is difficult to imagine political borders as serving any purpose other than to classify human beings as either locals or tourists. But to imagine a nation's borders as an intellectual tool for characterizing one human being as a local and another as a tourist is about as accurate as characterizing one human being as the product of nationalism and another the product of tourism. Nationalism only exists within an individual's psyche, and tourism is a petri dish for inflation. Which brings me to the other nice thing about illegal immigrants, which is that after they take the living expenses out of their $3.50 an hour paycheck, they send the rest home. When it comes time to pay off Obama's debt and there are no small businesses left to increase the value of the dollar, trillions of worthless Federal Reserve notes are going to be printed and dumped into the US economy. The only thing that will give the US dollar any value at all will be the labor of illegal immigrants who first and foremost work hard to give the dollar value, then stretch their earnings as far as humanly possible, and finally they will increase the value of the dollar by sending their surplus capital out of the United States thereby making the dollar just a wee bit more scarce domestically.

Not all of us are immigrants; some of us were born here. I for example live in Dare County, which was dubbed in honor of Virginia Dare. Virginia Dare was the first English child born in the New World; and in spite of the fact that when she was born she neither spoke nor behaved English, she was not the first child born here, and the world into which she was delivered was anything but new, the Progressives of English colonialism did not hesitate to regard Ellinor "Mom" Dare's labor as a testament to English greatness. Ironically, Virginia Dare was named after the colony in which she was born (Virginia) even though the political borders of today indicate that Baby Girl Dare was born in North Carolina. To revisit another portion of Dare County history, recall that the Wright Brothers are said to have flown their self-propelled heavier-than-air machine in Kitty Hawk, although the current political borders place them squarely outside my back window in Kill Devil Hills (and really they were from Ohio). Of course not everybody is familiar with the geopolitical setting of the North Carolina's Outer Banks, so consider the political efficacy of the borders of much of the Middle East. When I am feeling particularly redneck I like to blame the unrest of the Middle East on its lack of bacon. In reality the borders of Middle Eastern nations were drawn by a bunch of imperial European nincompoops who had absolutely no regard for the long-standing and distinctive cultures of the indigenous people who lived there. The Kurds for example, have been residing in the mountainous region of northern Iraq and southern Turkey for far longer than the Iraqi-Turkish border has been running smack through the middle of their homeland. But the disputes over political borders (*read* 'borders that are imaginary') are not confined to nations that dislike nomads.

The Mexican-American War extended the southern and western borders of the United States deep into what was legally Mexican territory. Like Obamacare, the Mexican-American War was legal because Congress voted on it. Today there is a modicum of self-righteous chest thumping by Hispanic activists about how a good portion of the United States actually belongs to them. The rationalization for this is based in the idea that prior to the Mexican-American War the Spanish-speaking conquistadors had won the land fair and square by implementing the genocide of the Mayans and Native Americans who lived there first. Ask any descendant of Spanish colonialism and they will tell you that they are by no means inferior to the descendants of English colonialism and that no civilized nation would ever annex them as if they were mere indigenous people. But since history is written by the winners, the United States got to put the spin of their annexation being met with an organized military defense thereby qualifying it as an actual war. Since the Mexican-American War was, in fact, a war, and wars are how civilized nations resolve real estate disputes, the land won by the United States belongs to the United States. A question more pertinent to the contemporary discussion of political property rights is why does it seem like the entire Spanish-speaking world is leaving the Spanish-speaking world as if they are fleeing an erupting volcano? Are they trying to get away from the places where Hispanic activists actually *are* in charge of the government? And why are none of the descendants of Mexican refugees who were annexed by the United States in 1846-8 trying desperately to escape the oppression of the gringos and return to the righteousness of the remaining Mexican territory?

Hispanic immigrants who are here to build a better life for themselves through hard work and character are more American than most Americans. Immigrants, legal or illegal, who don't play the Democratic Party's blame game are more conservative than most Republicans. They are appreciative of personal property, they love and respect the traditional family and faiths, they take care of themselves and they do not micromanage their neighbors. In fact they're a might bit better than the founding fathers because illegal immigrants don't own slaves. American citizens will always speak one of the languages of its colonial rulers, and it doesn't matter which one as long as everybody can agree on what the Constitution says. And as long as humanity remains too stupid to behave itself without the schizo-ethics of religion, as long as Americans remain so ignorant as to interpret "working smarter instead of harder" to mean "hard work is dumb", and as long as we have social programs that no person born in America ever seems to get off of, we will need illegal immigrants to quell this foolishness and keep alive the government that has prevented our land from sucking as much as that ruled by the Mexican government, drug lords, or whomever it is that's in charge down there.

Environmentalism

The men who penned the Constitution didn't have sewer and water. Their educations were not slowed by bitter cold, sweltering heat, corporal punishment, the teacher being reprimanded for the Marx brothers' grades, incandescent light bulbs, indoor plumbing, or a lack of cable in the classroom. It took weeks to travel from one nation to the next. The infrastructure of communication was sail and horseback. The procedures of the medical field were almost indistinguishable from those of the Spanish Inquisition. The most effective weapons of mass destruction were wintertime, drought, and communicable diseases. Only bits and pieces of the great outdoors were utilized for human existence and comfort, and the vast majority of nature was something that had to be constantly tended simply so it didn't kill you when you weren't looking. Then came coal, the steam engine, and the Industrial Revolution.

Believe me, I get it. Industry is good. In my own house we now have two rooms with that newfangled drywall stuff. We have a bathroom with tile, a kitchen with a groovy vinyl floor covering that the dog can both puke on and eat off of, and all of these products were made in a factory. We traded the mastodon on a stick for a Bissell upright. Thanks to industry I can drive my own car fifteen miles to my garden and I no longer trim the driveway with kitchen shears. We use air conditioning to keep the interior of our house comfortable and we justify it by saying that it prevents our manufactured books and furniture from mildewing in the humid Outer Banks air. But I also understand that just because the environment will still kill us if we give it the chance, that we do not need to continue treating it as if it's our enemy.

In spite of having grown up in the rural United States, I was thirty years old before I first saw a Bald Eagle in the wild. There were never turkeys in the woods when I was growing up. Or pelicans at the beach. I don't romanticize these critters as being anything nobler than a carrion eater, a Thanksgiving dinner, and a nice break from sparrows, respectively, but I think my kids should get the same chance to eat and observe them as I do. These birds are making a comeback due to the work of environmentalists, many of whom are hunters. Do you know what else I would like to see in person? I would like to see my uncle who died in Vietnam. To a far lesser extent I would like to see a passenger pigeon. Both my uncle and the passenger pigeon are gone because of the stupidity of governments at war; am I supposed to think *H. sapiens* are any less stupid for killing off the birds?

Here on North Carolina's Outer Banks, the size of bird populations shares a direct positive relationship with beach driving. As the number of vehicles driving on the beach has increased, the numbers of osprey, piping plover, brown pelicans, etc., have also increased. The same cannot be said for the populations of fish; pardon me while I wax Buzz Killington for a moment:

On the Nags Head causeway there is a bridge named in honor of Sen. Melvin R. Daniels. Senator Daniels was an outstanding person who came from humble beginnings in the fishing village of Wanchese. Perhaps it is appropriate then, that the bridge that is named for him has been a fishing landmark for decades. Everybody calls Sen. Daniels' bridge "The Little Bridge" because there are two bridges on the causeway and, well, you can guess what the other one is like.

Fishing on The Little Bridge used to be a bit treacherous. Only a thin metal handrail separated the hooks and lines of casting geezers from the antennae of passing Buicks. But the reward was worth the risk. In the old days of the 1980's and 90's people fished for dinner, and to that end the species known as *spot* and *croaker* were the staple food of salt-water anglers. When the spot were running at The Little Bridge people would run out of bait and continue fishing-- and catching fish-- with just about anything on a line. There were stories of the spot running so thick that they were biting cigarette butts, chewing gum, and even empty hooks.

When our mom took us fishing in those days we didn't go all the way to The Little Bridge. We went to the Kitty Hawk Pier. There were days that we would latch two bottom rigs together and catch fish four at a time as soon as the sinker hit the bottom. Once our mom took us on a whale watching trip on the headboat *Crystal Dawn*. We didn't see any whales, but we did troll through a school of bluefish that was ten miles long and spanned all the way to either horizon. A decade later, during the same fall that ECU went 11-1 in football, my sister and I chased the schools of blue fish as they ran the beach. All you had to do was cast your line into a vortex of diving seagulls and as soon as the spoon hit the water you would hook a bluefish as big as your thigh. Little fish were getting chased up onto the beach by the marauding hordes of blues. Fishing trips did not last very long that fall. Chasing bluefish consisted of driving down the beach until you saw a bunch of seagulls diving into the surf. The seagulls were diving to eat the smaller fish that were being driven to the surface by the blues. If the seagulls were within casting range you would run down the beach, hurl your spoon into the swarm, reel in a giant flipping sea monster with gnashing teeth on one end, admire it for a moment, throw it back, then run down the beach to follow the school. You repeated this process for about 45 minutes until you got tired and needed a break or until the school swam out further than you could cast. At that point you'd walk back to your car all covered in little scales. Your hands would be tired and fishy, and you might have a cut or two from the line or where you got finned by a particularly ornery blue. You'd open up the cooler and find that you still had a whole 12-pack of Rolling Rock left. Sometimes that would be the end of the fishing for the day.

Beach fishing has slowed significantly since then, but not because Generation X caught and ate all the sea creatures. The Little Bridge is still steady, but the days of filling your cooler in an hour are gone. The Nags Head causeway is now an environmental ghetto populated by people who are so enamored with the wetland setting that they've filled it with asphalt, sod and concrete. There is also a golf course up the road now, and if the number of loose Slazengers is any indication of the volume of pesticides and herbicides that are also rolling into the Sound it's surprising that there are any fish left at all.

I don't know what environmentalism means to a person who is from an urban area, but it has got to be more idealistic than realistic. Do city folks see a picture in a magazine and read that without their donations there will be no new pictures for them to look at? I appreciate the fact that anthropomorphism of nature runs so rampantly in America-- it shows that our economy is robust and our people are kindhearted-- in that order. What I don't like is that environmental charities have tapped into the same lucrative divisiveness that televangelists have engineered and perfected. It doesn't matter whether you fail to give money to Greenpeace or to Creflo Dollar Ministries; either way your inaction is paving your own descent into hell. The problem is that if you don't give to Greenpeace you are made to believe that you are taking everybody else to hell with you. There was a time when people donated to the church and to environmental organizations because they were good; today they do it because they are *better*. Republicans have seized and embraced this divisiveness and made it part of their identity politics.

For Republicans it is no longer enough to side with the logging industry; you also have to actively hate spotted owls and want them dead. To truly be a Republican you have to believe that it is better to kill off every pelican in the universe with DDT than put forth the effort to help developing countries afford mosquito netting, which is the most effective method of preventing the spread of mosquito-borne illnesses. It's not a requirement of the RNC to believe that every animal in the ocean is magically replenished by the same fairy that fills one's underwear drawer, but it helps.

Look, I know that urban environmentalists are more detrimental to the environment both in legislation and in personal behavior than anybody who actually lives in the places that urban environmentalists are trying to save, but these people aren't stupid, they're just sheltered from reality. Around 80% of the US population resides in urban areas, and those urban areas comprise about 10% of the total area of our nation. If we can agree that there are no natural resources in urban areas other than the same ones that will remain here when all life on Earth comes to a crispy end, maybe we can also agree that urban environmentalists only know what they have been told by people who take their money for a living. Those of us who live outside the hive know that animals in the wild die either by starvation or by being eaten alive by other animals. We've watched as the fad of recycling paper has converted tree farms into housing developments. We know that without logging we'd all be wiping our asses with plastic. We know that if it isn't farmed it's mined. We know that ethanol causes engines to wear out more quickly and forces everybody to use more of other natural resources. We know that it is just as detrimental to a population of animals for them to have no predators as it is for them to be overhunted. We know that covering every inch of the Nags Head causeway with housing developments produces runoff that kills the fry and eggs of indigenous fish. Rather than simply being the polar opposite of people who regurgitate the talking points sold to them by the six-digit magnates of wildlife nonprofits, take the time to explain to these people what nature is all about. Be their guide as they tippy-toe through the environment and teach them that the most important thing for a healthy ecosystem is a healthy economy. Urban environmentalists need to understand that nobody cares if the fish they catch is of legal size when they are starving. Nobody cares if the water is clean if their children have never seen a Capri Sun. And nobody cares if the flora they use for heat and shelter is endangered if they are dying of exposure.

I implore those of you who have been screwed by urban busybodies to be mindful of our environment when disposing of your emotions because it is *our* environment, not theirs. We are the ones who actually live and work outside in reality, and those who are ignorant of life outside of nonprofit propaganda deserve to be nothing more than ignored. Spotted owls are just a tool of those who dislike the aesthetics of logging. The piping plover was used for the sole purpose of clearing the imaginations of people who do not like the idea of other people driving on the beach. Sea turtles are just as much victims of environmentalists who are offended by plastic bags as those of us who are now stuck schlepping groceries in the rain in paper bags that tear and dump your soy milk and OJ down the steps of your house. Hate the game, hate the players, but don't hate the poor dumb animals that are used as pawns in the urban environmentalist's crusade to give their imaginations a legislative boob job.

Poverty

Just for fun let's pretend that the world is only 7,000 years old. For the first couple thousand years the descendants of Adam & Eve played *Land of the Lost* with dragons (or "dinosaurs" as the heliocentric crowd likes to call them). Then came Noah and the sea level rise. Since the gentle brontosaurus couldn't fit on the Ark it just didn't seem right to welcome the more vicious and brooding dragons on board, so Noah made an executive decision: any ruminant reptile under three cubits in height with cloven hooves could stay on the Ark and everybody else had to swim for it.

The immediate postdiluvian period brought about the settlement of the continents and experimentation with domestic architecture. After centuries of building houses out of grass, sticks, gingerbread and shoes, God's ant farm invented concrete. Concrete gave rise to the era of castles, large gaudy fences, and anything else that could be made by sticking rocks together with mortar. Playing with rocks ultimately led to the discovery of coal, and the Industrial Revolution followed shortly thereafter. Humanity thus liberated itself from the Stone Age literally by burning rocks.

For 6,800 years a banner day for *H. sapiens* was one in which you got a handful of berries and nobody died a premature and gruesome death. Wealth was defined by the possession of so many shiny objects that you could afford to give some of them away as payment to thugs for their protection of the rest of your shiny objects; and it was the person who had both the ability and stomach to do the most violence who had the most bling. Living in filth and

142

violence used to be normal. Today the people with the shiniest objects identify poverty as living the way that we did for almost all of human history, even if that history is only 7,000 years. If you are a round-Earther, poverty is how we lived for the two-hundred thousand years that preceded the Industrial Revolution. This is to say (if you are a hellbound heliocentrite) that the time since the Industrial Revolution is so brief that it is statistically insignificant and that humanity has been 'impoverished' for the entirety of its existence.

In industrialized nations poverty is measured by the accumulation of shiny objects. To be an American is to be so materialistic that you gauge another American's happiness by estimating how much money they have spent; and those who are pitied have a duty to spare higher society the burden of feeling sad by lamenting their own relative impecunity on behalf of the bourgeoisie. The existence of poverty is the most conclusive indication that a society has escaped the wetland of hunting and gathering and stumbled into the wasteland of civilization.

Booker T. Washington wrote of freedmen who elected to return to the plantation because they did not know how to survive on their own. Allegorically, government welfare in the form of EBT, Social Security, Medicaid and unemployment rations is the rebirth of the slave plantation. This time however, there are freemen of all skin colors who do not know how to survive on their own. The narratives of Frederick Douglass and Malcolm X are completely reborn with the poor being slaves, the welfare office being where the trusted *house negroes*-- the

Uncle Toms-- dispense the rations to the *field negroes*. The *master* is the state government which is responsible for providing the rations, and the *slave owner* is the Federal Government which dictates and enforces the hierarchy. A good slave is one who believes that they cannot live off of the plantation; but this is merely a cruel allegory. In reality every person who is in favor of this system belongs to the same political party that was in favor of it prior to the Civil War.

The culture of American poverty is a lifestyle revolving around the acquisition of wealth. The wealth that is acquired by the poor is either found or is exchanged with them for the social merit of almsgiving. You are not truly poor in America until you give up hope of ever providing tangible goods or services to your fellow man. To be poor in America one must surrender to the self-identification of being the creator of jobs within the government offices, churches, and nonprofit organizations that underwrite your hangover treatments. The mind of an impoverished American is broken down to a state in which they are either content to be detached from society, or they substitute their hope of economic advancement with blame for economic stagnation. Blame is the best psychological defense against the displeasure that accompanies one's unrequited love of material things; but make no mistake that it is material wealth that defines American poverty. Americans place no value on wealth of character, intellect, experience, or interpersonal relationships. A person can have all of these things, but as long as they lack hope of ever increasing their collection of shiny objects then they will define themselves as poor and promote themselves as such to the rest of society. Is there anything more delightfully ironic in American culture than a person who plays a musical instrument exceedingly well but whose life is nonetheless "a waste" because they are not able to surround themselves with shiny objects?

Every person who gives money (even if it is not their own) to the idea of the poor recognizes the meritorious feeling that they get in return for their assumed generosity. If these "generous" people, through hard work and a positive attitude, actually earned the money that they gave away, they would not only feel a greater degree of concern about whether or not they had actually helped whomever they were alleged to have been generous to, but they would also be far less likely to do it again when they discover that their hard-earned money was spent frivolously, as given wealth always is.

The intellect of a poor American is wasted on appeasing those who trade wealth for social merit. An impoverished American can be a genius, but as long as they spend their time trying to fit the American stereotype of a poor person instead of on improving themselves they will remain poor. In essence, the career of an impoverished American is to make as much money as possible by capitalizing on the generosity of others.

Wealth that is won or gifted is almost always spent frivolously. I, for example, squandered $4500 of my inheritance on running for Congress. But this is not to say that impoverished Americans are poor because of frivolous spending; rather it is the opposite. Frivolous spending is the result of being poor. In America we brainwash our poor into placing all social value on material wealth. In exchange for their hardship they are given money. Our poor are then spiritually broken because no matter how much money they are given or how many things they buy, it is never enough to get them out of poverty. Being "poor" is the only way that they know how to make money, and thus they are forced to become masters of the craft of being "lower class". What else is a poor person going to master in their free time? Playing an instrument? Pursuing the perfect cuboid Euler brick? Finding a shovel-ready job in Boynton, Oklahoma? None of these things permits you to forget the fact that you still need money *now*, and it is far easier to get a ride to the welfare office once a month for a sure thing than it is to go wherever the GED classes are being held three times a week and risk yet another embarrassment in the eyes of "the rest of" society. Any poor person will tell you that a welfare check is no substitute for dignity, but that it is infinitely better than failure. Just as a person is not a failure until they give up trying to accomplish something, an American is not poor until they give up hope of ever having enough money to fulfill the materialistic fantasies that they have been brainwashed to believe. Consequently, poor people in America see no reason to invest money, save money, or even to spend conservatively. Poor people in America know money to be something that always leaves them, and they feel that they have to exchange it for whatever they want at the time-- quickly before it disappears like Cinderella's dress and coach and whatever other stuff that materialistic wench dreamt about.

Although my depiction of the mental state of the American poor appears as a caricature of ignorance and thus seems to be little more than an insult, make no mistake that being born in the United States to a parent who depends upon the government for their survival is the closest thing possible to being born into slavery. Only in America do people cry over being poor even though they have more stuff than 99.999% of the rest of the people in the world; and this is because they are slaves to American materialism. Being poor is a miserable experience, and when somebody says that a poor person should "get a job", they are showing that they are just as ignorant about the American poor as the American poor are about everybody else. Poor Americans are so because all of their role models spend all of their intellect pursuing the trickle of wealth that the government plantation rations them. The first generation that lived off of welfare undoubtedly needed help, but their children had some very difficult choices to make. The third generation that lived off of the government had no decisions to make at all because by that time American poverty had become as much a culture as slavery. Now that we are on the seventh or eighth generation of people who live off the government, we have literally paid to institute a subculture of people who resent education, who distrust anybody who does not talk in clichés and simple metaphors (read *lies*), and who have no idea how to live on their own. Do you remember that person in college who didn't know how to do dishes, use a vacuum, hold a job, cook Ramen noodles, pay a parking

147

ticket, or figure out why no amount of phenolphthalein would turn his base solution pink? Imagine that person without supportive parents, without a high school education, and pretty much without anything except a TV and a free ride to the voting booth and suddenly you have a poor person. It's frustrating being ignorant; trust me, *I know.* Now imagine how emotionally screwed up that person would be if he had to live in a cardboard box instead of the dorm. Imagine thinking "I need money, but I don't have a job" and not having any idea how they guy behind the counter at the gas station got there. Now imagine being that person and having a role model who lived off of welfare, in government housing, and who got a raise for getting knocked up with you. Imagine that this is not just how it is with your role model, but with your entire family tree all the way back to the 1940's. Poor people in America have absolutely no idea how to apply for a job, how to budget their time or how to study. All they know is what they have been taught by their peer group, which is that if you want money you have two choices: you can either sell drugs or you can live off the government-- the latter of which is accomplished by telling anybody who works for the government that their clothes are beautiful. To a poor person, the choice between selling drugs or living off of welfare is as much a reality as going to college or learning a trade is to everybody else. It is no joke.

A powerful, compassionate person cannot observe the habits of impoverished Americans and not consider using social engineering to force these people to tap their latent potential. But there should be some tremendous concerns regarding the use of social engineering to eliminate poverty. For example:

- o Is poverty strictly financial? If not, how can poverty be quantified? Happiness is obviously out of the question. How about IQ? Hunger? Skin color? Child-to-income ratio? Unwed motherhood? Education? If we pick a social method of quantifying a person's poverty then aren't we really just using the government to institute a social hierarchy based upon our biases against people with different skin colors, BMIs, IQs, diplomas, marital status, or number of children? No, better we assume that if a person doesn't make a lot of money that they are pitiful: 'cause *that's* not culturally biased.

- o How forceful are we going to be with this social engineering stuff? Forcing kids to go to school is obviously not doing anything except wasting a bunch of money on kids who don't care about school to the detriment of those who do. One could argue that the reason that people do not appreciate perfunctory education is *because* it is perfunctory. Nonetheless, something needs to be done: should we expand on this silliness and impose mandatory military service on our citizens so that everybody can learn a trade? If so, what will we do with the people who have gone through mandatory military service and still wind up poor? Wouldn't it just be easier to simply give people money and hope for the best?

- What if we went Soviet Union on anybody who wants handouts from the government and chose career paths for these people? If you are a kid who is growing up on Social Security you could be taken to whitewater kayaking camp and train for the Olympics or something. Or if you're not athletic you can be programmed to be a computer programmer. If you're neither athletic nor smart you can be trained to be a poetry critic. No, no-- the right of a person to fester in government housing in front of *Wheel of Fortune* shall not be infringed.

- Well then, what about not doing anything? People from other countries don't seem to have a problem getting jobs in America, even if they are here illegally and don't speak English. These same people don't seem to be raising children who grow up and live off the government. And what do all of these people have in common? They have the common experience of poverty sucking. Maybe if poverty sucked again in the US people would again look to themselves for a solution to it, like picking up a leaf blower and breaking a sweat. Only in America is labor something that is beneath the American poor. In a way, the American poor are the only inklings of nobility left in this country.

Having grown up poor, I don't believe that poor people are the reason for poverty. At the very least it's circular logic. In America poverty is due to drug use, mental illness and social engineering; and the government fails miserably in its attempts to ameliorate each of these things. All social engineering is founded in the stereotyping of the people that it is intended to help. Social engineering requires laws, which is to say it requires the invention of crimes and punishments to inflict upon the citizens. Fighting poverty with social engineering does not work because you cannot force an individual out of a life of poverty and/or crime by threatening them with monetary fines and/or the label of 'criminal'. I have personally struggled with the relative appeal of being labeled a criminal versus the misery of being labeled poor. The only way to get poor people in America to make the most of themselves is by leaving them alone. If you know a specific poor person and you want to help them out, *that* is the attitude that changes things. By all means *do it*. But if you want to hand out money to strangers (especially if the money isn't yours) and call it progress, you're a Marxist in the nuttiest and most religious sense of the term. We all make mistakes, but it is inexcusable for any intelligent person to force a public policy of pushing the same glowing elevator button to Marxist utopia that 75% of the human population has been fruitlessly pressing since 1848.

Poor people in America are poor because of their behavior, and their behavior is learned. Much of human behavior is directed by the path of least resistance. In other countries being poor is difficult. In the US our government makes *damn* sure that being poor is as easy as voting; but it remains as intellectually and emotionally difficult as being a child who loses their parents.

Energy Independence

A policy of US energy independence seems to be a policy that conservatives and liberals agree on for different reasons. In short, liberals want us to commute on wind-powered trains and (ironically-called) conservatives want to burn every last drop of our own oil rather than have it imported. The latter idea is far dumber than the former if for no other reason than the fact that liberals are at least asking what's possible rather than what's easy. When Sarah Palin says "drill baby drill" she may as well be saying "self-imposed oil embargo". Drill and cap: yes. Drill and store: maybe for stabilizing the price of imports. But drill and combust? Don't be an idiot.

Energy independence is a political catch phrase that is vague because it is a political catch phrase. True energy independence would mean using blankets and screens instead of heat pumps, sunlight instead of lamps, bicycles instead of cars, and pretty much living like most of the people in my neighborhood growing up. There is a word for true energy independence but politicians refuse to use it. That word is *poverty*.

Energy independence is about the alleged danger of importing fossil fuel, primarily crude oil. What is the danger of importing oil other than both Conservatives and Progressives agree that it is a bad idea? Oil spills? The Pirates of Lake Huron? Import tax?

Actually the danger resides in Americans' inability to stop purchasing the same amount of fuel when the price goes up. In economics this is called *inelasticity of demand*. When a person's demand for something does not decrease as the price goes up, their demand is said to be *in-elastic*. The responsibility of an employer is to find the line where customers stop complaining about prices and walk away from a purchase, and to stay beneath that line. It is a customer's responsibility to cultivate elasticity in their demand for products and services. In psychology inelasticity of demand is called addiction.

Much like the war on drugs, the war on foreign oil focuses on the supply of a substance to which Americans are addicted. But the danger of a substance rarely originates from its supply. The danger of firearms is not that they are present; it is that they are used to implement the demands of those who hold them. The danger of tobacco and cocaine is not that they are available; they only become dangerous after you take them into your body. The danger of a car, swimming pool, ladder, road, or nuclear weapon lies in the willful use of these things, not in their mere existence. The danger of gasoline is that people build an entire way of life around its being supplied cheaply, and then they have no recourse but to pay more for it when the price goes up. What is a person to do when they drive an hour to work and the price of gasoline goes up? Stop driving to work? Drilling and refining our own oil will not change the danger of inelasticity of demand. If we are not going to improve ourselves by decreasing our addiction to fossil fuel, then it is in America's best interest to use up somebody else's supply of it first.

When we purchase foreign oil, we exchange relatively cheap digits in a computer for a product that is extremely valuable. We also get a trade partner who is going to want to remain on good terms with us or risk losing American dollars. It is to America's benefit to purchase foreign-- particularly Middle Eastern-- oil because many of the nations that trade oil with us hate Americans and would otherwise love to see video of our Infidel corpses burning on *al Jazeera.*

Allegedly if the United States continues to purchase oil from Middle Eastern nations those nations will be able to raise the price of oil on us and we will have no recourse but to continue printing money to pay the higher price. This is complicated by the fact that the largest consumer of oil in the world is the US military. Imagine the danger of sending our American men and women in uniform out to quell the problems of some pseudo-republic and having some evil Muslim nation price gouge us over the threat of our troops not being able to refuel in-between invasions and whatnot.

Well that is all nice to imagine, but now let's dabble in reality. The majority of foreign oil that we buy comes from Canada. If the United States is at war we don't want our oil fields and refineries, or those of our friends to the north, being targets for the enemy to blow up. If we are at war with North Korea, Kim Jong-un will not make additional enemies by bombing the oil fields, ships, and refineries of Middle Eastern nations. Furthermore, the US dollar is the gold standard of Middle Eastern currency. Nobody-- not even Iran-- wants North Korea to be their best customer. The inconvenient truth is that the only nations which would present the United States with a likely military threat are those in the Middle East. Saudi Arabians hate us and would like to see every last one of us burned and crushed beneath a million tons of concrete, but as long as we are trade partners with the Saudi Government they are not going to side with any like-minded terrorist organization.

It is not a coincidence that many al Qaeda lemmings are from Saudi Arabia. Saudi Arabia is a Monarchy ruled by the Saud family. A large portion of the Saudi citizens are oppressed by the royal family, but the royal family is far too powerful to be overthrown due to the money it receives from the United States from the sale of oil. Thus it is not a great extrapolation to recognize that the United States is the biggest enabling force behind the Saud family's ability to oppress the Arab people. In a sense al Qaeda is kind of like the Tea Party. Al Qaeda is angry at the intrusion of the progressive Saudi government into their lives. Unlike the Tea Party, al Qaeda can neither protest nor vote against the government intrusion that they suffer.

It is imperative to understand that oil is the single greatest substance required for the implementation of an effective military. Now consider the fact that the military with air superiority is the military that dominates its opponents. Since airplanes do not fly on batteries and airplane factories do not run on patriotism, the last nation with the most jet fuel, *i.e.* with the greatest oil reserves, will either have the superior air force or will be the ally of the nation with the superior air force. Contrary to what conspiracy theorists say about fossil fuel, there is no equal substitute for it. Indeed there are substitutes for liquid petroleum, but you cannot begin the manufacturing process for any of them by simply sucking the product substrate out of the ground. In the future combustible fuels will be manufactured from sources that are grown, such as algae and switchgrass. But a military which mobilizes based upon the benevolence of a growing season will never defeat a military that has energy at the turn of a pump.

At some point it will become cheaper to grow fuel in vast fields than it will to take it out of a pipe. Only then will the transition to alternative fuel sources become an endeavor in which the entire international community becomes involved. I have no idea how this is going to progress, but it is going to suck for everybody who is not a government official.

If humanity's transition from fossil fuel to alternative sources of combustion-based energy is moderated solely by nations that adhere to a constitutional-republican form of government, then the transition will be peaceful but will primarily serve the nations involved. If the United Nations attempts to redistribute the world's oil reserves there will be worldwide violence with most of the traumatic deaths occurring in the oil-rich nations, while the citizens of poorer nations will suffer mass deaths due to a reduction in what few medical resources they already have. But there is a possible outcome for America that is even worse than these. The transition from fossil fuel to an alternative will happen long before the untapped fossil fuel reserves run out, and as long as the United States is governed by representatives who understand that the reserves are, in fact, running out, we will be OK. But lurking within our midst are people, some of them in public

156

office, who believe that the Earth is only 7,000 years old.

Under household conditions, believing that the Earth is only 7,000 years old is only as dangerous as believing that women have more ribs than men or that days weren't created until Thursday. But if enough legislators believe that fossil fuel was formed naturally in the last 7,000 years from existing carbon sources within the Earth's crust, then America will end up being the largest third-world country on the planet. Some conservative Christians are literally 7,000 years behind in their geology studies, and 100% of them are Republicans. So when it comes to energy policy America is screwed. We can vote for the Democratic Party's hysteria of CO2 as Apocalypse, which at least has a foundation in science and will leave our military with oil reserves when the environmental apocalypse fails to happen. Or we can vote in favor of the Republican Party's 7,000-Year-Old-Earth policies which start out L. Ron Hubbard wacky and go downhill from there.

Alternative energy

In 1901 Wilbur Wright said "man will not fly for 50 years". He was 34 years old at the time, and the life expectancy of an average American male was only 46 years (his brother Orville only lived to 45). After Wilbur grumbled his infamous quip he and Orville did not even hesitate to continue pursuing their dream of flying. Two years later they safely flew an airplane 120 feet-- roughly the wingspan of a Boeing 737. Sixty-six years after that the American government either put men on the moon or got close enough to it to realize that it would be safer to fake a video of landing on it; either way America had once again affirmed its pride of being the undisputed overachievers of humanity. So every time some voice on the radio bemoans the inconsistency of wind and solar power I feel the United States turning just a little bit more into just another Spanish-speaking nation. It makes me want to dress up in colorful handmade clothes, perform a commemorative dance in celebration of some battle in which we didn't attack first and still won, and then eat something made with corn and a mystery vegetable.

The physics of harnessing wind power is exactly the same as that met by the Wright Brothers. For talking heads who contribute absolutely nothing to the development of humanity's future sources of energy to say that wind power is not worth pursuing, is short sighted and frankly un-American. Whether the 7,000-year-old-Earth crowd likes it or not there will come a point in time when it will become cheaper to illuminate the world with the unreliable energy of windmills than with fossil fuel. There will be period of time in which no amount of money will facilitate the export of fossil fuel, and those who have fossil fuel will only exchange it for the services of the most effective and loyal forces of security. These developments will display with brilliant clarity the difference between the power of a dollar to turn a generator and the power of a real source of energy. Only then will Americans become interested in harnessing our potential to once again lead the world in the development of the technology that will take humanity out of its fossil fuel pubescence and into the grown-up world of budgeting beyond the imaginary realm of the dollar.

If we wait until wind, geothermal, and solar power are all cheaper than fossil fuel to switch over to them, we will be stuck using these relatively puny energy sources to perform the research to perfect them. If we wait until we are dependent upon algae for power we will add decades to the process of finally harnessing fusion as an energy source. What would the Wright Brothers do? It is better to do the research now while our dollars can still be easily printed and traded for the fossil fuel that is essential for high-end R&D.

Guerilla Marketing for Dummies

After I registered as a Republican candidate and vowed not to take campaign contributions, I was confronted with the challenge of getting my name out to the voters who don't really pay attention to politics. I decided to use a tactic that has spelled success for dozens of companies across the beaches of America.

If you have a little bit of money and malleable ethics, you can make a bit more money by tapping into the market for surfwear. The surfing lifestyle is an image that need not be exclusively for the athletic, pelagic, or Californian trust funders. If you want to pretend that you have the 'surfer attitude', all you have to do is purchase a t-shirt that has the name of a bona fide surfwear company on it. And how do you know if a surfwear company is authentic? Easy: whichever company has the most stickers on the dumpster by your apartment is the brand that the cool kids are wearing. Choosy posers and your author choose Birdwell Beach Britches.

That's right, I chose stickers as the primary medium of my political campaign. I thought about scribbling my name on rocks and throwing them into people's yards, but alas, we have no rocks in coastal North Carolina, which makes them more expensive than stickers.

I went to Staples and had a roll of 200 rectangular yellow stickers printed up for me. The stickers had black lettering which read "If you're ready for a middle class politician vote for Jim Miller on May 4th". My hope was that by stating that I was middle class, as opposed to a traditional politician with lots of rich friends seeking tax write-offs in exchange for porcine entrees, that potential voters might forgive my vandalizing our district with my 2" by 3" adhesive tabs. I stuck those suckers everywhere: gas pumps, trash cans, underneath the drive thru window at fast food restaurants, on the little plastic thing that flaps down on shopping carts, next to the dollar-bill eater on soda machines, above door handles on windows of store fronts that were up for lease. I even stuck them in the bathroom stalls in Lowe's and Books-a-Million. For my entire life I've had to look at everybody else's decals stuck all over the world; now it was my turn. I had absolutely no idea why anybody would stick a *Local Motion* decal on the McDonald's drive thru menu, but when I stuck my name smack in the middle of a NO LEFT TURN I was filled with the hope of saving my nation from either massive inflation or full-blown depression, one of which is still

161

imminent.

I was enabled to participate in littering my beloved environs with propaganda by a (I don't know the correct adjective here) timed $10,000 check from my grandmother's estate. My grandmother had passed away a few months earlier of lung cancer at the age of 88. I am embarrassed to admit that I did not know my grandmother very well. My parents were separated before my father died, and I don't know how much of my not knowing my dad's mum was due to the awkwardness of that situation. The easiest excuse for my not really knowing Grandma Nell was that she lived in Twin Falls, Idaho. I saw her a couple of times growing up and since then we had mostly only communicated via snail mail.

So in addition to being an introvert I have other character flaws that make me a lousy politician. Specifically, I absolutely loathe those cardboard political yard signs that have nothing but a candidate's name on them. Cardboard political yard signs are a monument to the stupidity of the American voter. If by some miracle human society becomes smarter in the future, our great-great-great-great-great grandchildren will look back on our era and say "How did they think that they could borrow a trillion dollars a year, spend 75% of it on entitlements, and not expect to have inflation when they printed the money to pay it off?" To which they will respond "Well their selection criteria for leadership was based almost entirely on the bandwagon effect of cardboard political yard signs. Obviously they were morons."

Think about this for a minute: what is the most pervasive form of political advertising? Not the most *in*vasive-- that would be telemarketing. Not the most annoying-- that would be smear campaigns on TV that start with "Candidate so-and-so is up to his old tricks . . ." The political advertising to which we are most frequently exposed is simply a name on a board on the side of the road. This is called *reminder advertising*. Reminder advertising serves the purpose of placing a thought in the mind of a person who is going to thoughtlessly purchase (or vote for) something. The textbook example of reminder advertising goes as follows:

Your boss has just been proven to be not-the-father of his ex-wife's child and you want to celebrate by throwing him an office party. As you contemplate what munchies to serve at your workplace soiree you recall that Alice is allergic to peanuts, Judy doesn't do gluten, Brad is Vegan and does not eat anything pre-packaged, Seth is kosher, Chris is on a diet, Monica is taking a monoamine oxidase inhibitor and you know that she can't eat a whole bunch of stuff but every time you ask her what she *can* eat she starts crying, Joe's fat ass looks like he's one hot dog away from a coronary, Betty is afraid of uncooked food, Larry doesn't do refined sugar, Mitt is Mormon and can't have caffeine, Barry says pork is the worst thing the white man ever gave the black man and everybody is afraid to ask him which color cake he finds least offensive.

The only normal person you work with is an illegal alien named Bergljot who straightens up around the office and waters the plants. You decide that Brad is only a Vegan for the attention and that secretly he would enjoy being excluded. Monica knows what she can and can't eat; she's a big girl and she's just going to have to deal. You know for a fact that Mitt sneaks over to Starbucks in the afternoon while his wife is with the girls at ballet. Larry is just a sissy and his liver works fine. Diets were made to be broken, kosher is easy to work with, Barry is going to feel oppressed no matter what you bring, Betty is an idiot, Judy is too much of a pleaser to complain, Alice carries an epi pen and Joe will eat everything that doesn't get eaten anyway. You decide that none of your coworkers are worth feeding, but you've gotten them all psyched up for an office party and you must deliver.

"What of snacks should I pick up at store" asks Bergljot, whose lower lip protrudes slightly toward you as she gazes at your mouth in anticipation of your response. It's a look that you've gotten to know rather well over the past few weeks; Bergljot's large blue eyes sparkle with hints of both innocence and simmering ferocity, of both longing and familiarity. It makes you feel like a dirty old man, which is pretty much why she does it.

You break your gaze with a blink requiring both eyebrows and you return your mouth to its more professional, closed position. Taking a deep breath you look around the office at your tedious coworkers and say "Just get a 12 pack of Coke and a bag of Lay's potato chips". And thus, with one mindless decision you have joined millions of other burned-out office-party organizers who don't give a fiddler's fart what kind of junk food gets purchased. In the land of plenty people frequently purchase
164

things that they have absolutely no opinion about. They say the first thing that comes to mind, and when the topic is soft drinks and potato chips American repetition advertising makes you say "Coke" and "Lay's". Once again Brad's Drink and Pigsah Wild Herb potato chips remain on the shelves while Joe and the gang get just-a-little-bit-more-brainwashed into blindly selecting Coke and Lay's the next time they are charged with spackling the carping maws of a phalanx of coworkers, a colon of book critics, or an upheaval of tweens.

Yes friends, repetition advertising is the modus of American ascent into political office. Yes friends, repetition advertising is the modus of American ascent into political office. When Joe Voter goes to the ballot box he doesn't carry with him a satchel of note cards that remind him "Congress 1st district: Miller- brooding with spurts of hyperbole, unqualified to coach a soccer team of seven year olds, tends to insult Democrats". All they come with is what they've been told by the TV and seen on the side of the road. It is your responsibility as a candidate to fill the void left in our society by ignorant voters with your smarts by repeating, repeating, *repeating* your name in as many media as possible. When being quoted by a newspaper, frequently refer to yourself in the third person. Don't just litter the roadside of your district with your surname: purchase radio announcements that mention your name as many times as possible too. Incorporate what is known as *association advertising* by playing patriotic-sounding music while somebody chants your name or slogan. Marches are good-- consider something by Sousa. People who get their political information from mass media may forget what country they are in, so show the American flag whenever possible. Remember: in Washington you manufacture bureaucracy; on the campaign trail however, you are selling hope.

After some very painful rationalization of priorities I caved and decided to give in to the ignorance of the crowd. I got online and compared prices for large, billboard-sized banners. By that afternoon I'd ordered four banners with dimensions of 8' high and 24' long, and three more at 4' by 8'. I figured if I was going to do something stupid I may as well do it big. I chose these particular dimensions because most lumber is sold in lengths divisible by 4', thus the signs could be placed on a frame erected with minimal carpentry. Then I had them shipped to Jason's house.

Since Jason and I are male and consequently never talk to one another, I didn't tell him that I was having ginormous banners sent to his house. A couple of days later when I returned to New Bern to work I was surprised to find a huge wooden frame erected in my drinking buddy's yard. The frame was v-shaped and on either side of the v was hung one of my ginormous banners for the passing traffic to savor. The traffic going toward New Bern got to read:

Middle class, fed up, over-taxed, *but with your vote*
<u>DOING SOMETHING ABOUT IT!</u>
Jim Miller   US Congress
NCDistrict1.com   Please vote **May 4th**

The traffic going toward the Weyerhauser plant got distracted with:

smaller budget . . . BIGGER IDEAS
Jim Miller, [blah-blah self-promoting propaganda]

The feeling I had was inexplicable. My drinking buddy was so supportive of me that he put up gigantic tacky signs right in his own yard, and built frames to do it on. I have always been blessed with great friends, and I know that any of my friends would have done the same thing for me, but for some reason it always makes me feel jittery and scared when it is obvious that people care about me.

About a week and a half later I was contacted by the district engineer of the North Carolina Dept. of Transportation. His name was Smith and he was the bearer of unfortunate news. Somebody'd been complaining to the DOT about the big sign in Jason's yard poking out into the right-of-way. For those of you who are unaware of what a right-of-way is, it's property that is yours insomuch as you pay taxes on it and are required to maintain it, but you aren't allowed to actually do anything with it because it really belongs to the government. The most common way that the government seizes the property of law-abiding citizens is by claiming it as right-of-way. After the Progressives of the world are done taking their right-of-way from your property and giving it to a corporate donor or turning it into a road, the government will delineate another right-of-way on "your" property, thereby giving you fair warning that they can take *that* whenever they want also.

This would be followed by their marking out another right-of-way, and so on until you have nothing left. Although it was irritating that somebody was utilizing Progressive legislation to hinder the election process, at least this was consistent and I had to respect that.

What was more disturbing than not being allowed to do as you want on your own rural property was the rest of Mr. Smith's email. Particularly the part which read:

> *I have searched around the Internet and made a few calls (local election office, NC GOP, Republican Party Craven County) but have not been successful in finding a phone number for either you or your campaign, hence this email.*

Although this answered the age-old question of who had better investigators: the 2nd district of the NCDOT's 2nd Highway Division or the *Washington Daily News*, it raised more troubling and far less important questions. Perhaps Mr. Smith was an astute observer of political paraphernalia and recognized the talking points of the Republican Party; but nowhere on any of my signs did it say that I was a Republican. How did he know? The fact that I had not flamboyantly announced my Republican affiliation might have had something to do with why I was not being thrown any coming-out parties by the GOP. However, I knew for a fact that both the NCGOP and the Craven County Republican Party knew who I was and had all of my contact information. I'd been receiving almost daily emails from the NCGOP ever since I notified them of my candidacy, starting with this:

FROM: NCGOP info@ncgop.org

TO: Jim Miller
DATE: Sat, Feb 20, 2010 at 2:03 PM
SUBJECT: Thanks for signing up

Thank you for signing up to keep in touch with the NCGOP. We appreciate your dedication to bringing back good government to North Carolina. We hope you will consider donating to the NCGOP as we work to elect Republicans from your local courthouse to Washington, DC. Thanks again!

But the NCGOP is a pretty big organization. It must be difficult to keep track of the candidates who don't bring money into the party. But in addition to notifying the NCGOP of my candidacy I'd also notified the Craven County Republican Party (CCRP). In fact I'd spent over $150 introducing myself to the CCRP partisans at their annual Reagan Day Dinner. I even had an invitation:

Jim,

Congradulations [sic] *on becoming a candidate. We are having our annual Reagan Day Dinner Sat nite at the Flame Banquet Center on Neuse Blvd. We hope to have 400 or so republicans attending and it would be a great way for you to meet some active republicans. Tickets are $40 each and if you want one or more let me know. We will also have a table for campaign materials to be displayed. Please go to our web site www.cravengop.org and you can get dates off the calendar for the Mens and Womens Clubs and also our monthly Executive meeting which is open to all. Please attend these events so we can meet you and vise* [sic] *versa.*

Good luck indeed. The Reagan Day Dinner had been on March 6th, and I was there. I had utilized the campaign materials table. I also made a spectacle of myself at the dinner by chasing the microphone all the way around the banquet hall as I attempted to join the other candidates in being video recorded while introducing ourselves to the other guests and stating the respective offices for which we were running. When I'd finally caught up with the mic everybody in the room stared at me like I was crashing a wedding or something. In their defense I was still wearing my uniform from work; maybe I looked like a Democrat. Nonetheless, most people clapped politely when I was finished. Of course the high point of the Reagan Day Dinner was a brief speech by NC Senator Richard Burr who, in between Republican clichés, said the following:

This is not one of those elections where any county can sorta take a pass and say 'well we really don't have competitive races'. If anything, all of the sudden the Republican Party has become a party where we've got a primary in every office: something we've never been used to. And I'm here to tell you today, work extremely hard for your dog that's in the fight. And after the primary come together again and support whoever wins and forget about the losses.

At the end of the dinner I'd posted myself at the exit and handed everybody who passed a pamphlet that contained my name, phone number, picture, email, proposed legislation and my political viewpoints. I also gave about 300 pamphlets to the woman from the CCRP who was manning the table of campaign materials. This person allegedly took my pamphlets to display at the CCRP Headquarters for all to see and take and discuss. She had even agreed to give me a call if my pamphlets started to run out. I guess I should have been tipped off that the CCRP wasn't interested in me when I had to talk them into taking my paraphernalia rather than being asked for it.

Damn you Craven County Republican Party! We exchanged numbers! You invited me to dinner! I bore my soul to you! I let you videotape us! How could you be so cold? (the author bites his fist)

Let me reiterate dear reader, that having a platform is a waste of time. What you should do is to raise a lot of money by offering tax-deductible festivities and reciting a catchy, three-word slogan that people can remember. If you do have a platform, make it about something that only a handful of people actually care about and convince the rest of the voters that it is important. Like gay marriage, or the location of a mosque, or how offensive it is that Mexicans are doing all the jobs that Americans feel are beneath them. This way if you get elected and you end up doing nothing about these issues, only a handful of people will actually be upset at you. The rest of the people who voted for you will want to vote for you again as a way of proving to themselves that they were right about you the first time. Plus, you'll be an incumbent so you will have myriad businesses to invite to highfalutin' tax-deductible events in which they can be propositioned to subsidize your political propaganda. This is how the successful politician protects his place in nobility. Spend as much money as you can on two-dimensional roadside litter and post it so far into the right-of-way that it scrapes the sides of cars as they pass. In order to be popular with your political party, your ideology and character do not matter. What matters, as in any fraternity, is that you are able to put the fun in fundraiser.

The right-of-way problem at Jason's was no big deal. The signs had to be 60' from the center of the road, which meant that I had to move them back about five feet. This only took me three hours on one of my days off and I got some sun in the process. I then turned my attention to the other billboards that I had to put up. And so it came to pass during the ides of March 2010 that I would again have to talk to women. The hospital at which I worked was like a small community in itself and it was there that I would pursue leads for locations to put up my 4' by 8' propaganda. The problem was that Southern women are very hard to read politically.

I decided to narrow the field of whom I had to talk to by figuring out who lived next to a large road and had a yard in which I could put up a 4' by 8' sign. The first woman I approached with the proposition of putting up a big, gaudy sign in their yard was Ann from ED registration. Ann was from my home town of Elizabeth City. She had been a couple of years behind me in school, but I remembered her because I always thought she was kinda purty.

I asked Ann if I could put a sign up in her yard and she said yes. I put the 4' by 8' sign up next to Ann's horse fence. The sign was posted on two-by-fours that went down about two feet into the ground. The sign read:

The government will never serve the middle class . . .
UNTIL IT *IS* MIDDLE CLASS!
Elect Jim Miller

I put it up on Saturday evening after dark and by Monday morning the entire sign had been stolen, two by fours and all. They could have just stolen the sign and left the wood for me and Jason to burn over a six-pack of Duck-Rabbit beer but *nooooooo*. The theivin' bastards had to take the whole frickin' thing. Ann and her husband felt that they were somehow responsible for somebody else's larceny, and I felt bad for how bad they felt. Ann's husband was particularly upset that somebody would hop over the ditch into his yard and steal something. And we're talking about people who live in the country. Ann and her husband had chickens. In the South you're taking your life into your hands when you fool around with people who have chickens. Whoever did the stealing was lucky they didn't get shot. Apparently nothing is sacred to whatever sort of person feels that the concept of private property is meaningless when it comes to working extremely hard for their dog.

Four days after putting up the sign at Ann's I put on my gonna-to-talk-to-women pants again asked one of the ED nurses if I could put one of my large, obnoxious signs in her yard. Her name was . . . let's say it was Bindi. That is correct: she was named after the Crocodile Hunter's daughter. Bindi gave me permission to put a sign up in her yard, and Bindi's yard was a little easier to work in than Ann's. Most prominently, Bindi's yard already had a billboard in it. All I had to do to avoid any harassment about the right-of-way was put my little billboard underneath the great big billboard. This was also an excellent spot because it was adjacent to US Hwy 17, and there were no trees or horses between the barrel of Bindi's husband's .30-06 and any low-down, triflin' sign pinchers.

I arrived at Bindi's house after work and met her husband and their kids. They were super nice people and very supportive of my sign-putting-up. After some pleasantries Bindi's husband asked if I needed any help and he offered me his tools. I declined with many thanks, and reported that I was pretty much ready to go with everything I needed in the Matrix. I set forth putting up the sign and I did not finish until after dark. While shuffling dirt around in the dark, Bindi's father-in-law (who lived next door) came out to ask me if I needed to be shot or anything. I told Mr. Bindi-in-Law that I had obtained permission from his son and daughter-and-law, and since it was already obvious from the sign I went ahead and told him that I was running for Congress. He was happy that I was not with the big-billboard people, because apparently they had not paid him in almost six months for the monstrosity that towered over my little sign. We had a brief chat and I decided that if I ever died and was reincarnated as a golden retriever that I wanted to live with the Bindis because they were such good folks.

The sign at Bindi's stayed up through the primary, after which I returned and took it down. I went up to the house to thank Bindi's husband again for granting me permission to clutter up his yard for a couple of months.
174

Mr. Bindi's truck was in the drive but when I knocked on the door nobody came. Later I learned that Bindi and her husband had split up. I also learned why Mr. Bindi didn't come to the door.

After the election Jason and I returned to our weekly routine of friends, bonfires and microbrews. One night Bindi arrived at the gathering late and was behaving in a decidedly helpless and questionably intoxicated manner. Through the fuzziness of springtime inebriation I suddenly noticed that Bindi was standing very close to me as we talked. She was upset to the point of crying. Bindi got all up in my grill and was doing that thing that women do of somehow making their breasts the center of attention even though they do not seem to be aware of them, and she sadly confessed to me the state of her relationship with Mr. Bindi. Bindi told me that before she was separated from her husband-- nice Mr. Bindi-- the man who had offered to help me put up my sign-- who had offered me his tools no less-- Mr. Bindi had accused his wife of clearing the snorkel with "the sign guy". After dropping this little daisy cutter Bindi slipped away into the bathroom as women do at parties. I opened up my phone and stared really hard at my pictures of Kelli for about 0.68 seconds, then I drank a bunch of water and hid in my car until I fell asleep. I woke up shivering a few hours later, relieved that Kelli was not going to leave me. That was the end of that, but I felt awful that nice Mr. Bindi thought that I'd screwed him by proxy.

The inventory of my three, 4' by 8' signs at this point would yield the following count: there was the one that got snatched from Ann's, there was another that somehow wound up imputing me in cuckoldry at Bindi's, and the final one was at my mom's in Washington. I had the intention of propping up the last sign in a friend's yard somewhere in the district the following week, but the mom had other plans. My mom commandeered my remaining sign and posted it on an A-frame in the rear of her pickup truck. This could have been pretty cool, but in addition to Mom being struck with the same affliction as myself of not really caring how things look as long as they work right, Mom is also not the best carpenter. By the time the billboard was erected in the rear of her '96 Chevy 1500 both she and the sign were slathered with duct tape, the A-frame was in cursive, and the whole thing looked like it might fly out into traffic at any minute. But what could I do other than strap the contraption down with a come-along and pray that when the sign ripped off that it didn't cover some unsuspecting independent voter's windshield and cause them to die in a fiery explosion like on *CHiPs*? It was me mum. She gave birth to me. She'd changed my diapers. She'd held me tightly as I bled all over the front seat of our neighbor's Oldsmobile as we drove to the hospital after I bit my tongue halfway off. She never told me how much she disliked my first girlfriend. She made up stories about the disappearance of my cat, which got crushed in the rear of a garbage truck; and about my gerbil, which I mortally wounded when I accidentally cupped my hands over him too forcefully during a high-speed chase through the living room-- to this day I don't know where you get a new gerbil at 8PM in Elizabeth City-- maybe I really did pray Brighteyes back from the light as Mom suggested. Anyhoo, she was my mom and I was obliged to humor her. Everything Mom does is a little different. I'm a little different too. I wouldn't be who I am without her so I was going to have to accept the rickety A-frame and duct-tape-covered campaign sign. And although our house in Washington was the most stolen-from, loitered-upon and vandalized place that we'd ever lived *and* we had to park on the street because we had no driveway, the sign in the bed of Mom's pickup remained untouched through the primary election. We'll never know for sure why nobody bothered my sign; perhaps it had something to do with the truck looking like there might be somebody sleeping in the cab with a sawed off 12-gauge. And maybe there was. Mom also shares my inclination for snoozing in parked vehicles.

Putting the Pain in Campaigning

That which I liberally call my campaign was hindered not merely my being a naïve, middle-class introvert. I was also oppressed by being gainfully employed. When you work a job that revolves around 911 calls you can't just ditch work and take Air Force One to Sioux City on a popularity quest.

As a consequence of my being a blue-collar schlemiel I was going to miss a meeting of the West Bertie Concerned Citizens. This may sound like no big deal, but I really wanted to meet these people. For one thing, the Concerned Citizens had actually invited me to visit with them. This was more than I could say for the Bertie Co. Republican Party, which was having a convention on the same day as the meeting of the Concerned Citizens. When it came to my candidacy the Bertie Republicans were pulling a *Washington Daily News*. As much as I would have liked to have met with the Concerned Citizens and crashed the convention, both of these gatherings were scheduled for an hour before I even got off work, and they were both over an hour drive away.

Some of the less sophisticated readers are probably wondering what a *Bertie* is. Bertie is a County, and it is one of my favorites. Windsor is a small town in Bertie County, and it is the County seat.

When I was growing up in Pasquotank County, Bertie County was the area that I identified as being the closest place to home with topography that wasn't absolutely flat. Pasquotank County is in the Great Dismal Swamp; and if there is one thing that you should know about swamps it's that they are flat. Eventually the swamps of Pasquotank County were drained in order to make extremely flat farmland, and that is what the majority of the Great Dismal Swamp is today. Bertie County began on the west side of the Chowan River and the very first thing that you noticed when you came across the Chowan River bridge was a ribbon of golden cliffs that plunged down into the brown water. For someone who was raised in a swamp even a fifteen foot cliff is a tremendous novelty.

The cliffs of the Chowan River mark what is called the Suffolk shoreline or Suffolk *scarp*. The Suffolk scarp is where the shore of the Atlantic Ocean used to be, and will be again. It is a geological formation that is not only visible from the Chowan River Bridge, but from space. Between 80,000 and 125,000 years ago the glaciers of Greenland and northern Canada melted due to the carbon dioxide released into the atmosphere by factories owned by a man known only as Mr. Slate. The smog from Slate's factories caused the sea level to rise as much as 25 feet. Everything to the east of the Suffolk shoreline is very flat because it used to be the bottom of the ocean, but we didn't know anything about that stuff growing up. All we swampdwellers knew was that hills were loads of fun. With changes in elevation came the possibility of riding your bike without pedaling, seeing farther than the next line of trees, and if it ever decided to snow you could presumably slide from place to place without being towed by somebody's sadistic older brother on a four-wheeler. On the way to 4-H functions from Elizabeth City the bus would always stop and pick up people in Bertie County. The Bertie kids were always friendly and smart.

I do have one unfortunate memory involving Bertie Co. In 1981 my sister and I went to 4-H camp somewhere along one of NC's low-lying coastal tributaries. This was the year that our mom came along as a camp counselor, and as fate would have it, it was also the year that 4-H happened to accommodate the largest collection of good-naturedly foul-mouthed campers to which I'd ever been exposed. Somehow on the bus ride to camp the catch phrase "suck the peter" was not just learned but embraced by what seemed like the entire bus. Within the span of a few hours 'suck the peter' had become the equivalent of a Southern *fahgettaboudit*. Ever other sentence was ended with it and every interrogative statement was answered with a postscriptual 'suck the peter': "Mike, what time is it?"

"Two-forty, suck the peter". If somebody was reading a book or watching the trees go by outside the bus for more than a few minutes they would inevitably be hailed:

"Hey Bobby!"

"Huh?"

"Suck the peter!"

"Aww man!"

And everybody would laugh except me because I didn't want my mom to catch me. From my perspective the use of such language was particularly dangerous behavior. At my school there was a very strict policy regarding the words that came out of your mouth. My teacher Mrs. Oldham had a jar on her disk filled with the nickels of students who used the words "ain't" or "dude". Any stronger language than that cost you a trip to the office for a 'spare the rod spoil the child' discussion with our Principal Mr. Parrott. If the discussion was relayed to your parents, you usually got a good old fashioned beating when you got home as a reminder of how much your parents hated being talked down to on the phone by Mr. Parrott's secretary Mrs. Bohannon.

Don't get me wrong-- at eleven I had an extensive lexicon of taboo words and phrases, and although my prepubescent intellect prohibited me from understanding what most of the expressions meant it didn't prevent me from using them whenever possible. But the whole joy of cussing and being generally vulgar hinged upon the fact that it was off limits because we were kids. To talk like an adult around adults and get away with it sort of defeated the purpose, and under no circumstances did I want to be caught swearing by my mother. Suddenly on the bus to 4-H camp I'd found myself surrounded by public school kids who not only found the phrase 'suck the peter' to be meaningful enough to repeat, but they said it in front of grown-ups and they said it *a lot*. Equally bewildering to me was the fact that the grown-ups just ignored it. In retrospect I suppose there was no rapport between the counselors at that point. Mom after all had never even been to camp, let alone been a camp counselor, and there's no telling how experienced any of the other counselors were. Failed authoritarianism so early in the week may have yielded disaster for the rest of the time at camp, so I guess the grown-ups were just waiting for this obnoxious spell to pass.

Normally the goofiness that develops when kids travel long distance on a bus dissolves within minutes of stepping out into the parking lot of their destination, but 1981 was different. This was the year that my 4-H camp got dumped on with rain from Hurricane Dennis almost from the time we unrolled our sleeping bags. Hurricane Dennis came up the North Carolina coast and flooded every part of our camp except the dining hall and the bunk houses. The activity field became a giant patch of black mud and drowned grass. The activity hall was literally half-submerged in the center of a three acre bay and had been deemed off limits to everybody, possibly forever. The ecology and marine biology activities were still being held, but we only had to step outside of our bunk houses to see every critter that eastern NC had to offer. Reptiles of all species were trying to dry off, mosquitofish were swimming up to the steps of the bunk houses, and aquatic birds were hunkered down on picnic tables that had turned into islands. One day we had a rather painful snowball fight with the frost that was building up in the cafeteria freezer due to the humidity. With most of the activities being cancelled, camp that year became much more about sharing space and resources and about developing relationships. With these lessons 'suck the peter' spread like wildfire from the Pasquotank-Bertie campers and contaminated the rest of the 4-H-ers.

On the fourth day inside, the counselors had grown so desperate for activities that everybody was taken to the dining hall to be taught how to make dinner rolls by the camp cook, whom we called Frenchie. Frenchie was a man with a French accent and he didn't seem to mind being called Frenchie even though I thought that most Americans used that name as something of an epithet. The first thing we learned at the bread-making sessions was how to understand what Frenchie was saying. Up to that point in the week the counselors had been translating what Frenchie had made for us for dinner, and it was usually something like "possum pot pie" or "skunk loaf". The nightly entree translation would cause all of the kids to look over at Frenchie to see if the counselor was kidding, and with a flourish Frenchie would say something that sounded like he might be making fun of us, but since we couldn't tell and we were hungry anyway, we poked at our dinner and ate what he had made, which always turned out to be tasty in spite of what it was called. For some reason Frenchie was the only person who was spared from hearing an impulsive 'suck the peter', and at the bread making class he patiently taught us how to mix flour, sugar, salt, yeast, warm water and wait. Later we came back and formed our dough into different twists and clovers and whathaveyou, then we covered them with towels and waited some more. That night we had at least seven different types of rolls to eat, and the fact that they tasted just like Frenchie's was especially rewarding because everything that Frenchie made tasted good. For the rest of the week Frenchie was given a level of attention and respect from the campers that I suspect few camp cooks ever receive. Frenchie took the attention in stride and continued to spend the latter part of every meal standing stoically at the door of the kitchen in his white hat and coat with the most subtle hint of pride on his face as he quietly watched us eat.

By the end of the week the remnants of Dennis had dissipated and we had safe, dry roads to ride home on. As fate would have it the home of one of the campers was located on a stretch of Highway 17 east of Windsor that was on the way to the pick-up location in Elizabeth City. The boy, whom I will call Rusty, had freckles and red hair that was long and slightly wavy and parted to one side as boys did in those days. Rusty was a nice kid and everybody liked him. His home looked as one might imagine a nice, red haired kid with freckles would come from. Rusty was a farm kid. His home was a modest, two-story white house with big oak trees around it. Because Rusty's yard frequently had farm equipment driven in it, there was a very

184

large area which, even after being flooded by Dennis, was passable by the bus without bogging down. Rusty's family straightened their piles of branches that had fallen during the hurricane as if to make even more room for the bus to pass, and in the hot August afternoon we all poked our faces out the windows of the bus to watch as they smiled and waved at us, scanning each of our faces for recognition. The bus doors opened and Rusty emerged to be hugged by what looked like his entire family-- parents, grandparents, sister, dog-- all took turns hugging on him and looking up into the bus as he pointed people out. Rusty's belongings were removed from beneath the bus, and within two minutes the bus doors were closed and we were heading back to the edge of the highway. There was a brief pause, then as the bus lurched out of the driveway onto highway 17 without any warning Rusty and his family were struck with the mightiest *suck the peter* ever! It was as if a thousand obnoxious kids had been trained by the Mormon Tabernacle Choir to shout in harmonic unison without the need of conduction. The bus was a riot of laughter as we sped away toward our flat, swampland homes. I had to hide because I didn't want Rusty's family to see my face and think that I had been in on the farewell, and because of that I didn't get to see the looks on the faces of Rusty's parents, sister. . . grandparents. *Egad!* To this day I can't drive down highway 17 through Windsor or by Rusty's house without being embarrassed and thinking that somebody will look out the window, see my face passing by in my car and say "Hey! That's one of those vulgar Elizabeth City kids that you went Hurricane camp with!"

I am inseparable from by 4-H brethren, even the hooligans with whom I attended Hurricane Camp. To that end their liabilities are my own, and almost 30 years later it looked like I was going to miss my opportunity to apologize to the West Bertie Concerned Citizens for the crudeness of my cohorts on that sunny day in August 1981.

Since having a job was interfering with my need for self-promotion, I had to come up with a way to establish a presence at the shindigs that I was going to miss. I asked myself what an entrepreneur would do: how could I survive in spite of my shortcomings and use my environment to overcome adversity? I had to be crafty. I had to use me brain. I had to take advantage of 21st Century technology as best I knew how.

A more connected candidate would have sent a reliable pledge to Bertie County to speak in his stead. But being a Republican candidate doesn't mean that the Republican Party is interested in helping you with your campaign. I had to do things myself. I started off thinking I could rap with the Concerned Citizens of West Bertie via Skype, but my computer was unreliable. I downgraded to making a DVD of myself as a talking head, but my Motorola RAZR only recorded video for about eight seconds at a time. Having no sensible way to video myself eliminated my next idea, which was to address the Concerned Citizens via YouTube. In the end I again tapped the technology of the 18th century and published more pamphlets which outlined my values, viewpoints, and the ways one could obtain more information about my candidacy. Alas the presentation for the West Bertie

Concerned Citizens for which I'd held such grand visions ended up being nothing more than an email and some propaganda that I'd sent via post. The email went as follows:

Dear Members of West Bertie Concerned Citizens,

I sincerely appreciate your invitation to visit with you tonight and I wish I could be there. As some of you know, I am a paramedic in Craven Co. and it is kind of tricky to adjust a schedule around 911 response. Out of respect to the person reading this, I will be brief.

I grew up mostly in Pasquotank County, although I lived for a year in Woodville in Perquimans County. I spent much of my youth volunteering with the agricultural extension agent doing surveys of potatoes, cabbage and insects for local farmers. After high school at Northeastern, I went to College of the Albemarle for two years then transferred to UNC-Wilmington. I did not have enough money to keep going to school. I spent many years saving money, followed by spending it on completing my degree in philosophy & religion at UNCW.

I did my concentration in religion because after the first World Trade Center bombing in 1993 I wanted to do intelligence analysis for counterterrorism. However, after volunteering with Easter Seals, and then experiencing the confusion and helplessness of a loved one having a stroke, I decided that I wanted to go into health care. I moved to Greenville and started college at ECU majoring in chemistry. After finishing my prerequisites for medical school at ECU, my wife and I moved to Beaufort County. After the birth of our second son, I realized that it was more important that I spend time with my kids than go to medical school. I took a job as a paramedic in Pitt County and started graduate school at ECU in technical and professional communication.

After a couple of years working in Pitt County, I took a job as a paramedic in Craven County working for a hospital. It was also about this time that I took an elective in graduate school about how to write public policy. The class was taught by Dr. Catherine Smith, who in addition to being a professor at ECU gives seminars for members of Congress who get elected but don't actually know how to write legislation. It was in this class that I learned that many of the people who intend to write public policy also intend for their legislation to be paid for by raising taxes.

The reason that I want to represent our district is because I have lived, worked and attended college in a great deal of it. I can't call any one county my home because I have numerous, unique and wonderful experiences in every place that I have lived and worked in our district.

Although there are a number of problems that are ongoing in the private sector, I am more interested in righting the injustices that have crept into our government. In our republic, the government is not supposed to have any rights; all rights are reserved for the people who comprise our republic. Some of the things that I would like to implement are:

Congress should not be able to give themselves raises when there is a deficit.

The government does not have the right to force any individual or entity to accept funds as in the *Stimulus Package*.

The government does not have the right to force any business to sell their stock to another business.

The government does not have the right to pressure lending institutions to write sub-prime loans.

The government does not have the right to force annexation.

The government does not have the right to raise the taxes on the market value of your home if your home is not for sale.

Members of Congress should not have the right to continue receiving federal benefits if they run a federal budgetary deficit.

And-

Congress does not have the right to use reconciliation to pass any bill that costs more than 5% of the federal budget.

I have a great deal more to say to all of you, but for the sake of brevity I am going to stop here. I thank you for your time and I encourage you to learn more about all of your candidates.

Please visit my website at NCdistrict1.com and feel free to contact me about anything that is on your mind.

Sincerely,

You Know Who

After a cooling off period of a couple of years, reading my letter to the West Bertie Concerned Citizens sounds like Sean Hannity wrote it for any Republican running for office. Thus, in order to be fair and balanced I've taken the liberty of rewriting my letter from the perspective of an MSNBC on-air personality:

Dear bumpkins who are too stupid to know that they're actually tea party scum,

First of all I must point out how desperate it makes you look to stoop so low as to invite a loser like Jim Miller to one of your little shindigs. Miller is an ambulance driver from a hick town and he is far too dense and slow to survive in our nation's capital. The reason that he can't get off work is because he hasn't raised one cent for his campaign and he would rather collect his paltry $15 an hour than spend an hour with you. Maybe if Jim were a little more Progressive he would see the value of taking a little time off from work once in a while; but as Jim will tell you, poverty follows stupidity, so you really can't blame him for having a wallet full of moths when his head is full of cobwebs. As if to illustrate his ignorance, Jim's going to tell you everything he knows-- in about two paragraphs.

He grew up outside some crossroads town blah-blah-blah; the bottom line is he's lived in more undesirable places than the flu. It took him ten years to get his BA in religion, he flunked out of two different colleges in the process, and this is supposed to be a *good* thing?

In the 90's Jim wanted to be Harrison Ford in *Clear and Present Danger*. When that didn't work out he wanted to be Zach Braff on *Scrubs*. And when that didn't magically happen (big surprise) he settled for being Nicholas Cage in *Bringing Out The Dead*. It's too bad that Jim is too young to have grown up watching *The Andy Griffith Show*-- he could kill two birds with one stone by getting elected to be the redneck sheriff of his TV dreams. Don't they get "TV Land" in the sticks? It might not be too late for Jim to strap on a billy club and push some people around. And what's this about some college letting him major in technical and professional communication? Once again it took Jim longer to figure out that he was dumber than the rest of the people in the program-- it took him what, *three years* to finally drop out of a two-year graduate program without a diploma? You've got another winner there North Carolina. First that decrepit bigot Jesse Helms and now Jimmy Jimbob Millikin or whatever his name is. What is it you people say? Yee-haw?

Now it sounds like Jim did have one valuable lesson in grad school, he took a class on how to write public policy and he was surprised to learn that legislation is paid for with taxes. Well, now Jim knows, and knowing is half the battle. It's too bad that he dropped out of

191

that program; he might have learned that it's cheaper to prevent illness than it is to try to fix it and that's why the *Affordable Care Act* is going to save money.

You should be happy to know that Jim thinks his district is awesome. Well, not so much *his* district as *your* district. Jim lives in Kill Devil Hills, which is actually in district 3, but whatever. He thinks your town is great: not great enough for him, but great enough for you, and that's all that matters. And it's understandable that he wants to get elected to Congress. It's free money, who wouldn't want to get elected to Congress; especially a chronic loser?

Jim isn't going to deal with the private sector. Since he's a loser and all, the private sector isn't really his forte. Instead Jim is going to pretend to write amendments to the Constitution which will be magically passed without anybody else having any sort of conflict with them. What sort of legislation is Jim going to pass all by his lonesome? Let's see:

He's going to cut funding to Congress during a deficit, as if what we need is less leadership during a time of crisis.

He's going to cut off funding to underprivileged children and to municipal utilities that are going bankrupt, so entire cities of children will have to starve to death in the dark.

He's going to let businesses do whatever they want.

He's going to let our country go bankrupt by letting our banks fail.

He's apparently going to get an amendment to the Constitution that prohibits local governments from collecting taxes from areas that they serve.

Jim Miller is personally going to tell you how much your house is worth and then tax you according to that figure, which he just makes up out of thin air.

And he's going to cut benefits to our hard working leaders in Washington during the most stressful times that they could be in office.

And finally-

Jim is going to prevent budget reconciliation from being used to reconcile the budget.

If you think that this all sounds like Jim has been listening to the filth that is spewed from right wing radio, you're right. Feel free to email Jimbob if you want to hear him recite more transcripts from the blabbermouths of the GOP.

If you want to visit his website do so at your own risk, it's almost entirely tea party clichés. If you want to actually advance your intellect afterwards, visit nbc.com and open your tiny little minds.

Congratulations on inventing the tooth brush,

You Know Who

*　　*　　*

The first political get-together that I was able to attend was the March 6th Reagan Day Dinner in New Bern. I was scheduled to work that day until 7, but fate was shining on me because the dinner was being held at a banquet hall directly across the street from work. Another good thing was that it was being held on a Saturday. Saturdays in New Bern were usually less busy-- EMS-wise-- than the rest of the week. I attribute this phenomenon to the doctors' offices being closed and to weekends being the days when family members visit their loved ones in nursing homes. I hoped that Saturday would be its usual slow self and maybe my shift supervisor would let me clock out early and go across the street to do a little campaignin'.

It turned out to be a lovely day at work. The thousand natural shocks to which the body is heir could apparently wait until Monday when the doctors' offices opened again; and enough families showed up at the nursing homes to provide the arms and eyes needed to keep the residents from touching the floor with body parts other than their feet. I finished my last EMS call a half hour before shift change. My supervisor gave me permission to clock out and go across the street with the caveat that if I noticed the remaining two ambulances going out before 7PM that the next time I came to work I'd better bring fudge.

I scampered across Neuse Blvd. to the Reagan Day Dinner in my EMS uniform. I kept my hospital name badge on . . . you know . . . so people would know who I was. Since I was thirty minutes late, the dining room was already full of dressed-up people seated at round tables with white tablecloths set for eight. I counted forks to see how late I was. I found a table with only a family of four at it and asked them if I could join them. Naturally they said yes. As I recall, the family consisted of a registered nurse from the hospital, a quiet gentleman in a tie, a boy who looked bored and a girl who looked beautiful. For dinner we had the standard political fare: pork. There were also steamed vegetables that may have been frozen since the Clinton administration. The beautiful girl was reportedly experimenting with vegetarianism and her parents were trying, as good parents do, to refrain from showing support of their otherwise intelligent daughter's pursuit of an identity which required no intelligence. I was trying, as good political candidates do, to refrain from asking her if I could have her pork medallion since she obviously wasn't going to eat it. They were nice people.

I did my best to meet all the big-wigs, but mostly I just shook their hands. The keynote speaker was Sen. Richard Burr. I did not get to press palms with Burr for he was only produced from behind a curtain like a prop at a magic show long enough to give a speech. I met my competitor-for-Congress Ashley Woolard and learned that he was as much of a celebrity at the dinner as Senator Burr. I also introduced myself to New Bern's neophyte Mayor Lee Bettis. Bettis entered the dinner as a lifelong Democrat and die-hard liberal and was apparently so moved by the Republican milieu that he publicly renounced his Democratic affiliation and vowed to start telling people that he was a Republican for as long as it remained to his benefit. This was followed by a rush to the bathrooms as partisans attempted not to pee themselves with excitement. I shook hands with Tom Fetzer and Steve Tyson; the former had been sending me near-daily emails about Governor Bev Perdue and the latter had been forwarding me near-daily emails about anything and everything Republican-Party. I shook hands with Scott Dacey, who looked familiar but I wasn't sure why; and I met some skulky candidate for sheriff who would not make eye contact with anybody and had the handshake of an uncooked chicken breast. I wondered, briefly, if the corruption implied by the sheriff candidate's demeanor negated the inaccuracy with a handgun that his limp-wristed handshake implied.

Maybe it was my hospital ID badge that made it difficult for me to meet people. Maybe hardcore partisans were like a flock of birds, frightened to scattering by objects that flapped in the breeze. There was a full bar in operation at the dinner and I would have loved to have tied one on, but I had to drive home to Kill Devil Hills so inebriation was out of the question. The evening started to wrap up quickly at around 8:15. The Duke-Carolina game started at 9 and people wanted to be home in time for the tip-off. I grabbed my still-full box of pamphlets from the propaganda table and parked myself at the exit of The Flame. I handed fliers to everybody who passed. Some people refused outright; others tucked my pamphlets with the other paraphernalia they carried. The half-dozen or so members of the Woolard camp took one pamphlet collectively, which was civil of them. A few people looked at me and stated that they lived in the wrong district to vote for me.

Suddenly there was a break in the crowd. The chatter of the exiting partisans faded to a silence broken only by the sound of a needle dropping onto the edge of a record. Everything sharpened and went into slow motion. The room filled with brilliant red and blue streams of light and bits of glittering confetti began fluttering down from the ceiling. The Flame quickly filled with the clean power of a saxophone croaking out Enur's *Calabria*, and out from the dining room floated a vision in a white scarf.

Her dark eyes flashed. Her auburn hair bounced engagingly as she took long, powerful strides toward me. Her smile was enormous and sincere. It was Ann Marie Calabria: incumbent Judge running for re-election in the NC Court of Appeals. My head swam as it filled with lines that would never work in a zillion years: *Is it the law that the Appeals Judge has to be so appealing? If justice is blind it's missin' out! You rule!* and so on. Suddenly I was very glad that I hadn't been drinking. I settled for telling Her Honor that I'd "Liked" her on Facebook (but left out the part about it being Doris Day's suggestion). Judge Calabria had been running a Facebook campaign to get some large number of constituents to "Like" her by the end of the month. Her eyes sparkled in the twilight as she said "thank you" and I watched, transfixed, as her lips pressed together sensuously as the *u* in "you" melted into a smile. What a fox! *Whoop whoop* indeed.

After the shindig was over I made like a moth and went back inside The Flame to talk with the wait staff. I left them some of my pamphlets and told them that I was far more comfortable with them than I was with a bunch of suits, but they probably thought I was just being a politician. I also spoke with the woman who was running the propaganda table and asked her if she would take a bunch of my pamphlets back to the Craven County Republican Party Headquarters. She said she would, and I left $80 worth of pamphlets in her possession. I asked her if she wanted help loading her vehicle. She said no. Then I scampered back across Neuse Blvd. into district 1, fired up the Matrix and drove back to the beach.

The Reagan Day Dinner was pretty much like any other banquet. While it's possible that banquets are like fruitcake, I'm compelled to assume that most people enjoy dressing uncomfortably, choosing between two options for sustenance and masticating them in unison while somebody recites contrived reasons to celebrate behavior that should be normal. A banquet is quite different than say, a business meeting-- which was what I attended two weeks later in Greenville.

In Greenville the monthly business meeting of the Pitt County Republican Party was held at a family-style restaurant that I'd frequented during my undergraduate years called Parker's Bar-b-que. I don't remember what happened, food-wise, at Parker's during the meeting of the Pitt County Republicans, only that I didn't eat near as much as I had in the past. I couldn't: I had a ton of papers and I didn't want to get BBQ sauce on them.

It was my first Republican Party business meeting

ever, and I was surprised by what I heard. I must preface this with the fact that Greenville, and much of the rest of North Carolina, was built with tobacco money. Farmers are usually Democrats due to their conservative pursuit of tax breaks; whereas the tobacco industry is typically a Republican-backed entity due to . . . the Republican denial of tobacco killing more Americans than the entire Muslim faith *I guess*. Thus both Democrats and Republicans have something to agree about in North Carolina. But I've never understood the Republican love of tobacco.

Republicans also think that alcohol is OK. It's no big thing to Republicans that booze causes people to misuse everything from cars to cows, that it is the biggest gateway drug of all, is involved in more preventable deaths than all other legal and illegal drugs combined, it destroys livers, kills brain cells, and tears families apart. The Republicans of Pitt County were not only in favor of lowering the taxes on alcohol, but they thought that it was atrocious that anybody would want to raise taxes on something as simple as two carbons six hydrogens and an oxygen. Why do Republicans think that alcohol is OK? Apparently for no other reason than because it's legal. Personally, I love getting drunk. If I didn't have kids I'd probably be an alcoholic. But if you ask me, for all the damage that alcohol does to otherwise contributing members of society, alcoholic beverages don't cost enough. The tax rates on alcohol should be experimentally raised and lowered until alcohol-related deaths and injuries reach their lowest possible rate.

So Republicans like cheap liquor-- so do I but that

doesn't make me right. But then inexplicably, the Pitt County Republicans were adamantly against gambling. Granted, gambling is not my preferred form of entertainment, but it doesn't destroy your lungs, heart, arteries, brain, liver, kidneys, esophagus, skin, mucous membranes and vocal cords like tobacco and alcohol do. Lottery tickets are about the only government program that provides people with something that they actually want, and thus it is about the only one that actually makes money. I mean *yes*: indentured voters *want* welfare, government subsidized health insurance, Medicaid and Medicare-- but only so they can purchase more lottery tickets. A lottery ticket is hope that pays off far more often than anything offered by the Obama Administration. Let people have their fun.

The Republican Party's hatred of lottery tickets and love of tobacco and alcohol was clearly and deliberately conveyed to all in attendance at Parker's that evening. It was almost like we were being reminded what to believe. Then the topic turned to the midterm election. The gentleman conducting the meeting stated that this was a particularly important election because the 2010 Census was underway, and whomever was elected would get to redraw the political districts when the census was complete. For over a century the political districts of North Carolina had been drawn by Democrats and it had left the state looking like a cryptograph from a Dan Brown novel. By chance, our gerrymandering was particularly detrimental to my campaign. As a political candidate is apt to do, I'd been going around telling everybody I knew that there was an election coming up and convincing them to participate. Only too often my endeavors were followed by one's finding that they lived on the wrong side of the gerrymandering to vote for me.

The orator of the meeting of the Pitt County Republicans spent a significant bit of time talking about how North Carolina was one of the most extensively gerrymandered states in the US. I was pretty happy to hear this because gerrymandering is one of my pet peeves. It is my belief that congressional districts should be drawn based upon existing political lines (as in townships), and should not divide more than two counties. The speaker pointed out how we have endured over a century of Democrats being in power and how the Republican Party has suffered incessant gerrymandering unanimously in favor of the Democratic Party and its candidates. I was genuinely filled with hope that gerrymandering, at least in North Carolina, was seeing the beginning of the end now that somebody who wielded a podium was finally admitting that it actually happened. The speaker began to wrap up his critique:

"That's why it's so important that we, the Republican Party, take back the North Carolina State Legislature this November so that we . . . "

Can return justice to North Carolina I thought.

"so that we . . . " he repeated.

Can redraw the districts fairly I thought.

"can do it to them. To the Democrats."

NOOOOOOOOO! I felt like I was going to turn into Munch's *The Scream* right there in Parker's.

Did we learn *nothing* during the century that we were gerrymandered by the Democrats? Gerrymandering is a disservice first and foremost *to the voters.* Is *nothing* sacred?

Ten days earlier at the Reagan Day Dinner I'd learned that everybody wanted their dog Woolard to win without even hearing what I had to say. At the meeting of the Pitt County Republicans I learned that gerrymandering was only bad if it wasn't in favor of your Party. It was at this point that I realized that I was not a very good Republican-- or perhaps the more appropriate word is *partisan.* I wanted to hear what *all* the candidates stood for, and I wanted to do what was best for representative democracy. I had no interest in perpetuating or hindering *any* Party by way of gerrymandering; what I wanted was to make elections simple and fair *for the voters.* Don't get me wrong, I think most voters are too ignorant to vote; but that doesn't mean that politicians should yoke the ignorance of the populous merely to perpetuate the cause of the minority that is their Party. That's *Progressive* ideology. When it came to gerrymandering though, the Pitt County Republicans were apparently quite forward-thinking in their desire to turn the corruption in their favor.

At that point the speaker yielded the podium to the candidates who were present. I confess that I don't remember what the local politicians said; I was busy reviewing my notes for what I was going to say. Then Jerry Grimes got up. Jerry dramatically set out five, three-ring binders containing the entirety of the text of the *Affordable Care Act*. Then he alleged to have read every last page of it. If he *had* read the *Affordable Care Act* in its entirety this would have probably made him the first person in the universe to do so. If he had not, he was fairly safe from being called on it because certainly nobody else had. Personally I had more important things to read. The Speaker of the House was right: we'd find out what was in it after they passed it. In the mean time I knew that the Obama Administration had grossly miscalculated where, if at all, the supply and demand curves for health care intersected. It didn't matter what the remaining four and nine-tenths of Grimes' binders said, the economics of requiring insurance companies to provide insurance for people after they got sick made it a disaster waiting to happen. Grimes spoke clearly and deliberately. His tie was a perfect Windsor. His pants were immaculately creased. And he even finished up with what was possibly the worst (and therefore the most professional) example of political humor I'd ever heard:

"And if you don't like gerrymandering, remember that my name is Jerry."

Oy vey! It was as bad as the "termite walks into a bar and asks is the bar tender here" joke. Jerry'd hurt my brain; but maybe that was his strategy because next it was my turn to get up and speak.

I introduced myself as a former ECU student and Pitt Co. paramedic. I told everybody where I'd worked in Greenville and what I'd done in school. Then I got down to the BBQ and cornbread. As a candidate I was mostly upset about *TARP*, so that's where I started my speech. I talked about how I was one of those people who had qualified for a sub-prime mortgage, but instead of bailing out on my mortgage when I couldn't pay it I instead rented my house out and moved into my car. I divulged how I had lived in my car for two whole years to make my mortgage payments while finishing college and paying for it myself. Being familiar with the liberal portrayal of Republicans, and having never actually been to a Republican meeting before, I took a moment to look out into the audience for some stereotypical, pasty-skinned debutante who refused to make eye contact with me for being whatever inferior class it was that lived in vehicles. There was a Hispanic man with a video camera who never moved. Jerry Grimes sat with an expression of contemplation and genuine interest in what I was saying. The entire audience was simply sitting there looking back at me. There were no contemptuous, Southern, holier-than-thou expressions of disgust that Hollywood portrays Republicans as holding for the homeless. Nobody pretended I wasn't there. Nobody was primping in their compact. Nobody got up and left. The room was silent, so I continued.

I pointed out that after doing whatever it took to get my education and pay my mortgage, suddenly the government decided to give Mulligans on the mortgages of every schmuck who was unwilling to pay the price that they had agreed to pay. I was not so much perturbed by *TARP*'s real purpose of being a legislature-wide shopping spree for campaign donors; what infuriated me was that I KNEW that since I was the taxpayer who was willing to live in my car to pay my bills, it was inevitable that I would eventually wind up paying off the loans that the Federal Government took out to pay for *TARP*, *Stimulus*, and whatever other Keynesian wild goose chases they would come up with if Congress didn't get some new blood in it.

That was it. My first real political speech and as far as I could tell it was neither moving nor compelling. Nonetheless, everybody clapped politely including Mr. Grimes. After I was finished the meeting was adjourned and the room slowly began to clear. A woman approached me and asked for one of my pamphlets. I opened the brand-new box of pamphlets that I had picked up from the copy store on the way to the meeting and found, much to my dismay, that every last one of them was overexposed. I had a box of 250 pre-folded pamphlets of super-dark and smudgy ink. On the cover of the pamphlet my face was a thumb-shaped silhouette against a dark gray background. I was too embarrassed to give the lady one of my pamphlets and promised to mail her one instead. I asked for her address and she gave me a sealed envelope with my name on it. In the upper left corner of the envelope was one of those rectangular, return-address stickers. "Just send it there young man" she said. "Yes ma'am" I replied.

When I arrived home three hours later I opened the envelope to find a check for $20. The memo, written in elegant script read "for your campaign". My first campaign donation. For the first time since registering as a candidate I actually felt pressure to win. The date was March 16th. I set the check aside and wondered if I'd get to use it after the primary.

Eight days later I put in my 12 hours at work, got off at 7PM and started driving toward the northwestern portion of the district. I was on my way to the Lewiston-Woodville Perdue food processing plant in rural Bertie County. I'd been in contact with the Warren County Republican Party and I wanted to deliver some of my pamphlets and *curriculum vitae* to them in time for their County Convention on the 26th. I was going to miss the Convention due to work, but rather than mail my paraphernalia to the Party I decided to drive and meet a contact known to me only as Rory.

The Perdue plant was some 90 miles from the hospital. To me, the size that a rural district must be to encompass over 600,000 citizens presents one of the biggest problems of Representative Democracy. North Carolina's first congressional district for example, contains around 620,000 citizens and is about 150 miles wide and 150 miles long. This seems bad, but when compared to Wyoming's first congressional district I suppose I should feel lucky. The entire state of Wyoming has only about half-million people in it, and thus it only has one congressional district. The Representative of Wyoming is elected for two years at a time, is outnumbered two-to-one by senators, and his district is 97,000 square miles in area. Are we really expecting the citizens of Wyoming to know, or even *see* their congressman when town hall meetings are literally held hundreds of miles away?

The other problem with Representative Democracy

is that gerrymandering is legal. North Carolina's 12th congressional district for example, contains roughly 620,000 citizens, is about 100 miles long, averages eight miles in width, and transects three of the five biggest cities in the state. How is a middle-class person with a job supposed to canvass such an absurdly shaped district comprised of people who live so far apart that they have almost nothing in common with one another? The tail of the 12th district lies in Charlotte, which is our state's largest city. Charlotte has 750,000 residents, 45% of whom are white, 35% are black, 13% are Hispanic and the remainder are merely human. The 12th district is 47% white, 44% black, and 7% Hispanic. Check those numbers: why isn't the 12th district completely confined to within the City Limits of Charlotte? Seriously. There are fewer white people and more Hispanics in Charlotte than there are in the 12th district. If there are still too many white people for comfort, there remain an additional 130,000 people in Charlotte neighborhoods for the politicians to cut-and-paste into and out of the 12th district until the numbers fit their corrupted version of reality. In populated areas you can have your gerrymandering without making the state look like Keith Richards' cheeks.

The Lewiston-Woodville Perdue plant was enormous. It was at least three stories in height and comprised of several large buildings clumped together like somebody had taken an industrial park, painted it white, and then scrunched the whole thing together neatly into one spot. The plant was surrounded by a ten-foot-high chain link fence with barbed wire on top. Access to the plant was granted via enormous, industrial-strength gates to give it that prison-ey feel. I parked in the parking lot and wondered why such a formidable cluster of huge buildings required such a huge and formidable fence. It seemed like it would sort of defeat the point of being a vagrant if you infiltrated a factory full of dead birds and workers with sharp objects. Maybe they wanted to keep out PETA or something. My contact Rory was supposed to go on break sometime in the next few minutes so I kept an eye on the giant gates as I put on more comfortable clothes and organized the things I had to give him.

The break at the poultry processing plant began shortly after I arrived. I walked up to the gate and suddenly realized how much I stuck out by putting on a nice shirt. The plant workers weren't covered with feathers or chicken guts or anything, but it was obvious that they all had been working hard. I rationalized this as being to my advantage since I did not know what Rory looked like, but all he had to do to recognize me was come outside the factory and see the only person wearing a seersucker within a twenty mile radius. I waited. Employees smoked. The evening wore on. No Rory.

I had Rory's cell number but could not reach him. Eventually the crowd of breaking Perdue employees began to thin until only the most dedicated smokers were left sucking every last bit of nicotine out of their squib o' choice before bending toward the pavement to crush out the butts and toss them into the grass. In desperation I went up to the guard house and asked if there was any way to get up with Rory.

208

"Are you Jim?" asked the gate guard. "Rory said you'd be here. He couldn't come out because he's doing battle with the vicious chicken of Bristol . . . HA! I'm just Joshin'. But Rory does have some work to catch up on so he asked me to meet you. I have to say you're better looking than I thought you'd be-- you know, for a Republican!"

OK so the real experience with the gate guard was not worth revisiting. Let me reiterate that it's a very big plant. The guard said that he would hold on to my $100 worth of printed, folded and sorted crap but if it was still in the gate house at the end of his shift the oncoming guard was going to throw it all out. The break was over, I was tired and still had to drive home, and I felt I had no other choice but to leave my rather expensive paraphernalia with the gate guard who was pleasantly frank about his not caring whether or not it got where I wanted it to go. The guard received my pamphlets and shoved them up against the window of the gate house on top of a pile of other unwanted things. I then sent Rory a number of texts and voicemails stating that the stuff I'd brought was with the gate guard. I left the plant frustrated, drove the hour and a half back to Jason's and went to straight to bed.

Less than five hours later I was back at work. Eleven hours after that my supervisor was again kind enough to let me leave work early so that I could get a head start driving to a *Meet the Candidates* function in the town of Hookerton, NC.

Hookerton turned out to be one of the most

tranquil places I've ever visited. Around every turn you could find another large open field bordered by giant oaks and pecan trees. The churches were modest and the homes were neat and cared for. Hookerton was perhaps my ideal eastern North Carolina town.

The beauty of Hookerton continued after I entered the community building. The inside of the community building looked like it had previously been a church: the floors were wood, the walls were white, and the sunshine flowed through the openness and spilled warmly onto the tables where the citizens of Hookerton sat. The people looked straight out of a Norman Rockwell painting. There were folks of every epithelial tint, but we were all dressed the same, groomed the same, seated the same. It was beautiful. We were Americans, one and all. The men had short hair and the women had their hair tied up. No brand names glared obnoxiously across anybody's chest. Hats were removed, backs were straight, and everybody had hands that reflected years of work. I love people who work. They give you faith in humanity.

At the front of the room a person spoke from behind a podium. I was trying to listen as I looked for a place to sit, but before I could determine the topic I was surprised to recognize a person whom I'd never met before. Near the rear of the community building sat a gentle-looking-man with short, gray hair and light blue eyes. I immediately recognized the man as my competitor John Carter. He smiled at me and scooted his chair over to make room for me at the table. We shook hands quietly and he whispered that I should be the next up to speak since everybody else had already gone. For some reason it had never occurred to me that a Meet the Candidates event would involve public speaking on my behalf. I had barely sat down when the speaker asked me if I was Jim Miller, followed by his opening the podium up to me.

Again I crossed a room full of people in my EMS uniform with the hospital badge flopping on my chest. There was no microphone so I knew I had to speak up, but even as I settled in behind the podium I had no idea what I was going to say. I looked around the room for a moment for inspiration and then I said the first thing that came to my mind.

"If the rest of America looked like the inside of this room I'm not sure I'd be running."

I heard a couple of people blink. For my entire life, speaking directly from my heart has been invariably followed by silence on behalf of my audience. This is why I prefer to write instead of talk: because when I talk I don't really make any sense. After a pause I continued.

"Our nation is dying."

It felt sad to hear myself say this, but I believed it. I'd barely finished speaking when somebody in the audience hollered out "YEAH!" which caught me off guard. I did not see who my fan was, but I thought it peculiar for somebody to get wound up by hearing a stranger say "our nation is dying". When Ann Marie Calabria had come powering out of The Flame in slow motion with her hot self, if somebody had yelled "YEAH!"

then I would have thrown up the rock horns and been all about it. This was not that sort of moment for me. Maybe political speeches are actually impromptu Pavlovian doggerel in which the speaker blabs out gangsta rap flavored nonsense and if the audience likes the sound of it they howl in approval. Maybe I should have put a ball cap on sideways, leaned forward and thumped my chest.

I don't remember much of the rest of what I said-- I was busy listening for more shouts of approval. I remember saying that I'd like to eliminate the taxes on all fuel used for farming until the recession was over, because somebody later asked me to "say that again". Being the anti-politician that I was, I said that just because I would write a Bill to suspend taxes from fuel used in farming vehicles does not mean that I knew which congressmen required naked pictures of my wife to keep the Bill from getting stuck in committee like so many socks in the legislative dryer. Nonetheless, the gentleman seemed excited to hear that I wanted tax cuts for farm fuel.

Cutting fuel taxes during a recession didn't seem like a groundbreaking idea to me. North Carolina has one of the highest fuel taxes in the nation. As a consequence of our high fuel taxes we also have some of the nicest roads in the nation, but farm equipment is rarely driven on the road, and even when it is, the tires only do as much damage to the road as they do to the crops that they drive on. The added expense of such a high fuel tax merely makes it harder for NC farmers to compete with farmers in states where the taxes are lower. Not that we needed to lower the price of tobacco to compete, or even that lowering federal taxes on fuel for farming would make NC more competitive (it wouldn't: it's the *state* fuel taxes that are higher), but everybody likes to keep more of their money, so why not offer to help the farmers of district 1 keep more of theirs?

After talking at the podium I thanked everybody for their attention and within a few moments the room turned into more of what I expected a Meet the Candidates event to look like. Hot dogs and two-liter bottles of soda were available, and being the foodservice guy that I am I checked with the people in the kitchen to see if I could be of assistance. We talked a bit, but like all foodservice people they did not require the help of a stranger. I returned to the common area of the community building and again had the experience of recognizing a person whom I'd never met before. The man was younger than me and he had the hair of Billy Dee Williams. It was Chad Larkins, Democratic candidate running in the primary against the incumbent Butterfield. Larkins was a nice guy: good handshake, made eye contact, listened thoughtfully and spoke respectfully. I asked him to take some of my pamphlets back with him to Warren County to hand out because "I'd be a lot easier to beat in the general election than Woolard".

While Larkins and I were talking we were approached by a gentleman who introduced himself as Larry Linney. Larkins and I both looked up at the man who towered over us. Linney was running against Senator Burr in the Republican primary, and he made an excellent third in our discussion. Linney and I were Republicans, Linney and Larkins were running against incumbents, and Larkins and I were running for congressional seats. The conversation that I had with Linney and Larkins was by far the most engaging one that I had in all of my time as a candidate. It felt that if Larkins, Linney and I were together in Congress that there would be nothing that we couldn't work out. After talking for a little while we realized that we should get out and Meet the Voters. We exchanged information and spread out into the crowd to meet other people. My entire experience in Hookerton was very positive: I could not tell who was a Democrat and who was a Republican. Everybody was civil and engaged. I just wish that I'd prepared something to say to those great people so that I hadn't gone and dumped "our nation is dying" onto one of the only thriving corpuscles of Americanism left.

A fortnight after my awesome evening in Hookerton I drove to the campus of Pitt County Community College (Pitt). Pitt is located in Winterville, NC; but there are so few gaps in development between Winterville and its larger neighbor Greenville that many people mistakenly think that the community college is in Greenville.

Pitt was where I'd taken all of my EMT classes, so it was a familiar spot for me. On the evening of April 12th I'd returned to Pitt to observe a scheduled debate between two of the candidates for sheriff. Unfortunately the debate was cancelled at the last minute. As I roamed the campus of the only school that had actually landed me a job, I caught wind of some eyebrow-raising rumors as to why the debate was cancelled. These included allegations that one of the candidates had been doing the Hale-Bopp with the other candidate's wife, as well as some chatter about a murder investigation being deliberately botched because it involved associates of one of the candidates. I concede that I don't know enough about law enforcement to know when the police do or do not act stupidly, but I couldn't help but wonder if the debate was cancelled due to there not being enough bulletproof vests to go around.

The very next day I returned to Pitt County to do a solo video presentation followed by an off-air interview with a reporter, both for the Greenville newspaper *The Daily Reflector*. For the video I brought an economics book as a prop and talked for pretty much the entirety of the two minutes that I was allotted. After the recording was finished I asked the people working the video equipment what they thought of my little speech. They quickly said that my clip was probably too long. Apparently viewers lose interest after about 30 seconds; but the recording people did send me off with a positive note by saying and that *they* thought what I'd said was interesting. I love people at work. They make ya' feel like you aren't completely wasting your time.

After I recorded my three-times-too-long video presentation I went upstairs in the *Daily Reflector* building to meet with reporter Ginger Livingston. I had barely settled down into a chair in the whatever-an-upstairs-foyer-is-called before she came out and shook my hand, followed by her finding an empty conference room for us to sit down in and talk. I'll spare you the details of the interview since it is pretty much more of the same stuff that you've already heard from me, although I did augment my answer as to what made me run in this election. I gave the perfunctory "the government is becoming an autocracy" factoid that has had so little impact during the Obama Administration. I also added "if Al Franken can run for Senate then why shouldn't I run for Congress? I mean it's bad enough that we had to put up with him when he was the worst player on *Saturday Night Live*, but now he's trying to turn the rest of our week into a testimonial for incompetence and cronyism". I followed this up by stating that my Minnesotan in-laws were Democrats who were unanimously good people who were hard-working, intelligent, educated, and self-supporting and that if I lived in *Franken-Barre* I could probably be a Democrat because (unlike in NC) they ask *not* what their country can do for them; but I swore that Minnesota would probably elect Corky from *Life Goes On* if he ran for office.

At this point Ms. Livingston conspicuously placed her pen and tablet face down on the table between us. Her legs were crossed, her back was straight, and she folded her hands neatly in her lap. Ms. Livingston then asked me levelly what I thought of the other candidates. She pointed out that her tablet was down and whatever I said was off the record. I briefly considering making up a story about dating Woolard in college and how it's not gay if you're pitching, but, as usual, I opted to make the mistake of telling the truth instead. I stated that I figured Woolard would win the primary because he had the most rich friends, but that he would have the smallest chance of beating Butterfield because he was a preeminent good-ol'-boy from what everybody knew to be one of the most racially divided towns in the free world.

216

I expected Ms. Livingston to ask me to substantiate my obviously-biased views with at least some anecdotal evidence, but instead she asked me what I thought of Jerry Grimes. I stated that I had no idea how difficult it must be to be a black man running in the party that has been effectively stereotyped as being a bunch of racists.

"He seems . . . guarded" I'd told Ms. Livingston. Again, no explanation was sought for my assessment. Then we were done. Since the day was still young I seized the opportunity to visit my favorite Greek Restaurant: Marathon. Props to Perry, he's my gyro. After dining in I got a spanakopita to go for my honey and I headed back to the beach.

Two days later on tax day I was again in Greenville for a luncheon with the Republican Women of Pitt County. The luncheon was held at Brook Valley Country Club, which was a familiar place for me. When I was a student at ECU I had a roommate who worked at Brook Valley doing something involving moving golf carts around. My roommate did not have a car, so on afternoons when he worked I would drive over to Brook Valley to pick him up and we would squeeze in three or four holes before dark. Almost twenty years later I found myself again at Brook Valley to attend the Luncheon of the Republican Women of Pitt County.

Kelli had to work that day, and I'm not sure why, but I felt like I should have a +1 for the luncheon. Maybe my attraction to independent women scared the married guy in me and I didn't want to go stag to a meeting of

Amazons. Or maybe I needed an anchor to keep me from turning into a lying, schmoozing antithesis of myself.

By chance I learned that a couple of friends from my earlier ECU days had gotten married and were living in Greenville. Since my friends are now grown up and professional and stuff I'm gonna use pseudonyms to spare them the embarrassment of being associated with me. Before my friends Sandra Bullock and Ryan Reynolds were married, we were part of a drinking platoon at ECU that was quasi-spearheaded by Ryan and my roommate Christian. In those days Ryan and Sandra hadn't even been dating or hooking up or anything, so to see them not just together but married was pretty neat.

In college Sandra had been far more Republican than I. Those were dark days for Republicans. It was fall of 1992. Sandra had a bumper sticker for Dad Bush on her car and as a result she was constantly being given the finger wherever she drove. I wondered why she didn't just take the bumper stickers off her car so she would no longer be a target of the jerks of the world, but Sandra was good natured and didn't let people bother her. At the time of the Republican Women's Luncheon Sandra had been teaching in Pitt County for almost a decade. I wondered if she had been worn down by all the Democrat administrators who blame Republicans every time a student doesn't do his homework or pay attention in class. I hoped she hadn't fallen prey to the game of blaming Bush for signing *No Child Left Behind* even though 95% of the Democrats in Congress voted in favor of it. But I didn't ask her.

Sandra met me in the parking lot of Brook Valley and I couldn't believe my eyes. She was beautiful. It always amazes me how women get better looking with age whereas men start off looking like shaved chimps and go downhill from there. The last time I had seen Sandra she'd been in a tepid jihad with ache and was having problems with thinning hair. That day, in the parking lot of Brook Valley, if Sandra was wearing makeup it wasn't obvious. Her skin glowed, her hair was thick and blonde, her jaw was squared and smooth beneath her sparkling blue eyes, and she had always had a pretty smile. It felt awkward bringing such a nice-looking woman . . . who wasn't my wife, to the luncheon. On the bright side perhaps I could get a little free publicity from being seen out-and-about at a luxurious country club with some blonde beauty while my hard-working spouse was back in Kill Devil Hills, where it was raining probably, and there was a nor'easter blowing 40 and the locusts were eating the siding off the house and pirates had taken over the neighborhood and both of my kids were crying due to having some sort of fungal infection that I likely acquired at the Chicken Ranch or something.

The luncheon was like a hybrid of the business meeting of the Pitt County Republicans and the Reagan Day Dinner; the biggest differences were the food at Brook Valley was superior, the decor was lovely, and I'd actually memorized a brief speech. After all the candidates had spoken, we (the candidates) all sat down in a row at the front of the Republican Women of Pitt County and had questions thrown at us. It was interesting, because the questions that came from the Republican Women seemed to be more philosophical in nature than the questions asked at any of the other gatherings that I attended. I liked that. We discussed the impending inflation that would come from paying off the deficit and I said that the money that the government prints has no intrinsic value until it is validated in the private sector by people who put forth the effort to earn it. We also talked about how pop culture was attempting to devalue the role of mothers by spreading the belief that it takes a whole village to raise a child. I stated that I had taken my share of anthropology classes and given a great deal of thought about the role of parents and families throughout history as well as in the contemporary world in all of its diversity, and that it was my assessment that it does indeed take a whole village to raise a child-- if you live in a village. I then gave an extremely truncated lecture about the roles of pasteurization, canned food and capitalism in women's liberation and how it is ironic that so many feminists are adamantly against the very capitalist system that provided them with both the free time and opportunity to think about what else they wanted out of life, if not a family. I noticed some furrowed brows in the audience, but no condiments or baked goods came whipping at me so I optimistically assumed that I'd merely spoken beyond the 30 second window of interest.

Afterwards the woman who organized the luncheon pulled me aside and said that of all the candidates in attendance she was the most impressed with me because I had memorized my speech. She said it just seemed more professional. I thanked her and she thanked me back and Sandra and I exited the Country Club. I'd just spent more time sober with Sandra that I ever had in college and we'd hardly caught up at all. When Sandra and I had walked into Brook Valley we'd been asked a variety of questions including the perfunctory yet awkward "how long have you been married". Once we were seated we were busy ordering and answering questions about salads and beverages and whatnot. The meeting started immediately after we made entree selections so we were stuck paying attention to our hosts rather than to one another. I'd then sat down in a line with the other candidates, answered a couple of questions, and then the meeting was adjourned. I still had to drive to Elizabeth City to see if I could catch some of the Tea Party that was being held there, so I never really got to talk to Sandra. I never even got to find out if she was still a Republican. We said good-by in the parking lot of Brook Valley and I haven't seen her since.

From the Luncheon with the Republican Women of Pitt County I drove to my home town of Elizabeth City. The Elizabeth City Tea Party was being held at a place called Waterfront Park, which is a nice enough place during the daytime. At night however, Waterfront Park became a rookery where everyone who probably shouldn't vote went to compete for mate selection, copulate, and purchase recreational drugs. It was a wasted trip for me. The Elizabeth City Tea Party appeared to be run by Jerry Grimes and his campaign committee. Real Tea Parties do not permit politicians to speak, but the only speaker I saw was Grimes. This illustrates both the beauty and the problem with a true grass-roots movement: rules are spoken but there is no hierarchy to enforce them. There was only one table at the Elizabeth City Tea Party, and it was set up smack in the center of everything and being manned by the Grimes Camp. To Jerry's credit he was reciting passages from the exact same essays from the *Federalist Papers* that I'd been studying over the past weeks. In reality Jerry was probably the only one of us who could have pulled off a Tea Party in Elizabeth City because he is black. Waterfront Park is within rioting distance of a black college called Elizabeth City State University, a school which is perhaps best known for being discriminated against by local election authorities who refused to let students living in the dorm vote both in local elections and in the elections at their permanent addresses. I like to imagine that ECSU students showed up at the Elizabeth City Tea Party to fight oppression but when they saw a black man leading things they realized that prejudging a group based upon its portrayal by the majority is a bad idea.

Eight days later it was Friday again, and I was officially on the first day of my scheduled vacation from work. Kelli and I were supposed to leave on a 7-day cruise on Saturday, and in order not to expend all of my vacation hours at once, my scheduling goddess Beth let me complete all of my hours earlier in the week. On Friday I'd gotten up bright and early and driven to Greenville, this time to have a lighthearted chat with Henry Hinton, host of Greenville's public cable access morning show called *Talk of the Town.* Mr. Hinton had scheduled me to sit down and talk with him at 8 AM at yet another location that I knew well. *Talk of the Town* was being broadcast from none other than the Krispy Kreme store.

I'd spent many a night doing homework and grading lab papers at the very table from which Mr. Hinton was addressing Greenville. Admittedly I didn't know much about *Talk of the Town*. Every time I'd seen it Mr. Hinton had been talking about ECU football with some other gentleman that I didn't know. My interest in football extended only as far as the tailgating, and since Mr. Hinton and his guests never seemed to discuss how to run a full Solo 16 between a gas grill and the winch of a '76 Ford Bronco during a ketchup fight without spilling, I'd never really paid them much attention. In fact, I didn't even know *Talk of the Town* covered politics: I thought all they talked about was ECU sports. I'd assumed it was the Greenville version of *Superfans*.

I stood in Krispy Kreme and waited in line to talk with Mr. Hinton. Ahead of me there was a woman seeking volunteers to help feed somebody or something, and behind me were some kids who were having some sort of fundraiser. When my turn came I sat down with Mr. Hinton, who immediately began asking questions in a rather lighthearted tone. This was fine; it was his show and all; but when somebody asks about earmarks with a pleasant smile on their face it sends the message to not say anything *disruptive*. I wanted to be disruptive. Tolerance and complacency are the reasons that we have scumbags and morons running the nation in whatever way benefits them most, and that needed to be shaken up, *hard*. But what could I say about earmarks in the middle of Democrat country?

"Well Henry" I said, "it's tricky because one man's

earmark is often another man's job. We all remember the days when the tobacco warehouses in Greenville were full and people came from all over to bid on what the farmers of Pitt County had grown, and today those warehouses are gone. And why are they gone" I asked, "because nowadays farmers have contracts with the tobacco companies and they are stuck attempting to work within a budget or lose money. Today the tobacco industries control the farmers, and unless the tobacco farmers have enough money to buy the equipment needed to start growing different crops they're stuck working for the tobacco industries."

Mr. Hinton said something through his smile but I don't recall what it was. It was fluff and I was on a roll.

"I think that a good program for the government to fund, an 'earmark' you might call it (I didn't use air quotes), would be research to genetically engineer tobacco to be a precursor to pharmaceuticals that people need. Tobacco has dozens of chemicals in it that affect our metabolism, and I think it would be a kind of poetic justice if we could turn tobacco into a crop for treating things like blood pressure disorders or Parkinson's disease. Then, if a tobacco farmer doesn't like the deal that he is getting from the tobacco corporations he might have the option to sell his crops to a pharmaceutical company."

Mr. Hinton didn't cut in, so I just kept on goin'.

"Now giving a grant to NC State or to some company in the Research Triangle Park would seem to many like an earmark because it is helping the state that I live in, but the fact of the matter is that if you want Ag research or pharmaceutical research performed then NC State and the RTP are the place to do it, and the products of this sort of research would be universal and not confined simply to North Carolina."

My 30 seconds was up. Mr. Hinton smiled and said "Well that's interesting Jim, and the topic that seems to be on everybody's mind these days is unemployment. The unemployment rate is 9.3%, what do you say about that?"

"I say we better get used to it. The Obama Administration seems to be using France as its economic model, and the normal unemployment rate in France hangs around 10%. As long as we have the Health Care Act forcing employers to provide health insurance to their employees, businesses-- especially small businesses-- are not going to hire any new employees and unemployment is going to remain high."

At this point the cameraman, who had been looking through the camera with his right eye and squinting with the left, unwinked and removed his head from behind the lens. He started glaring like he was trying to kill me with mind bullets. I had to fight the urge to laugh at him outright. What was camera-guy going to do: jump from behind the equipment and slap the business sense out of me?

Later I realized what a political chach I'd turned into. In just over three months I had gone from being a slow-talking, honest person who spoke in specifics, and turned into someone who was quick to make Clintoney generalizations and Hannity clichés.

In my five minutes on *Talk of the Town* I'd mislead people without a second thought in the following ways:

- *One man's earmark is another man's job* is just a rationalization of voter exploitation. An earmark is nothing more than political corruption with a human shield. Some federal programs benefit all Americans either directly or indirectly; but it should be the case that *all* federal programs do this. The fact that some individuals depend upon the government's fiscal waste as their source of income is the reason to eliminate that waste, not an excuse for preserving it. If Americans ever realized how much money EMS costs to Medicaid and Medicare for example, and then found out that almost all of the 911 calls for EMS could be accomplished by a cab driver I would be out of a job and have nothing to say about it except *what took you so long?*

- While the poor-little-farmer stuff will certainly fly in a bipartisan manner there is no such thing as a poor farmer. There are poor *gardeners*; the folks who from the bed of their pickup sell watermelons in the summer and collards in the winter, are not rich people. I will also concede that there are a handful of farmers out there who aren't George Soros. But there are not any farmers who are scraping by in an 800 sq. ft. apartment using plastic lawn chairs and the base of a *USA Today* box as a dining room set. Farmers work hard for their money, they possess knowledge that is not common and which literally keeps people nourished, and the income of a farm can vary greatly from year to year; but farmers are not *poor*. The farming industry is changing and there is a great deal of unhappy chatter about it, but the last time a farmer had to move into a smaller house was when President Carter said "if you grow it, you'll get rich" and those who were greedy and/or dumb enough to believe him lost everything.

o When I said the Obama Administration was using France as its economic model I was lying. Worse, I was lying in order to make fun of our Administration. The truth is that I don't think the Obama Administration has any economic model at all. They are literally making everything up as they go along. Being liberals, they like to "think outside the box" and do things in new and different ways. This is an admirable thing when people do it with their own money and succeed, but I just don't know how else to convey Obama's incompetence when such incontrovertible failure in policy is so blatantly obvious. The Emperor and his Administration have no clothes. What is left to do other than to simply make fun of Obamanomics? Perhaps with extended ridicule some of the liberal elite will go George McGovern on everybody and use their own wealth to start a business and learn firsthand how the government screws them every step of the way. Americans cannot go on imagining that economics is just some sort of right-wing conspiracy that forces people to save money by going to Wal-Mart. Continuing with that vein, economics will *never* favor the *Affordable Care Act*, borrowing your way out of debt, taxing a nation into prosperity or any so-called Stimulus Packages in which state governments are forced to assume a loan and spend it on vague, faux-Keynesian projects of *you know, infrastructure and stuff*. I mean, there may be precedents for whatever Obama's economic model is, but they weren't recorded because no dictatorship ever wants documentation of the times when they did something stupid.

o *Unemployment is going to remain high.* Anybody can assert this because both the terms *unemployment* and *high* are open to interpretation. An unemployment rate of over 5% is "high", so even if *Stimulus* had worked and Obama's unemployment rate dropped four percentage points in a year, technically the unemployment rate would still be high. Furthermore, the unemployment rate is based on unemployment claims, not on the number of people who are actually out of work. If Republicans cut unemployment benefits so that only 3% of the population was receiving them, then unemployment would technically be 3% (or "low") even though the actual number of unemployed citizens in 2010 would remain around 17%. My statement was that of a typical politician in the most derogatory sense of the term, and I would apologize for it if not for the fact that I was well beyond the 30-second window of viewer-voter interest and thus nobody other than the cameraman even heard me.

And as if Being a Wallflower Isn't Enough

Legislation is trickier to write than most people realize. Let me give an example. Imagine you were raised by urban hippies. Since birth you've been indulged in every manner possible and after 26 years of life you have emerged from your chrysalis a full grown toddler. You find most things about the United States to be utterly horrid abominations to humanity, but there is one cultural matter that turns your stomach more than *Repugnicans*, more than people who worked their way to the top, and even more than people who are happy. That's right, you hate sausage.

Since your open-mindedness makes it OK for you to tell other people how to live, you decide that legislation should be passed making it illegal for other people to have sausage. Being educated, energetic, and smarter than everybody else, you decide to sit down and pen the anti-sausage legislation yourself. You start by giving your Bill a name that reflects your enlightenment by calling it *The Healthy and Ethical Americans Act*. Then you hit your first snag. It becomes apparent to you that you can't just write "From this day forward, sausage is illegal". Obviously the law won't go into effect until it is passed, so starting out with "from this day forward" is a little too vague. You decide that in order to be clear you should specify a date for when the law is to take effect. Then you think a little more. You have an uncle who works in a supermarket and you realize that although he works in the produce department, the day that sausage becomes illegal he may wind up selling fewer onions. You don't think that onion sales comprise enough of your uncle's salary to cause him to lose his job, but you do realize that making sausage illegal will negate the need for the second butcher in the meat department, and one of the butchers is your uncle's husband. Although you do not approve of your uncle's husband's profession, you'd hate it if *The Healthy and Ethical Americans Act* caused him to become unemployed (you're conflicted like that-- it means you're intelligent), so you tighten up your thinking cap and really start utilizing the brain cells.

You realize that if sausage became illegal on the day that the law was passed then by the end of the week tens of thousands of people would lose their jobs. Of course the workers who made sausage would be out of work, but there would also be a surplus of hogs, causing the smaller hog farmers to have to either sell out or lose their farms. Then the people who provide food for hogs would have to raise smaller crops or, if the hog feed was a by-product of some other industry, then the industries that produced the feed would simply have to throw out their by-products, thereby increasing the load on our landfills as well as causing a reduction in salaries, benefits and possibly even jobs of the employees of those industries. And of course there would be the loss of revenue for all of the peripheral businesses such as gas stations, convenience stores, supermarkets and various other small businesses which depend upon the patronage of those who labor in the agricultural and meat processing industries to keep their doors open.

Being accustomed to always getting your way, you realize that your ethics are far more important than anybody else's livelihood, and you smile to yourself in recognition of how lucky everybody is that you are such a compassionate dictator. You generously decide set a date for your legislation to go into effect which is far enough in the future to give farmers, small business owners and your uncle's husband ample time to find better careers.

Next, you have to define *sausage*. You know that sausage means the links and ground patties that you have for breakfast. But what about hamburger? Hamburger is a ground patty, should it be illegal? What about other link-shaped meats like hot dogs, pepperoni, bologna and salami? What about Slim Jims? Should these products be defined as sausage? What about the sausage that comes from the butcher on a flat, rectangular Styrofoam plate like ground

231

beef-- is it really sausage even though it has not been placed in a casing? People make sausage out of deer, turkey and soybeans, are those forms of sausage going to be illegal too? If it isn't the casing that makes sausage sausage, then can pork products packaged in a can be considered sausage? It's essentially the same shape and same ingredients, so why not? What about Potted Meat? What about deviled ham? Is *Spam* sausage? What about deli meat? Deli ham is prepared and formed into a manageable shape just like sausage and it comes in a plastic casing-- is deli ham actually sausage? Maybe the problem here is that your spoiled ass isn't simply offended by sausage but by pork products in general. Maybe the legislation should read: On July 4th, 2015, all pork will be illegal, so make sure your hot dogs are kosher at that time.

So the next question is, what do you mean by *illegal*? How far does the pork ban go? Can I raise and kill my own hogs? Can I own a ham and just use it to flavor my collard greens? Is it OK to have mustard, coleslaw and teriyaki sauce in the hizzy, or are these now considered pork paraphernalia? Are pigs still legal? Can I still own a Vietnamese potbellied pig as a pet or will the government assume that I'm gonna smoke it? What about non-domesticated pigs? Can I still eat wild boar? What if a wild boar wanders through my yard, can I be fined for that?

Which brings us to the final consideration, which is what you are going to permit the government to do to a person who is caught with illegal pork. If a law isn't enforced then it isn't going to be followed very closely, especially if the law is stupid. So if you're caught with pig snacks, will the snacks merely be confiscated or will there be further punishment? What if a person survives on EBT rations and pork cracklins are the only things that they can purchase that they like? Are we going to oppress this person by forcing them to eat organic, free range, gluten-free lobster like others on EBT? And how are we to pay for enforcing *The Healthy and Ethical Americans Act* when the government no longer receives revenues from taxes on the price of the food that fed the pig, taxes on the sale of the pig to the processor, taxes on the sale of the meat to the supermarket, and taxes on every expense that was used to get the pork from farm to fork such as payroll tax, petroleum tax, road tolls, licensing, and energy consumption? Prior to being illegal, all of these taxes and fees were covered in the price that the consumer rendered in exchange for the sausage biscuit that they got at the drive-thru. Will that money be spent on something else now that pork is gone? If so, will the tax revenues be the same for that *something* as they were for pork? There is no way to be sure. However, if you put tens of thousands of people out of work it is a fair deduction that not only are these people not going to be paying income tax, but that they are also not going to be spending as much money on anything as they did when they were gainfully employed. More likely, with *The Healthy and Ethical Americans Act* the government will be assuming the liability of unemployment benefits as well as the inflation that comes from paying people to do nothing. On the bright side, giving unemployment benefits yields the exact same results as buying votes; which brings us back to the date in which the legislation should go into effect. It is imperative that *The Healthy and Ethical Americans Act* goes into effect as soon as (but no sooner than) the senator whom you want to introduce the legislation is presumably to be re-sworn into office; that way, *six years after that* when your senator is up for re-election he can campaign as the person who gave thirty thousand people unemployment benefits in their time of need rather than the person who killed thirty thousand jobs.

When writing legislation you are supposed to start out by clearly identifying a problem, and therein lies the problem. The things that furrow the brows of lobbyists and activists rarely have anything to do with the rest of us until they become law. Average Americans can have up to as many as 99 problems, but sausage isn't one of them. In reality the problem is that a person who wants legislation such as the *Healthy and Ethical Americans Act* just wants to impose their will on the general public by using the power of the government and the justification of ethics.

Voters need to become aware that just because a Bill is given a benevolent name and passed that it does not necessarily do what it is supposed to do. A bill may not do anything at all, and with time may even have the opposite effect of what was intended. Of the latter, the environmental lobby seems to be the entity which most often purveys legislation that does the opposite of what it intended (although Obamacare is going to make environmentalists look like a Mensa convention). Recycling paper and plastic for example, not only uses more energy and money than making these products from scratch, but it

234

keeps the hydrocarbons that comprise them exposed to sunlight and the atmosphere where they ultimately degrade into CO2. If these carbon-rich products were simply thrown out they would be sequestered underground where environmentalists would have us believe all carbon-rich things belong. But it's good that environmentalists think about garbage because frankly somebody needs to do it other than people who hide it for a living. It's just unfortunate that in addition to the environment, environmentalists do not think about things that are equally realistic and important when it comes to the environment, such as logistics and economics.

For example, due to environmental legislation America's greatest export is now garbage. After collecting scrap metal from all over the country we transport it to coastal ports where it is shipped overseas to nations like China and India. After our scrap metal is recast, it is put on another ship and returned to us, where we buy it back. Our recycled metal is then dispersed back into the interior of America. While this is a lovely case-in-point of how government regulation causes outsourcing, it is also a sterling example of how the purpose of legislation and the results of legislation can end up being very different things. The reason that America ships its scrap metal overseas is because environmental legislation has socially engineered us to do so. We cannot afford to recycle our scrap metal in the US any more. Due to the stringent environmental restrictions in the US, it is now cheaper to ship scrap metal across the Pacific where there are absolutely *no* environmental restrictions, as well as lower standards of quality. Thus, rather than decreasing the pollutants that arise from recycling metal, American environmental legislation has increased pollution on a global scale, caused us to use more resources in the process, and has left us with lower-quality metal that prematurely fails and subsequently winds up being recycled more often.

One of the reasons that democracies are so ineffective is because neither voters nor politicians seem to know the difference between a direct relationship and causal relationship. While nobody can prove whether or not causehead politician truly believe in the direct relationships that they use to stir up bandwagon support, the simple fact that the tactic works illustrates the ignorance of the voting populous.

The textbook example of the difference between a direct relationship and a causal relationship begins with the fact that there is a direct relationship between ice cream sales and drownings. Fortunately the dairy lobby is strong enough to prevent unscrupulous politicians from banning ice cream sales near large bodies of water. The fact is that drowning deaths increase when ice cream sales increase because both activities go up when the weather turns hot. While it is true that there is a direct relationship between the *number* of ice cream sales and the *number* of drowning deaths, purchasing ice cream is not causing people to drown and drownings are not causing people to buy ice cream. There is a direct relationship between these activities, but there is no *causal* relationship. Thus, an unscrupulous politician should instead focus his attention on cultivating a bandwagon for saving lives by banning nice weather. This, of course, has been accomplished by getting voters to believe that there is a causal relationship between nice weather, large bodies of water, and atmospheric CO_2.

I was watching a CSPAN program about Climate Change in which questions were accepted from the audience. A middle-aged man dressed like a stereotypical college professor stepped up to the microphone. He had the beard and the glasses and the herringbone wool blazer with the elbow patches, and his voice quivered with emotion as he addressed the panel of authorities. As calmly as he could manage, the gentleman asked the panel how "we" can get the people who do not believe in Climate Change to understand its importance.

The passion of this person struck me. It was like being in church. Just like in church I leaned forward in my chair a little. Maybe this was it! Maybe I was finally going to receive the testimony that I needed to make me start believing Al Gore's prophesies and repent by buying a Prius and some elbow pads for my flannel hoodie and start voting straight ticket Democrat. As a non-believer in CO_2 as Apocalypse, I swear on my life that if anybody can undo the things that the environmental lobby has done to me over the years then they will have my unwavering allegiance. Seriously environmental activists, if you want those of us who live outside in the environment to take your concerns about us seriously, you are going to have to do more than simply make our lives more expensive. Belief-in-climate-change is just as much of a generalization as Belief-in-the-Bible. When a Christian evangelist characterizes a person as 'not believing in the Bible', what they mean is that the person does not believe the same things that they do. It is no different with Climate Change.

When a Christian labels someone as not-believing-in-the-Bible, they imply three things:

- That one does not believe that there is a book entitled *The Holy Bible*.

- That one does not believe that the characters in *The Holy Bible* existed.

- That one does not believe that the stories of the characters in *The Holy Bible* hold valuable truths about human existence.

Most people do believe all of these things. What some people do not believe are the following:

- That the miracles described in *The Holy Bible* make the Jesus figure more charismatic or compelling than say, the Buddha or Vishnu figures.

- That they are bad people for disagreeing with you on that point.

- That they must repent for disagreeing with you or suffer the consequences of other things about which they disagree with you.

I know: Jesus only died for the sins of people who believe in circular logic. But you know what? If somebody needs to believe in wizards to be a decent person then good for them for at least setting a goal for themselves of treating others the way they want to be treated. Religion is a kaleidoscopic peek at what happens when the individuals of a species gain awareness of their mortality, and it only gets oppressive when zealots start trying to control those who disagree with them. For example, when an environmentalist says that somebody does not believe in Climate Change they imply three things:

- That one does not believe that there is such a thing as Climate Change

- That one does not believe that the net change in climate is an increase in temperature

- That one does not believe that the net change in climate is increasing faster than it should be.

Most people do believe all of these things. What some people do not believe are the following:

- That the faster-than-it-should-be net increase in global temperature is a bad thing.

- That the climate is warming up faster than it should because of carbon dioxide.

- That the CO_2 that is causing the faster-than-it-should-be temperature change is originating from man-made sources; and

- That once the man-made sources of CO_2 are eliminated, the climate *might* go back to normal.
  Let's break this credo down for the people:

There is such a thing as Climate Change

It would be really strange if our climate didn't change. The only places on Earth where the climate does not change are those where the sun don't shine. We have a different climate for every single position the sun holds in the sky. We have a daytime climate and a nighttime climate, which is why they get separate forecasts from the weatherman. We have a noon-day climate and a twilight climate. We have winter climate and summer climate. Our climate allegedly changes with the Milankovich cycles, and I believe this allegation to be true. The Sahara is in-between green cycles and North America is taking a short break from being covered in ice. It is just a matter of time before the Garden of Eden returns to the Iraqi desert. As long as Antarctica continues to hoard ice the overall climate of Earth is going to be a lot cooler than whatever is happening now. Climate change is a hypothesis that has stood the test of time even if you are a creationist and believe that that time is only 7,000 years. Climate change is an undisputed theory.

The net change in climate is an increase in temperature

I'm going to have to defer to the authorities on this one. As the worst chemistry student at ECU I don't even know where to start with measuring climatic temperatures. Do you measure the temperature at a standard air pressure, or at a standard elevation like soil level, sea level, or thermostat level? Do you measure it in the shade of a tree or on the sunny side of a leaf? Do you only gather data at night when the temperature plateaus out so that it won't be skewed by the activity of the sun? Are data collected using a standardized partial pressure of individual atmospheric gasses including water vapor, or are five different variables
240

measured as one? Do you measure the temperature over water or land? Do you measure it in cities or in the country? Do you measure it next to an exhaust pipe or a volcano? Do you measure it in deserts, tropics, the arctic, the horse latitudes, or what? Do you average the temperatures together, or are local temperature deviations adequate for determining that the world is coming to an end? And what about time-- how large does a data set have to be before you get to call it climate? Is it days? CO_2 as Apocalypse zealots (as well as the naysayers) never fail to pipe up whenever a daily temperature deviates from the norm in either direction. Is climate measured in weeks? We now blame the destructiveness of hurricanes on Climate Change rather than on the units by which we actually measure the destructiveness, which is in dollars. Do we measure by months? The coldest winters in recent years have been in recent years but that doesn't seem to matter. Do we measure by years? If the average midnight air temperature at forehead level over this year is higher than the average midnight air temp at forehead level over last year does that mean that the climate is changing? Decades? We seem to have minor climactic fluctuations over 40 year cycles, do those count for anything or should we ignore them? Centuries? The climate data measured *in-situ* only go back about 200 years and, not surprisingly, all of the record-breaking weather has occurred since we've been paying attention to it. I guess we're supposed to assume that all non-recorded weather was just like the week leading up to Woodstock. But riddle me this Batman, which is more of a change: breaking a weather record set a century ago or having a century-old weather record continuing to go unbroken?

Is climate measured in millennia? The most dramatic sea level rise in recent millennia was an average of half an inch per year over the 8,000 years following the end of the last Ice Age when there was no industrialization. Do we measure climate by eons? If so then the current warm climate that we are enjoying is the thing that is abnormal-- shouldn't we just enjoy it before the world goes back to its normal cold state? No matter how climate is quantified, I have faith that the scientists who do it have addressed these variables at least to the extent that further research grants will be required to better determine just how screwed we all are if we don't re-elect the politicians who allocate the money for the grants.

Although I am as ignorant as Al Gore about what the climate of the entire globe is doing, I can say with a fair amount of certainty that my winters seem to be getting milder. Nutria (giant South American water rats) have are destroying NC's wetlands almost as quickly as tourism Armadillo now have summer homes in Wyoming. Glaciers that have been around for thousands of years are receding to expose nice, fertile soil for us to grow sugar beets in. Atolls are receding back beneath the waters from whence they arose. Minnesota is now a corn state. And how do we explain the loss of jobs for those guys who spent their whole careers driving ice breakers on the Great Lakes: George Bush strikes again? If the authorities say that the net temperature of the climate is increasing, even if they have absolutely no idea what they're talking about there's still a 33% chance that they're right. The temperature is doing one of three things: it is going up, going down, or staying the same. I'm in. I'll assume that the temperature of the air at ground level is going up all around the world with the exception of Antarctica, because that's what the most pompous of the people with the PhDs in climatology insist upon, and frankly I stereotype them as being just as smart as anybody with a PhD in divinity.

> *The net change in climate is increasing faster than it should be*

Well it either is or it isn't, but what is this hypothesis based upon? The climatologists who preach Global Warming have just barely pulled the Global Warming data out of thin air and already they're building on it? The quasi-inductive reasoning of "our climate model doesn't work, our climate model was anthropogenic, therefore the discrepancy between the model and reality is anthropogenic" requires a leap of faith that only politicians and college students are willing to make. As my Christian missionary aunt told me about believing Christ's miracles, "you only have to believe in the first one; after that the rest are easy".

The data on climatic temperature have as many peaks and valleys as the Himalayas. Sometimes the CO2 levels rise before the atmosphere warms up, and sometimes it lags behind. Currently atmospheric CO2 levels are insanely high but the atmospheric temperatures are just as whacky as they've always been.

The Earth is in between Ice Ages. We do not have

in-situ temperature data from before the last Ice Age. Actually we don't even have *in-situ* temperature data from most of the time since the last Ice Age. Beyond a vague description of "an increase in temperature followed by a decrease in temperature", we have no idea what a normal change in climate is between Ice Ages. But absolute and total ignorance about what is normal for Climate Change does not prevent people from asserting that they not only know what it is, but they can tell us exactly how we were born of original sin and how we can repent for our deviance from the blessed norm. Global Warming zealots use the same sort of model-making technique as stock brokers.

Just as large cap stock values are going to rise as Obama's policies crush small business, atmospheric carbon dioxide levels are going to rise as deglaciation occurs. In order to make money on this, a stock or climate broker takes a raw data set and puts it on a graph. Then they flatten out all of the peaks and valleys until they get a nice smooth curve. Then they formulate an equation to describe that curve, and finally they sell their results to interested buyers. When the model fails to predict reality, the brokers cite the overwhelming complexity of the business/Global Warming cycle and then tell you that the important thing is that you continue to pay for their advice or you're going to lose everything.

But let's not be so hard on stock brokers; at least they start off with real-time data that is documented *in situ* even if the models that they make are as reliable as those of climatologists. It's pretty hard to deny that at time X, Y number of shares of GM were traded for Z billion of your tax dollars on the NYSE. Climatologists on the other hand are extrapolating climate temperature from samples of atmospheric gasses trapped in glacial ice. Don't get me wrong, that's brilliant. That is fascinating. I want to know more about it. Hell, I would rather collect and study glacial core samples for a living than tote drunks to the hospital in an ambulance. And do you know what else? I have faith that the climatologists' extrapolations of atmospheric CO_2 levels during periods when the glaciers were melting rather than growing are representative of the CO_2 levels of the area of the atmosphere at which the water vapor first froze before it fell and possibly melted and flowed into crevasses and mixed with the glacial melt that occurred during the warm years and became buried with snow on the cold years all the while gliding down the glacial slope to the sea. After all, CO_2 is heavier than air and dissolves readily into water-- especially cold water-- and then the water flows downhill until it vaporizes, so whatever CO_2 makes it from the ground into the snow in Antarctica is probably representative of something, right? But I'm not willing to assume that the CO_2 levels in Antarctic ice illustrate causation of increased air temperature of the entire rest of the globe when climatologists have shown that the variance between atmospheric CO_2 levels and atmospheric temperature is ± 1000 years.

The scientific community has absolutely no idea what a "normal" rate of atmospheric temperature change between ice ages is supposed to be. They are fanatics about their conclusions for the same reason that Christians are fanatics about the resurrection: because deep down inside they know that they are basing their entire identities on presumed events that raise more questions than they answer. There are people who use carbon dating to prove that the world is only 7,000 years old, and they are only slightly more eccentric than those who use it to glean air temperature from before the last Ice Age.

But you know what? I'm going to believe the climatologists anyway. What is life without just a little faith in the people who say that they are trying to save me personally from certain doom? You read right: I'm going to believe in Global Warming because I'm dumb. I prefer to think of myself as open minded, thank you. So now for the things that I'm *not* going to obsequiously believe:

> *The faster-than-it-should-be net increase in global temperature is a bad thing*

We're just under half way into the CO2 as Apocalypse creed and we're well into a chaos as disordered as the poets ever feigned. Let's bite the bullet and see where this line of speculation takes us. First we need to define *bad*. Personally, I feel that there was no time in the history of Carbon Dioxide as Apocalypse that was as terrifying as when I was in high school. It was the 1980's.

In high school we were told that *the Greenhouse Effect* was going to cause the polar ice caps to melt and the sea levels were going to rise a minimum of three feet and possibly as much as 30 feet by the year 2000. Sure enough, that very day the Atlantic Ocean rose three feet at the Outer Banks. Later that day when the moon was at a different position in the sky the tide receded back to where it had been.

As if humanity's imminent destruction by yet another flood was not bad enough news, not only did the doomsayers insist that we were the ones who needed to build an ark for them, but we were also told that a hole in the ozone was going to destroy the entire ecosystem from the bottom up by frying all of the bacteria in the Antarctic with UV radiation. It's kinda unrelated, but we were also told that AIDS was going to be the end of humanity and that one in three freshmen girls in college had HIV, and our stupid asses believed those lies too. In spite of our imminent destruction, over the next fifteen years the only major change that the world underwent was Al Gore inventing the Internet. One of the biggest-budget movies of all time, *Waterworld* was made upon the premise of the Greenhouse Effect turning Mt. Everest into beachfront property. Much like the movie, all of the Greenhouse Effect apocalypse scenarios were a flop. And then something even more unfortunate happened. With the invention of Al Gore's communication superhighway peons everywhere began to find out that even if the entire northern polar ice cap melted it wouldn't change the sea levels because ice (being H_2O and all) does not displace H_2O when it changes states. In order to explain this to environmental activists everybody had to take a deep breath and say "that's why your beer doesn't overflow when the ice melts in it sweety". It was also discovered that a good portion of the evil smog that collected around our cities was actually ozone, thereby making the hole in the ozone over Antarctica a rather awkward topic. An even more inconvenient truth was that instead of melting, the glaciers in Antarctica were getting deeper by the day. Thanks to Al Gore's interweb it was even discovered that greenhouses don't stay warm because of the carbon dioxide that's in them, they stay warm because the glass traps the air as it warms up. Yeah, we were pretty dense back then but we was wisin' up. And with our wisin' up the environmental lobby realized that it needed some New-Jack marketing to take down a New-Jack demographic.

With a total lack of sea level related disasters to cash in on, there was great fear that the Greenhouse Effect would cease to be taken seriously. It was time for our environmental apocalypse to get an extreme image makeover. In the 1990's Generation X was trying to outdo our hippy and yuppie parents by becoming citizens of the world. The cool major was international business. We were becoming millionaires on the World Wide Web. We figured out which troubled area of the world was the absolute farthest away from us and we made its spiritual leader, the Dalai Lama, a celebrity. We referred to ourselves as living in the global village. The only logical name to give our new political apocalypse was *Global Warming*. A greenhouse is a pleasant room that promotes plant growth and plays host to all sorts of little animals. And an *effect*, well that just sounds like something that you can observe in a detached and objective manner like Doppler or Success - N -. *Greenhouse Effect* sounded like an album by KC and the Sunshine Band. *Global Warming* was a cataclysm that cool kids could fear without shame.

While Generation X was rushing around paying $15 for compact discs and seeing how many times it could get its passport stamped, we were also getting additional phone lines and dedicating entire rooms of our apartments to setting up computer towers, phone modems, monitors and keyboards. We were energized by the technology boom, and in regard to it we optimistically thought of confusion as being the path between ignorance and understanding. This was sometimes to our detriment as occasionally Generation Xers would embrace confusion and attempt to take it to new levels. In college the more brilliant of the liberal arts majors strove to change by not changing; they overtly equated absurdity with profundity and were renowned for their doggerel style. Others, in what looked to be little more than an ignoramus' attempt at feeling superior, considered themselves to be open-minded simply because they believed in things that didn't make any sense, like crop circles and tithing-as-salvation. Perhaps most significantly, Generation X and our parents assumed that prolonged confusion over a product was an indication of that product's superior technology. A VCR for example wasn't "good" unless it was too confusing for anybody over 30 to program it. The best stereo systems were the ones with the most dials and little bouncing bars of light. And I regret to report that most of us chose Microsoft Windows over Apple II under the incorrect assumption that just because the former was harder to use that it was more technologically advanced. Confusion was the new educated, and in an appeal to our stupidity the Greenhouse Effect was given a new, counter-intuitive explanation of how it was going to be the end of the world as we knew it. The days of Noah and his greenhouse flood were gone. The disaster du jour was that Global Warming was bringing on-- wait for it-- *the next Ice Age*. Never mind the fact that we are due for another Ice Age, this Ice Age was going to be the fault of Republicans. Once again Hollywood made a movie to educate the public of the dangers of voting Republican called *The Day After Tomorrow*, and once again the end of humanity as we knew it failed to happen.

It's been another decade and now our premature end is called *Climate Change*. A trillion dollar per year deficit is unimportant, but an increase in sea level of as much as six inches by the year 2100 is a disaster. I hate to break it to everybody, but the richest nation in the world is going to have to "fix" Climate Change; and since we're broke, I hope the countries that sell oil are up to the task.

For most of my life I've heard that my home is going to be under water in a matter of years, yet the ocean is right where it was 25 years ago when the Greenhouse Effect / Global Warming / Climate Change hysteria began. I confess that our winters are pleasantly mild and our summers are still not as hot as they were when I was a kid, but maybe that's because now I have a heat pump. How is it that Global Warming tycoons can continue to tell the same story that doesn't come true over and over and over and over and over and over and nobody ever catches on? Two reasons: because CO_2 as Apocalypse isn't science, it's religion; and because every year we refresh our High Schools with new and gullible Freshmen who have been brainwashed with Climate Change dogma since they first emerged into our brave new world.

The climate is warming up faster than it should due to carbon dioxide

Even scientists have joined the Church of CO2 as Apocalypse. *Sciencemag.org*, the online version of one of the premiere peer-reviewed journals of the scientific community, publishes studies that give religious conclusions to otherwise scientific research. One study cited an analysis of gas samples from Antarctic ice which stated that that the last time that atmospheric carbon dioxide levels were as high as they are today was 15 million years ago. A review of the study subsequently reported that 15 million years ago the temperature of the Earth was 5-10 degrees warmer (Fahrenheit because it's more dramatic) than it is today and that the sea levels were 75 to 125 feet higher. Think about that for a minute.

So am I really the only one who sees that if all of these calculations are correct then there is not a direct relationship between temperature change, the ice melting, and sea level? And I'm not just talking about collecting glacial samples that froze at 5-10 degrees above normal or asserting that because the prehistoric climate is different from the contemporary climate that anthropogenic catastrophism is the logical explanation for lapses in uniformitarianism. Back in the prehistoric past when I was in school it only took one exception to a hypothesis in order to disprove it. How much of a difference between atmospheric CO2, sea level and air temperature does there have to be before the CO2 as Apocalypse hypothesis is disproven?

If the last time atmospheric CO2 levels were as high as they are now was fifteen million years ago,

and the last time atmospheric CO2 levels were as high as they are now the sea level was 75-125 feet above what they are now; *and* the atmospheric temperature was 5-10 degrees warmer than it is now,

then atmospheric CO2 does not share a direct relationship with either atmospheric temperature or sea level.

This is not a paradox. There are countless variables to consider when analyzing Climate Change and to reduce the entire field of climatology to "atmospheric CO2 level = sea level = air temperature" is frankly insulting to real scientists. But let's be honest, if you're going to believe that the creation and destruction of deserts and rain forests has nothing to do with the energy source for photosynthesis and everything to do with the inert chemical that photosynthesis converts into starch, then you're foolish enough to believe that the way to solve this imaginary problem is to vote for Democrats; and isn't that really the point of CO2 as Apocalypse brainwashing in the first place?

> *The CO2 that is causing the faster-than-it-should-be temperature change is originating from man-made sources.*

This is the point where imminent armchair environmentalists put down their copies of *Cosmo*, pause their gum-snapping, pick up their $8 latte and snuggle down into their leather couch as they turn up the volume on their 54" flat screen.

Believing that CO2 is evil is easy to do. First of all, CO2 is a bodily waste just like urine or poop. And since it's human waste it's particularly filthy. Also, since you were little you've been told that if you breathe into a plastic bag long enough the carbon dioxide will poison you. And when people leave their car running in the garage the carbon dioxide kills them. Carbon dioxide is dirty and evil and bad.

Actually the plastic bag thing kills you because you run out of oxygen. The car in the garage thing kills you because of carbon monoxide. True, carbon dioxide is a bodily waste, but it is also plant food, and every last bit of fossil fuel is the result of photosynthesis removing CO2 from the atmosphere. When you burn fossil fuel, you are putting CO2 back from whence it came before some fat, mosslike, prehistoric plant so greedily sucked it out of the air. Carbon dioxide causes a small amount of heat to be retained within the Earth's atmosphere, and although an armchair environmentalist may believe that CO2 only radiates heat back toward the Earth's surface, it actually radiates heat out in all directions including back toward space. Nonetheless, CO2 does retain some heat, but it does so at a far smaller rate than several other greenhouse gasses. Of particular interest are methane (CH4), nitrous oxide (N2O), and water vapor (H20). Even the Lord's own holy molecule of benevolence-- ozone-- is a GHG that comes out of our chimneys and tailpipes *ad nauseum*. Of the GHG's however, methane is probably the worst because it retains large amounts of heat, takes forever to break down, and when it does break down it turns into water vapor and CO_2. But while the EPA scrutinizes the relatively small amounts of CH_4 and N_2O that accompany the combustion of fossil and renewable fuels, it makes no attempt to regulate the water vapor which comes out of our tailpipes at about the same rate as CO_2. Water vapor causes the atmosphere to retain heat far more readily than all of the other greenhouse gasses combined, and it is so prevalent that it eventually clumps together and freezes, followed by scientists taking samples of it to look for traces of carbon dioxide. Deserts aren't cold at night because they don't have any CO_2, they're cold because there is no water vapor to retain the heat of the day. Given that the presence of atmospheric water vapor is an indication of precipitation, coupled with the facts that water vapor retains heat far more readily than CO_2 and that trees grow faster with more rain, it follows that if Al Gore's tree ring data indicate anything it is increased water vapor yielding additional rainfall. Perhaps this hypothesis could be refuted by comparing the growth of stalactites in caverns beneath the trees from which ring data were collected. Furthermore, during the beginning of industrialization the combustion of fossil fuel resulted in the production of a tremendous amount of soot. Atmospheric soot blocks the radiation from the sun and prevents it from reaching the Earth's surface, which is why all of the disaster scenarios about megafires such as nuclear holocaust or megavolcanoes warn of global cooling rather than warming. If both the soot theory and the CO_2 as Apocalypse hypothesis are to be believed, then having "clean" combustion of fossil fuels is making Global Warming worse because it eliminates the particulates that block out the sunlight which causes the warming in the first place. But the bottom line is, if you assert that the human combustion of fossil fuel is causing the temperature of the Earth's atmosphere to increase at a faster rate than what is assumed to be normal-- setting aside once again the fact that you have no idea what *normal* even is-- and you are not counting water vapor as part of the greenhouse gasses, then either by ignorance or arrogance you are kidding yourself about the relevance of your findings which, not surprisingly, never correspond with reality anyway. Remember when George Bush said that there were WMDs in Iraq and Congress went along with it and then no WMDs were found? This is the same thing. But the problem here isn't so much that CO_2 activists want to believe Al Gore's assertion that modern society is immoral and must change its ways and repent per his direction or we will have hell on earth; the real problem is that no environmentalist is going to call water vapor a pollutant no matter how many thousands of years of industrialization it would take to attain an atmospheric CO_2 level that yields a retention of heat equivalent to that which water vapor from our tailpipes is retaining *right now*. To a CO_2 activist it will never matter how much heat water vapor retains, how much water vapor comes out of our chimneys and exhaust pipes, how much CO_2 water absorbs as it cools, how much CO_2 water releases as it warms, how much the partial pressure of water vapor is increased as a result of whatever effect CO_2 actually has on local temperatures, or even how long it takes for CO_2 levels to return to "normal" after atmospheric temperatures return to "normal". By neglecting these variables and observations CO_2 activists attain the leap of faith that transubstantiates their hypothesis into religion; but because CO_2 activists regard themselves as intellectuals they must call their leap of faith something else. They call it open-mindedness. When a person advertises their open-mindedness, what they usually mean is that even though they cannot actually prove their lucrative and liberty-crushing hypotheses, they are nonetheless open to the possibility that the rest of us should do as they say without question.

I have to admit though, making CO_2 the culprit is one of the more rational assertions of the path to CO_2-as-Apocalypse enlightenment. Most people have no idea of the extent to which humanity depends upon fossil fuel, and when you do realize just how much CO_2 is returned to the atmosphere by the combustion of fossil fuel, an intelligent person can't help but think that it is going to have an effect on something. It is just unfortunate that environmentalists by nature have a proclivity to assume (in addition to water vapor being good) that any effect that humans have on anything is going to bear the moral label of "bad"-- hence the previous two mantras. To a CO_2 as Apocalypse zealot, man was born of original sin and any behavior that is not approved by the Society of CO_2 as Apocalypse is detrimental to the fabric of society. It is unfortunate that CO_2 as Apocalypse is a religion, for the message might actually be of value to humanity if the rhetoric of it was not so ensconced in moral judgment. Can you think of any other religions that do this?

> *Once the man-made sources of CO2 are eliminated,*
> *the climate* might *go back to normal*

The noble path to CO2 as Apocalypse enlightenment may be conclusively identified as a religion by the fact that your faith now requires additional faith. One hundred percent of the benefit that you gain by following the spiritual path of CO2 as Apocalypse and voting straight ticket Democrat is emotional, so congratulations: you are now officially just as whacky as the people who want *Harry Potter* banned.

All I ask of the environmental activists of the world is some rational prioritization of crises. Carbon dioxide? *Seriously?* I can understand why nitrous oxide isn't an option because let's face it, who doesn't love a couple of whip-its after an exhausting week of reading Margaret Atwood and memorizing the anatomy of a flower? And you can't really start a crusade against ozone when a lack of it is supposed to be destroying the Earth. Sulfur dioxide is a little difficult for the general public to grasp, and you don't want to compete for federal grants with the acid rain lobby since it might make things uncomfortable at university department meetings. But tell me armchair environmentalists, are you aware that of all the greenhouse gasses that come out of your car, carbon dioxide is not only the weakest heat retainer but is the most benevolent to the environment because photosynthesis, and therefore the entire food chain above the level of the deep sea vents absolutely depends on it? The reason there is oil in the ground in the first place is because plants and algae sucked up CO_2 and became the foundation of the food chain for almost every living thing on Earth. Terrestrial life is carbon-based because of carbon dioxide, and it literally makes more sense to worry about the decrease in the partial pressure of atmospheric oxygen which occurs when combustion converts O_2 to CO_2.

Look, if you want a GHG to stress over, at least try to look like you've done some homework and pick methane. Methane is almost impossible to dissolve into water over 60 degrees Fahrenheit, it takes forever to break down, it retains far more heat than CO_2, and when it breaks down it turns into two other GHGs. And it even smells bad: imagine the marketing potential! All your wealthy benefactors with their checkbooks at the ready would make even fatter donations to you if you extricated them from their 4,000 sq. ft. house, crammed them into your quaint environmentalist's status symbol du jour and drove them out to where I grew up and said "that's the smell of the world to coming to an end." Make methane the bad guy. Carbon dioxide just makes for thick vegetation and happy champagne.

In April of 2012 *SFGate.com* Columnist Mark Morford wrote an editorial entitled *10 Things You Need Not Worry About*. Morford's #2 thing that you need not worry about was none other than Global Warming. Morford's advice? I'll quote him:

"Here's what you can do about Global Warming: Vote accordingly. Change your personal habits.

Have fewer kids. Thank a scientist. Enjoy Earth Day."

That's right people who elected Nancy Pelosi: don't burden yourself by questioning pop science and leave the thinking to the *politicians*. You heard it from an e-columnist so it's gospel. Well, sorry Mark and Nan but I'm afraid those of us who think for ourselves are going to have to pass Climate Change in order to see what's in it.

Believe it or not I am a big fan of scientists. The study of glacial core samples is absolutely fascinating. Grants for climate research should be a priority among federal funding projects. I hope my kids grow up to be scientists; and if they use the tuition that Kelli and I spend on them to become climatologists and then proceed to tell me that my tailpipe is killing frogs faster than my tires, well then I'll have to adjust the way I get from place to place starting by not giving them rides back to the airport. But what is the current message of Climate Change? The message is: if I don't do exactly as some wealthy bureaucrat says (but not as he does) about every single thing from my thermostat to my lightbulbs to my car, then some time in the next hundred years or so something bad might happen. As a person who lives next to the ocean I can say with absolute certainty that in the next 100 years the most detrimental thing that is going to happen to our environment is our running out of money to protect it. We have a trillion dollar per year deficit: the only certain things in our future are a demand for cheap energy and lower standards for everything. Obama's deficit will kill our shorelines long before morbidly obese shrubbery ever will.

The Tea Party Chapter

If it turns out that the Tea Party was nothing more than a footnote of the 2010 midterm election at least it will have, by its opposition, brought to light the tremendous effect that propaganda has on modern society. Consider for a moment that the opposition to the Taxed Enough Already Party serves absolutely no purpose beyond raising taxes. What is the argument against being Taxed Enough Already if not *No, We're Not Actually Taxed Enough Already?* The opposition to "Taxed Enough Already" is "Raise Our Taxes". *Raise Our Taxes!* How on Earth do you get a bunch of taxpayers to rally in favor of being taxed more? I'd say that wanting higher taxes is like telling your boss to keep more of your paycheck if it weren't for the fact that wanting higher taxes is literally telling the government to take more of your paycheck. How does this happen?

Propaganda. As Charlie Rangel said "It's not spic or nigger anymore, they say let's cut taxes". Rangel is employing textbook examples of *transfer* and *name calling* propaganda.

Running for Congress has cost me my hope that America will stop becoming the soft, pathetic, incompetent, spoiled-brats-who-can't-take-care-of-themselves that the Soviet Union pegged us as being way back in the 70's. Naturally I don't like to think of my political memoirs as whining. I'm writing an epitaph for the next great republic to read. I'm trying to outline the small but pervasive flaw that caused our Great Experiment to fail. It is the same flaw that makes Marxist-type governments fail every single time they are attempted. The flaw is human nature. Government cannot be corrupt because government is merely an idea. Only human beings can be corrupt. Government fails when the humans who animate government begin to believe that they are entitled to things which the inanimate aspect of government denies them.

Greed used to be defined as the desire to possess more of something you don't need. Today the outspoken spoiled brats of America define greed as somebody else's desire to keep what is their own; with the emphasis always being on *somebody else's*. Just as with all other attempts at socialism, redistribution of wealth has no driving force beyond the Progressives' baseless faith in dictated morality.

In this chapter I am going to anger a lot of people who up until now have been supportive of me. That's OK though, because I don't actually know any of you. But since I'm on a roll I may as well preemptively burn any bridges that I may have someday held with Anheuser Busch, specifically Budweiser. As it happens, while I was becoming jaded with our electoral system I was smack in the middle of enjoying the daylights out of the renaissance of American beermaking. If you ever want to learn about brewing beer by watching TV, a good start would be to watch one of the documentaries about how Budweiser is made. Brewing for the masses is a fascinating process involving all of the hard sciences including organic chemistry, engineering, quantitative analysis, biology, economics, and logistics. And just when you think that all of these endeavors would have sapped any enjoyment that the final product may have held, the efficacy of every single field is tested with the nose, tongue and palate. Budweiser is a perfect mesh of the fields of science, business, and culinary art. And it's carp. For all of the exhaustive effort that is put into making Budweiser beer, as far as I'm concerned AB could save themselves a whole bunch of work by drinking a Fat Tire 1554 and micturiting the remains into bottles labeled 'Bud'. Do you know why they call it Bud? Because it only stimulates one taste bud in your whole mouth. Budweiser is merely the doorstep of an entire kingdom of beer gustation. But the bottom line is if you want to capture the hearts and dollars of the majority of the American public, be they beer drinkers or voters, your product must be bland and pale, somewhat bubbly with a soft white head, and most importantly it must offer the cool, crisp comfort of an invariably predictable routine. It doesn't matter whether you are selecting a beer on Election Day or a president during the World Series, the typical

American is going to choose a product that is simple and familiar.

Try to put a name with the following slogans:

This Budget's for you
Silver Bullets, and guns to put them in
If you've got the will, we've got the tax
Everything you always wanted in a president . . . and less
Head for the Mountains
The man who made Milwaukee famous
Always rich, even when you're not
It don't get more hopeful than this
O'bama: Irish for debt

* * *

In no small part I lost the primary because I was at first ignorant, and then dismissive of the cliqueyness of political parties. Although my platform was puny and nontraditional, none of the partisans particularly cared because their only real passion was vanquishing the opposing fraternity in intramural cheerleading. It was the Tea Party however, that opened my eyes to the extent to which politics depends upon propaganda and the stupidity of crowds.

During my brief stint as a candidate I was only engaged by one full-blown Republican partisan in real, man-to-man type conversation about why I was playing politician with the big boys. It happened on April 10, 2010 at the Rocky Mount Tea Party at Englewood Park. After a couple of hours of listening to speeches and potential supporters, I was talking with a woman about the usual stuff:

"Yep, it cost $1700 to run . . . the deficit is *definitely* untenable . . . *yes*, the fact that socialized health care only works in prison *is* a prudent analogy" etc.

After talking for about ten minutes the conversation changed. Suddenly the questions stopped and I was the one who had become the recipient of information. I was informed that I needed to meet a particular mogul of the Republican Party. I honestly do not remember the gentleman's name. I'm horrible with names. I'm going to make up a pseudonym that encapsulates both the respect and frustration that I incurred upon meeting this man.

"You really need to meet Mel Gibson. Mel's one of the most important campaign connections for Republicans in this part of the state. He knows all the candidates and keeps up with every candidate who's ever gotten elected."

This was just the beginning of the pitch. It continued for . . . well it probably wasn't that long, but it seemed like forever because I kept waiting for the woman to repeat the gentleman's name and the coordinates of the realm in which he appointed politicians, but she never did. Worse, after such a distinguished introduction I was too embarrassed to ask "*who* are you talking about again?" Apparently this was the person whom I absolutely *had* to meet if I was 'really serious about getting elected'. After all the buildup, when it was finally shared with me that this particular bigwig was at the very Tea Party at which we were conversing, I actually said "he's *here!*"

"Would you like to meet him" the woman asked.

"*WOULD I!*" I kicked my leg over my head and did the touchdown move with spirit fingers.

"I'll introduce you to him later" she said with a wink; then she left me to simmer in my glee.

I glanced around Englewood Park for a sheik's tent or some other opulent mobile refuge that I must have missed for the past three hours. It was very strange being informed that I would be *permitted* to meet somebody. It was like I was being pinned for a fraternity or selected to be Made or something. After a few minutes I realized what a dork I was being and I found that part of me was a little pissed that I needed to be fixed up to meet a fellow human being. I assumed I was just feeling the discomfort of an introvert swimming in a social circle. Still, I wondered why somebody who is so influential and important didn't just run for office themselves. No matter. This guy was probably just admired by his friends and there's nothing wrong with that. There were actually a handful of people looking up to me now that I was in politics, and I was just as much of a dud as I'd ever been. Celebrityism is bizarre.

Over the next hour I wandered around the Tea Party and tried to act like an extrovert. I met several good people, one of whom was the young man who was organizing the Greene Tea Party in Snow Hill, NC. He was sitting in a lawn chair away from the greater mass of people and was accompanied by a cooler and couple of regular-looking friends. They looked like my kind of people. They had the humility and easy-going character of folks who had held jobs since before they could drive. They wore t-shirts and flip flops. They smiled easily and gave no indication of being interested in either griping with, or enlightening me about the right way to be an American. Like most of the people at the Rocky Mount Tea Party they were merely enjoying their day off. It was nice to be around people whom you could trust not to think that the government should enforce your moral obligation to pay their mortgage, health insurance, retirement, unemployment benefits, disability for being fat, etc.

I was having a pleasant conversation with some representatives from a local veterans' organization when the woman who had pinned me for pledge status arrived and dragged me away in mid-sentence. I was ushered over to meet the man who apparently ran the northeastern region of North Carolina's Republican Party out what I imagined was a bunker underneath an abandoned Piggly Wiggly. Like all superheroes, Mel Gibson looked like a normal guy. He wore comfortable shoes and a loose-collared shirt. He even had a goatee and wore a baseball cap. Unlike other superheroes however, this one kept his sunglasses on as we were introduced. Then we shook hands, or so I thought. Mel Gibson took my hand in the handshake position but he just squeezed it and didn't let go. He even pulled it toward himself a little bit like he wanted a hug or something.

I didn't hug.

We stood there on the sidewalk next to the tennis

courts basking in the springtime sun. I held Mel's hand in silence as I stared into my reflection in his sunglasses. Maybe he was waiting for a secret handshake or something. Maybe I was supposed to ask him if he was a travelling man. Whatever Mel was waiting for it was obvious that he didn't regard making eye contact to be serious enough to remove his shades, so I figured it would be OK if I broke my gaze from his bug eyes and looked around to see what his posse was doing. They were just standing there with big grins on their faces. A slight chuckle rippled through us; it may have been initiated by me but I'm not sure. After another moment it became apparent that in addition to not taking off your shades when you meet someone, Mr. Gibson also had a very one-sided view of the meaning of shaking hands. His grip was good, far better than most in fact, but I was beginning to think that his firmness of grip was merely so I wouldn't slip away when I realized that his handshake was more of a show for his posse than it was for the American ritual of assumed mutual respect. In his defense he could have been looking at the Band-Aid on my face. Two days earlier I'd been working on my lawn mower and had almost gouged my left eye out with a pair of needle-nosed pliers and I figured that my face would look better with a Band-Aid on it than like I'd just undergone amateur Mohs surgery. Whatever the reasoning for Mel's freestyle interpretation our long-hallowed customs it was all very liberal. And since I wasn't the most iron-fisted Republican *and* I was pretending to be a politician, I concluded that I was just going to have to learn to put up with handshakes-for-show and other such BS.

Finally Mel started talking. Although he had the sunglasses and handshake etiquette of a celebrity posing for a photo he talked like a regular guy. We chatted for a minute, reciting from heart all of the staple "how 'bout that deficit" type ice breakers that we Tea Party folk share. Mel Gibson seemed to approve of my assessment of our nation's challenges. Then the real questions started.

"What are you doing for fundraising" Mel asked.

"I'm not accepting donations during the primary" I said. "The primary is for the informed voters and if the Party picks me then we can worry about fundraising after that."

Mel chuckled through his nose and glanced over his shoulder at his posse, who chuckled through their noses in response. Then he looked back at me and shook my hand with every other syllable as he spoke.

"I want to vote for you" he said "but I can't unless you can convince me that you can raise enough money to beat Butterfield".

This seemed like a fair statement, except that political fundraisers are a farce and they just piss me off. Was Mel asking me if I thought that I was able to throw a $5 an hour dining experience and charge $40 a plate for it like the Reagan Day Dinner in New Bern? I suspected that I had more foodservice experience than all of the other candidates combined. To ask a politician to throw a fundraiser is literally nothing more than asking him to throw a tax-deductible night out with friends. I pointed to a billboard across the street from where we stood and addressed Mel in a not-so-politically-correct tone, "If you want to vote for the person with the most rich friends then vote for Woolard".

There was no campaigning allowed at the Tea Party in Englewood Park, so the Woolard entourage had parked their ginormous mobile billboard with his name on it directly across the street. Mel turned his sunglasses to look over at the giant sign and the couple of guards who had been standing next to it all morning, and his mouth took on a slight look of frustration. For a split second I had hope that this political bigwig was about to recognize the fallacy of using fundraising as the deciding factor for party endorsement. But his expression could have been about something else. After a moment the look on Mel's face disappeared so completely that I thought that I may have imagined it. Then he set his jaw and redirected his sunglasses back at me.

"How are you going to let people know what you stand for if you don't have fundraisers?"

"That's what I'm trying to do right now" I said with a chuckle.

I thought that this should have been a slam dunk considering I was talking to the man who got Republicans elected with a phone call or whatever. I mean, if Mel Gibson was the politician-maker that his posse characterized him as being then he must be rich and able underwrite my campaign like he's Bruce Wayne or something. But asking me if I could come up with a fundraiser was like saying "I like you just as much as the other candidates, but Jerry Grimes promised me salmon puffs". Obviously Mel didn't view it that way, but that's how it is. I was too much of a libertarian to ask people for their money in exchange for their baseless hope of my someday writing legislation that favored them over other citizens. Asking for a tax-deductible bribe in exchange for heavy *hors d'oeuvres* just seemed to make the entire electoral process even more of a joke. Still, Mel did join me in a brief laugh.

A pause began growing in the conversation. I wished he'd take off his stupid sunglasses. Maybe he'd just had Lasik or something. Members of Mel's posse stood frozen in silence with awkward smiles plastered on their faces and their eyes darting between one other. I must have been something of a novelty-- not caring about the boost in social status that I'd get by overcharging for tax-deductible, mass-produced entrees and all. Then Mel asked me how I was paying for my campaign. I told him the truth: that my grandmother had just died and I had received $10,000 from her estate; I was using the money for a variety of things, mostly paying bills, but a good chunk of it I spent on registering as a candidate and on roadside advertising. Mel's smile disappeared and he stared at me in silence from behind his sunglasses. He released my hand. Then he scrunched his lips into a thin line, shook his head sadly and turned and walked away without saying another word.

Mel's posse didn't seem to know whether to keep smiling or not. With obvious uncertainty about what had just happened, the posse slowly stepped into line behind
270

Mel and left me to squander my money on faith in America alone. It was at that moment, as I stood there in the warm Rocky Mount sunshine with my mouth hanging open that I realized that the Republican Party has no interest in anything beyond throwing tax-deductible parties for their friends and calling it a fundraiser. The idea of believing in yourself enough to underwrite your own efforts was apparently just a fairy tale that poor people like my parents tell their offspring. Somehow, up until that exact point in time I had naively believed that roadside signs with nothing but a surname and some adjectives on them were for wooing the stupids who got their voting inspiration from name recognition and word association. As it turns out, fundraising for propaganda is the cardinal excuse for throwing tax deductible parties with your political cronies. It was like being in a fraternity all over again:

Step one: form a t-shirt committee over pitchers at Front St. Brewery.

Step two: have t-shirts printed with your slogan on them.

Step three: buy the t-shirts with your own money.

Step four: celebrate your successful "fundraising" over a keg.

What a disappointment. Not the fraternity part-- when I was in college I actually needed beer and t-shirts. I just couldn't believe that I was dumb enough to think that political parties were about the pursuit of a more perfect union and legislative QA/QI.

*   *   *

That same day in Rocky Mount, the young man whom I'd met earlier invited me to attend the next meeting of the Greene Tea Party. I said I would be there. The meeting was scheduled for Tuesday, April 13th. at the Greene County Community Center in the peaceful hamlet of Snow Hill.

The Greene County Community Center looked like it may have recently been a small church. It was a T-shaped building with the top of the T facing the road. It was clad in light-colored lap board siding with a parking lot on one side and a basketball court in the rear. Parked on the road in front of the community center was a gigantic fiberglass pig on a trailer. "Oh goodie" I thought, "bar-b-que!".

I parked the Matrix in the community center lot and yanked up the hand brake. I turned and placed my nekkid tootsies onto the asphalt and enjoyed the yellow warmth of the late afternoon. After a moment I put on some shoes and a dressier shirt. To this day I feel like my biggest lie as a candidate was putting on shoes and snug-collared shirts; but I reckon we all make concessions in exchange for popularity. As I mentioned before it was a beautiful day. I wondered what my kids were doing. Suddenly I was seized with an empty feeling like I was making a terrible mistake. My sons were seven and nine years old and you only get a handful of beautiful spring days to spend with your children before they want to go off with their friends. What lay inside the community center for me other than more people in shoes and tight-collared shirts talking about what we should do to make everybody else start taking responsibility for themselves? I didn't want to force anybody to do anything, which is perhaps what makes me such a lousy politician. What is the point of a political party *really*, if not for lamenting the behavior of strangers? I wanted the government out of my life, and to pursue this end I was pretending that I wanted to spend more time away from my kids so that I could be completely immersed in government? I'd passed on medical school because I didn't want to neglect my kids; and the difference between medical school and politics is as a physician I know for a fact that I would help at least one stranger have a better life before I died. This didn't make any sense. I'm not comparing myself to Thomas Jefferson but at least Jefferson's vision of a nation of self-sufficient people who let each other live in peace was possible. At the very least during Jefferson's time humanity had the common enemy of nature. At any time the weather could have literally swooped into TJ's life and killed him faster than a redcoat with an H-bomb. Modern society is invasive of the lives of individuals as well as codependent and malleable to the will of the mob. Worse, the typical American would think very long and hard if presented with a choice between living with no air conditioning or the promise of free air conditioning if they just let communist China be in charge. It just happens that I get along with partisans on both sides because I choose to live the life that Democrats want to force on us, and I do so because I actually embrace the values that Republicans insist are theirs. Was I really going inside on a beautiful day to be with strangers instead of with my family? If I left Snow Hill at that very moment and drove straight to the beach the kids would be fast asleep by the time I got home. I tied my shoes and tie, walked into the community center and closed the door on the sunlight.

It was comfortable inside the community center in a clean, carpeted, and climate-controlled way. People were setting up tables and I helped. I didn't spoil the feeling of community by mentioning that I was a candidate. It seemed like every time I told someone that I was running for Congress I was either sucked up to or not taken seriously, both of which were equally unpleasant. It was nice to simply be a fellow teabagger organizing chairs and tables to the ends of having no additional taxes and being hated for it by the television.

As if on cue, as soon as the rearranging-of-the-furniture was completed the community center began to fill with people. There was quiet chat and some cautious poking around to see if any social "victims" had shown up to harass us until we oppressed them by defending ourselves. I went over to the information table and said hello to the woman there as I took a plastic bag and stuffed it with paraphernalia for later reading. I asked the woman if she was giving out any pens that I could use for work and she offered me a copy of *Capital Connection* instead. Then I picked up a menu that outlined the evening's tea. We were going to hear from a local insurance agent, Americans for Prosperity, a North Carolina conservative think tank and education coalition called The Civitas Institute, and from the organizer of the Greene Tea Party whom I had met informally at the Rocky Mount Tea Party. Then I saw something that made my heart leap in my chest; my old economics professor from ECU was on the docket!

It had been almost 20 years since I'd seen Dr. Parker and I doubted he would remember me. In 1992 I was just another kid from the beach who showed up to class in flip-flops and an Al Merrick t-shirt and always sat in the back row. Dr. Parker had to be at least 120 years old by now. He was the person who'd opened my liberal dude-eyes to the role of interest rates and government spending in the economy. He described the behavior of taxpayers who purchase US savings bonds as "literally taking your money out of one pocket and putting it in the other". He made us aware (this was during Dad Bush's Administration) that the national debt which we were all so worried about was fairly benign when you compared it to our own credit card bills, college loans, impending marriages, rent, car loans and lack of gainful employment. He also pointed out that Dad Bush's tax cuts were actually an increase in the tax rate. The "decrease" was just a lowering of the rate at which our taxes were increased, and Dad Bush went on to lose the next election to a draft dodger because of it.

Dr. Parker taught us that John Maynard Keynes was in fact a brilliant economist and that it is those who blindly follow him (he named no names but called them "flaming Keynesians") who make Keynesian economics dysfunctional. Government spending puts more money into the private sector and will either boost the economy or cause inflation; whereas government hoarding of money leaves less wealth in the private sector and can have the effect of decreasing inflation. But what was perhaps the nail

275

in my liberal coffin was when he taught us how there is an optimal range for taxation. If taxes are too high then people have less money to spend on the things that they want, resulting in fewer sales and consequently fewer tax revenues are collected. If taxes are too low then the infrastructure that allows normal business to take place deteriorates and consequently businesses aren't able to reliably keep products on their shelves, again resulting in fewer tax revenues being collected. In the light of realization that tax rates and tax revenues do not share a linear relationship, one becomes free to watch the news and disagree with the talking heads that are really only there to sell you soap.

What made the Tea Party so exciting to those of us who weren't joiners of the status quo was that it was like *We the People* were finally getting a second option for representation in government.

It was true that I was disillusioned with the Party that I was supposed to be representing, as well as with our political system in general. I was disgruntled about having to represent the agenda of a national Party rather than the will of the people of my district. But in addition to my political concerns, the Tea Party seemed like something of a sanctuary from the chaos of the typical political circus. And now that I was in Snow Hill what I really needed to find out was where the bar-b-que was being served.

I'd already asked the woman at the information table if she was giving out pens so I approached her again and asked "So, uhhhmm, what's with the big pig outside there?"

"That belongs to Americans for Prosperity" said the propaganda woman, giving no indication about whether or not the ginormous trailer contained stores of tasty slow-roasted porcine goodness. I waited for further information but none came. The young woman continued to organize the things on her table in silence. Having no other choice, I had to ask.

"Is Americans for Prosperity serving bar-b-que?"

The leaflet woman squared the edges of a stack of postcards and smiled a little as she replied "No, it's one of their things for illustrating government waste."

I returned my gaze to the leaflet woman and was surprised to find that this time she was looking back at me and smiling. Suddenly I realized that the leaflet woman was hot! Of course as I realized this I froze up and my mind went completely blank. Within milliseconds I was rendered unaware of whatever expression was on my face-- I'd forgotten I even had a face. Fortunately all of those years being around Doris Day came back to me and my training took over. I took a deep breath, held it, and quickly turned and walked away with my arms hanging limply at my sides. Attractive women give me the munchies, as do the daydreams of slow-cooked pork that I get from giant pink fiberglass pigs. I had no choice but to search the community center for unsupervised snacks.

There were no foodstuffs to be found anywhere in the community center. If nuclear winter happened while we were having tea it was going to be a very short and uneventful fall to our collective demise. When I returned to the main hall I found that the party was about to get started. I ignored my churning stomach, diverted my gaze from the siren at the information table, and took a seat at one of the farther tables from the lectern. Momentarily the man who'd invited me to the Greene Tea Party stepped up to the podium and introduced himself. I'm going to call this gentleman Joe, because that may actually be his name but again, I'm horrible with names and I just don't remember. Joe welcomed everyone to the Greene Tea Party. He was wearing a suit instead of a t-shirt as he'd been in Rocky Mount and he looked a little uncomfortable in it. Joe looked like a man who is accustomed to working with his hands and his mind, but who had been propped up behind a microphone and forced to work with his clothes and mouth instead. Most of the people in the room looked this way in fact, and we were empathetic toward Joe. We all knew that if you wait so long that your problems have to be vocalized that they are already getting out of hand.

The Greene Tea Party was attended mostly by men. The majority of the room looked to be in their mid-fifties. Some were older, a handful of us were younger, and there was a kid or two present. Many of the men looked like farmers, which was encouraging since farmers in North Carolina were almost always Democrats. The Obama Administration might not be uniting the rest of the nation, but he was bringing the Tobacco State together for the first time in over a century.

Joe introduced the first speaker, who was the local insurance agent. This gentleman looked like most small-town insurance agents. He was about six feet tall, thin in

278

body and in hair, and nearing retirement. He was neatly-but-not-glamorously groomed and clad in a suit. He spoke clearly and sincerely, and he told us what we already knew--that you can't insure everybody regardless of pre-existing conditions without the cost of insurance going up. For the insurance company, accepting preexisting conditions was like being required to provide homeowner's insurance to somebody whose house has just caught fire, or has had termites for five years, or has gone without a roof for a decade, and not expecting the premiums to go up. The agent was not condescending toward the people who had medical problems but who did not want to pay to have them treated, or toward those who did not want to purchase insurance in preparation for a problem they could not afford. Expanding health insurance coverage to everybody and expecting your coverage and premium to stay the same was kind of like inviting five total strangers to move into your house and expecting to maintain the same access to and cost for utilities as you did when you lived alone. The increase in the cost for an insurance company to insure everybody can only be recouped by the adjustment of two things: the insurance company can either decrease coverage (*aka* rationing) or it can increase premiums. Essentially the insurance man didn't tell us anything we didn't already know, but it was nice to finally hear somebody report what the TV refused to.

The next person to speak was Dr. Parker. It was awesome! It was like returning to the back row of a classroom in Brewster Hall only without the hair and the hangover. We discussed the deficit and the level of taxation

279

and how America had been in a similar situation at the end of WWII. The difference between the US deficit today versus 1945 is that in 1945 about 75% of the federal budget was going to the military to fight the Axis powers. Once the war was over, almost all of that expense was eliminated and the budget shrank back to manageable size. Today about 75% of the federal budget is spent on entitlements such as Medicare, Medicaid, Social Security and the like. Current military spending comprises about 12% of the federal budget. Rather than fighting the Axis powers America is now fighting the generation whose greatest contribution to society occurred in 1969 when they advised one another that the brown acid was not particularly good (my words not Dr. Parker's).

Have you ever been in a class in which all the properties of reason, math and sociology came together to mesh harmoniously? That is how I feel about economics. When I majored in philosophy I was constantly confronted with the duality of a worldview as it is advertized by its followers versus how it is actually practiced. Al Qaeda and Sufism for example, are both Islamic minorities which claim to pursue purity in their worship of God; but the latter values peace and mysticism while the former worships mass murder and virgins. Economics has very few of these contradictions, and the contradictions that do exist are teaching points about society rather than lapses in logic and reason. Economics allows you to read statistics such as "43.8% of motor and jet fuel is purchased directly by consumers, while 41.4% is purchased by businesses, and the remaining 14.8% is purchased by the government to help fuel ambulances, police cars, F-18's etc." and amend it with the knowledge that 100% of the expense of running a business is paid for by the consumers, and 100% of the expense of running the government is paid for by consumers, thereby illustrating that 100% of the fuel purchased in the US is paid for by consumers, even if they do not purchase it "directly".

Another example of economic enlightenment is how packaged food corporations have found that if you manufacture a cake mix that only requires water and you sell it for a dime a box, people will not purchase it; but if you remove the protein and fat from the very same product, raise the price to a dollar and tell the customers that they have to provide their own eggs and oil, then people will purchase enough of the cheaper cake mix for the corporation to decrease unemployment.

Similarly, a particular yacht maker wanted to make powerboating affordable to more people, so he engineered and manufactured yachts that were far less expensive than anything else on the market. Nobody purchased his yachts. The man then raised the price of his yachts to that they were the most expensive ones on the market. Suddenly celebrities, politicians and dictators the world over were lined up to purchase the exact same boats that he had manufactured and priced for the middle class.

It is an absolute intellectual joy to see humanity's desires objectified and quantified in the demand half of economics. It is like somebody took the entire psychology department and went B.F. Skinner on it; there is no projection from deep within the dusty crevasses of your psyche as you speculate why people do the things they do. With economics you are simply a scientist who observes and quantifies from a distance. You can be detached. You can live and let live. You can mind your own business and remain worldly. With economics I do not have to try to understand and be compassionate toward the bullies on Bus 42 who demanded my ass get beaten every day, all I have to do is recognize that it happened because I supplied my pacifism for them to abuse.

Some people go to church to hear about how their enemies will burn in hell when they die. Some attend lectures on Climate Change to hear how they can save humanity from original soot. Some go to therapy to hear that their parents were only human. I love economics lectures because it lets me turn society into Schrodinger's cat, wherein I can determine the consequences of any demographic's demands simply by identifying what must be supplied in order for the demand to become reality.

After Dr. P had finished laying out the economic downfall of America in 27 PowerPoint slides with charts and graphs and a paragraph on the bottom of each one he attempted to end on a positive note. He broke out a graph which illustrated that every time America has deviated from its historical pattern of economic growth it has always managed to return to normal. We were pretty far from normal and things looked like they were only going to get worse, but the graph didn't lie. Every other time America got into economic trouble eventually the American people overcame whatever it was that was causing the problem.

Never has America's problem been its citizens' inability to give up government entitlements, but inflation was sure to make that meaningless eventually. It was ironic that we all clapped enthusiastically when Dr. Parker had finished scientifically illustrating that we were all economically screwed.

The next person to talk was the representative from Civitas. This was where the Greene Tea started to taste a little weird. To me, the Tea Party was a bunch of people who thought beyond the remote control and were gravely concerned about the direction that our government was dragging our citizenry. But the Civitas presentation seemed to have almost no impact on the attendees. The Rep. talked about the importance of getting involved in politics and outlined the research that the Civitas Institute performed. We were invited to partake of any and all of the Institute's research. We were invited to peruse the quarterly periodical *Civitas Review* as well as the monthly *Capital Connection*. Things went smoothly and professionally and when the Civitas talk was finished we were asked if we had any questions.

It bears stating at this point that the Civitas Representative was the woman from the information table. Her name was Jessica. She looked like a college cheerleader, spoke like an MBA and appeared to be as comfortable in business attire as Hillary Clinton only without all the smirking and condescension. She stood strongly with her feet together, she made eye contact with the audience, and she spoke both clearly and at a level that everybody could understand. Jessica was well prepared to answer questions about state and Federal Government, elections, grassroots fertilizer, Civitas, and a thousand other political things. What she did not seem to be prepared to do was supply her affirmation to a room full of middle aged men who suddenly demanded that she know that they were heterosexual. It was as if we had forgotten all about the imminent economic downfall of America, the degradation of republican democracy, and the implementation of legislation which mimicked both the depth and popularity of *General Hospital*, and switched topics to the importance of increased government regulation of gender-related cultural rites of passage. Almost the entire Civitas question and answer session consisted of middle aged dudes asking the Civitas representative about gay marriage. There were at least three men who had popped enough Viagra prior to the Tea Party to flat out ask Jessica how "we" can get gay marriage banned-- as if Civitas' political research was actually code for *political activism* which was actually code for *I desire a girl with a truncated skirt and a protracted jacket.* Every time another audience member took it upon themselves to enlighten Jessica about how bad gay marriage was the crowd would grow quiet and lean forward. Very diplomatically the Civitas Rep. would attempt to point out that gay marriage was the sort of thing that one could select a candidate over, and that if one wanted to look further into a candidate's background such as their voting record, rap sheet, legislative behavior, etc., then Civitas was there to help. At one point a man even compared gay marriage to illegal immigration because "they're both bad for our taxes". The man wasn't specific about exactly *how* illegal immigration or gay marriage were bad for our taxes, or even what *bad for our taxes* meant. Nonetheless, the assertion was followed by a great deal of supportive clucking from the audience. It was embarrassing. Somebody eventually asked Jessica a relatively easy question-- one that had the smell of being intended to return the discussion to something more reflective of people who had been taxed-enough-already. It was a marshmallow of a question about whether or not Civitas can tell us who voted in favor of tax increases or something, and of course the answer was yes. Then there was silence which lasted about five full seconds before somebody asked something else about gay marriage. The Civitas Rep., God bless her, smiled her cheerleader smile and actually said "Ah yes, gay marriage again. Well, I'm primarily here to talk about getting people involved in knowing the stances of their politicians, not about discussing individual policies, so if anybody has any other questions for me I will be at the table in the back." Then she offered us a believable "Thank you for having me" and she stepped down from the podium.

"Way to go, *fags*" I thought. "Now we have to look at another dude."

It was at this point that I decided not to tell anybody at the Greene Tea Party that I was a candidate. I kinda wanted to tell Dr. Parker but it wasn't like he remembered me from class, and Tea Parties generally didn't permit campaigning anyway. Although cultivating my anonymity was sort of like anti-campaigning I felt that it was somehow politician-esque of me to so blatantly hide the truth from my presumed constituents. By being quiet

285

during the gay-marriage-should-be-banned nonsense if anybody later found out that I was at the Greene Tea Party it would likely be assumed that I approved of banning gay marriage, which I don't. I have to say that I think that most of the people at the Greene Tea Party were concerned with state politics and had no real interest in pursuing a constitutional amendment that stated *We the Government of the United States reserve the right to tell our Subjects who may and who may not engage in certain cultural rites of passage.*

The final speaker was the representative for Americans for Prosperity. I like Americans for Prosperity even though the name smacks of propaganda and the guy that they sent to speak that day gave me the creeps. The Americans for Prosperity Rep. was some sort of Republican celebrity, whom I will call Vegas.

From the moment Vegas stepped behind the podium he reminded me of every morbidly obese fraternity-socialite-who-went-on-to-sell-used-cars that I've ever seen. His hair was feathered and pretty. His belt made a 45 degree angle as it went from above his ass to beneath his gut. He talked nonstop on a level of simplicity that made debate pointless, and he only offered original statements built off of things that other people said. In short, Vegas could be our next president.

From its very start Vegas' presentation paled in comparison to that of all the other speakers, and yet the audience ended up cheering, whistling, and completely enthralled. To recap the evening thus far, the first speaker provided us with official confirmation of what we already suspected about the future of health insurance coverage and premiums under Obamacare. Dr. Parker broadened our views of the deficit, budget, taxation, and economic history. Jessica offered us access to additional information on our politicians and legislation. Then Vegas got up and just started running his mouth. I will grant that he had something of a slow start. Prettyboy began his pep-rally by thanking Dr. Parker for coming to talk to us, as if he was somehow speaking on behalf of the audience rather than to it. Then Vegas informed Dr. Parker that he had applied for admission to East Carolina University and had been turned down. The room fell silent. I looked over at Dr. Parker who, like most people in the audience, was staring at Vegas with his mouth slightly open. Why, of all things, would Mr. Charisma divulge *that*?

It is common knowledge in eastern North Carolina that prior to 2008 *everybody* got into ECU. I first started at ECU while I was on academic suspension from UNC Wilmington. It was so easy to get into ECU that people called it *EZU*; but there was a catch. East Carolina would give anybody a chance to learn, but it also flunked people out at the drop of a hat. Any clown could get in, but if you made it to graduation you would have an education as good as any in North Carolina. So when Vegas said that he didn't get into ECU everybody knew that he was probably lying. We just couldn't tell if he was sarcastically making fun of our school, or if he was just trying to loosen us up with a Henry Youngman-type opener that bordered on making fun of the mentally handicapped. Nobody wanted to consider the possibility that Vegas might actually be telling the truth, which would mean that we had all gathered in breathless anticipation to listen to a complete moron.

Vegas deftly administered all the fluff found in a typical political rally. There was a three-word catchphrase: "November is Coming"; and it had the effect of transforming us into a bunch of little Obamaites who may as well have been chanting *Yes We Can*. Vegas worked his magic and converted the Greene Tea Party from an intellectual pursuit of liberty into a sing-along with Captain Feathersword. Naturally we were all supplied with free propaganda to take home and enjoy, but perhaps the high point of Vegas' pitch was when he passed out a bunch of red, five-by-eight-inch cards. We were instructed to scribble our respective Herbie Hancocks on the cards, slap a stamp on them and mail them to our representatives in Raleigh. The general message of the card was "we're not going to re-elect you if you vote in favor of any of the following things"; and the card listed four pieces of legislation. I don't recall what the bills were, but at the time I noticed that one of them had already been voted on and passed months earlier. Didn't the Greene teabaggers at least warrant fresh propaganda from Americans for Prosperity? How long had AFP been waiting to hand these cards out? I had received a couple of similar cards in the mail from some Pro-Life folks asking me to ban abortion, but none of them stated that if *Roe v. Wade* went in favor of Roe then I could count on them to vote for the Democrat.

Vegas seemed like a douche, but many people have thought the same thing about me. I dislike myself when I regard a stranger as a hygienic aqueous jet, so I decided that

I would talk to Vegas and try to get to know him better. However I decided to talk to him after tea was over so that I wouldn't get tarred and feathered if I disagreed with him in front of the *Price-is-Right* audience that he had somehow turned us into.

After the Americans for Prosperity presentation ended and the party was brought to a close, I helped put away tables and chairs. I talked with the young men who had organized the tea-vent for us and I thanked them both for putting forth the effort to try to save our nation. I stated that I thought they were doing far more to save our nation than any politician; then we half-heartedly joked about how the government does not *yet* completely control the peoples' right to peaceably assemble.

Moments later I again found myself standing at the main exit shaking hands with people as they left. I guess I learned this trick from my pastor. After a few minutes the flow of people leaving the center began to slow and I heard the nonstop rambling of the representative for Americans for Prosperity. As I waited for chatty to exit the building I had a brief conversation with a gentleman who reminded me of my stepfather. He was tall, bald, pear-shaped with khaki pants and ruddy cheeks that scrunched his eyes into slits as he smiled, which he did freely. He wore large, thick-rimmed rectangular bifocals. The man mentioned that he had been on the presidential campaign committee of some guy in California in 1964. I confessed that I had never heard of his candidate-- my having not been born until 1970 and all. The gentleman smiled his big, sincere grin and seemed pleased that my ignorance gave him a chance to reminisce. He chuckled a little bit and said that the man for whom he was campaigning "was so conservative that he made Barry Goldwater look like a communist". He followed up with a good-natured "you know who Barry Goldwater was don't you?" I gave him my worst-chemistry-student-at-ECU answer of $AuH2O$ and he said "there ya go" and chuckled some more. The gentleman was a good fellow, but his statement left me confused. What is one supposed to think when somebody says that a candidate made Barry Goldwater look like a communist? How is that even possible? Am I misunderstanding communism? Am I misunderstanding Conservatism? What am I doing here? Jeepers Wally, I don't know *anything*.

The twilight was giving way to mercury vapor lamps and dew was setting on the grass. I imagined my kids getting ready for bed. Vegas was saying nothing nonstop and I had to stand within his airspace for several minutes just to catch a pause in his gabbing. I outstretched my hand to him as he turned and walked right past me. I followed and excused myself for interrupting his walk and said that I wanted to ask him something about the red cards that we were supposed to mail out to the candidates.

Vegas blinked slowly before looking at me with a slack jaw and his eyelids half shut. "What's that" he said dryly.

"Well" I said, "if you tell a candidate that you are not going to vote for them if they vote in favor of *any* of these bills, and *one* of the bills has already been passed, then the candidate really has no reason to do what you want on the other three bills because you're not going to vote for him anyway."

I thought this was a reasonable thing to point out and I sincerely hoped that Vegas would finally say something intelligent. Instead he said: "Those are for the people not the candidates" and he turned and walked off, immediately yapping away about something else. Then Vegas and Jessica, and the white rabbit and the Cheshire Cat all piled into the pigmobile and rode off together.

After a while I blinked. I turned and started unbuttoning my shirt as I walked through the dark toward the Matrix. There was only one other car left in the parking lot. Clicking the fob to the Matrix I walked around to the relative privacy of the passenger's side of my car to change clothes in preparation for the three-hour drive home. I pulled my feet out of my shoes and kicked them into the floor of the car. The pavement was still warm. I quickly replaced my pants with shorts and tightened my belt. After years of parking-lot changes out of wet wetsuits and into dry skivvies I can accomplish this maneuver with dry clothes in about four seconds flat. There was a basketball court behind the community center and the flickering of the old street lights gave the court the look of being underwater. Sharks glided out of the shadows to congregate under the far hoop as the last person out of the community center started walking toward his car. The man's car was a '68 Camaro-- one of my favorites. I admired the car in silence and thought that the Tea Party would fail for the same reason that GM, Marxism, subprime loans, and the American Experiment have all failed-- because the greatness of humanity lies in the character and accomplishments of individuals, not crowds. Crowds are incapable of doing anything other than destroying one another, and our government is elected by crowds. Nancy Pelosi was right: the Tea Party was just a bunch of Republicans pretending to be a grassroots organization. If we weren't Republicans we wouldn't all be running *in the Republican primary*. The Tea Party was probably America's last blossom of liberty, and it would die quickly and quietly because it was filled with nobodies like me instead of with winners like Vegas.

Cruisin'

The knockdown blow to my chances of winning the election came when I went on a Caribbean cruise during the week leading up to the primary. Perhaps the reader can glean from my actions the authority by which I criticize others who fail to achieve higher standards of living: I know all about failure because frankly, due to my behavior, I am one.

I feel uncomfortable confessing that we go on cruises. Although I enjoy roaming the Caribbean on a floating mega-mall chock full of things that I have almost no interest in, it just isn't consistent with the mindset that I grew up with. My sister and I didn't know that we were poor, but we were aware of a certain worldview that had been pushed on us. Our parents seemed to be against any sort of activity that might be considered relaxing. Even baseball bordered on being taboo. No sport was ever spoken of in the Miller household, and when I was dropped off for knee pants it was a solemn and somewhat confusing affair that was more like being driven to the abortion clinic than to the Boys Club. Comfort and leisure were bad words in our house, and we regarded anybody who indulged in things like games, air conditioning, or especially vacations to be of a somehow inferior class. Cruises, being the epitome of R&R, were for rich, lazy people who never lifted anything heavier than a pair of maracas. Like Charo. Even watching *The Love Boat* bordered on being an indulgence deserving of guilt.

Kelli and I had booked our 2010 cruise a year in advance. Every year we go on a cruise with friends from college and we book the cruise for the following year while we are together. In 2009 we'd been worried that we wouldn't have enough money to afford the 2010 cruise. The economy was puny and was being made even worse by politicians who found that they accrued more votes if they instituted the economic policies of celebrities, trailer trash and third world dictators rather than that of business owners and economists. The future looked grim for the middle class. Those of us who already paid all the bills of the Fortune 500 magnates by purchasing their products looked as if we were about to get stuck with even more bills as we paid back China for the deficit and suffered inflation as money was printed to pay back that borrowed from Social Security in order to subsidize Medicare. In short, the good days of knowing that if you worked hard and saved your money that eventually you would get ahead, were being systematically eliminated by the greed of almighty politicians and the new government class. Fortunately there was still alcohol.

On our 2009 cruise we discussed the deficit in the Schooner Bar. We voiced our concern about the gap between functional unemployment and unemployment claims over a Boddington's at the Hoof and Claw. At the Sky Bar we lamented the government destruction of small businesses over shots of Jäger. Finally we went back downstairs to The Catacombs and attempted to establish whether the typical voter even knew what Fascism was. Alas the Catacombs were too loud to discuss such things verbally and we resolved to continue our discourse via a tricotee of the Sprinkler, the Cabbage Patch, and the Cactus Dance. When we found ourselves at the On Air Club singing *Let's Get It On* rather than Ranking Joe's *Cold Blood*, it became apparent that we might be taking the downfall of American liberty just a little too seriously. Yes, alcohol is truly the devil's beverage.

Thus, in April of 2009 we decided that there was still hope for America. We knew that Obama and his followers were intelligent people-- it was just a matter of time before it became obvious to them that America was not going to get out of debt by borrowing more money. Although liberals found the 'ivory tower' portion of their handle a little too *Venere con lo Specchio* for their liking, they were undoubtedly intellectuals. No matter how sequestered from reality they were, eventually their objectivity would overwhelm their faith in Obama and they would concede that *maybe* the economics department wasn't entirely filled

295

with troglodytes. Watching the Obama Administration assert that the *Stimulus Package* was going to decrease unemployment was going to be like watching Oral Roberts prophecy that if he didn't raise a certain amount of money God was going to take him home. It would be heartwarming to watch the rest of the nation finally learn economics. *Expensive*, but heartwarming. It would be like sending our Goth teenagers out of state to James Madison University and watching them major in business. They would stop getting the same old boring tattoos of skulls and Celtic knots and start getting stamped with supply and demand graphs on the small of their collective backs. They would get the katakana symbols for *employee morale* and *customer satisfaction* on their forearms. They would start understanding statistics instead of depending on innumerate J majors to tell them what the numbers meant. Obama would unite the country by proving once and for all that social prosperity absolutely never comes from going into debt in order to let the people eat cake. We had hope. Change was looming. And as long as the whole swine flu thing that the cruise line told us had broken out in the 'States didn't kill us we figured that the Obama people were destined for an economic epiphany. We bit the bullet, assumed we'd still be solvent in a year and booked a cruise with our friends for the end April 2010.

It was March of the following year before Kelli and I realized that we'd booked the cruise for the week leading up to the primary. For about a month there was some nail chomping as I debated missing our third vacation ever just to become more disappointed with our electoral process versus abandoning my idealism about being a candidate that is dedicated to having a platform rather than advertising campaign. Since I'd already been approved for the time off from work I could have used the time to do some last-minute campaigning around the parts of the district that I'd not yet visited. For example, I really wanted to go to Gates County.

When we were kids our family would take trips to the Gates County landfill. At the landfill my dad would repair the heavy equipment that was used to dig trenches and bury trash. While my dad made ratcheting and swearing noises in the still of the Gates County wilderness my sister and I would try to identify the artifacts that emerged in alto-relievo from the hills and trenches of the landfill. Gates County was the kind of rural setting that I loved and regarded as home. In addition to meeting with the NO OLF people, I wanted to simply spend a day out in the country. I wanted to visit Merchants Millpond State Park. I wanted to try Gates County truck stop food. I wanted to see the John Deere sign in Sunbury that I'd only ever seen while riding with my family-- my whole world-- in the car as a kid.

Of course there were other areas of our enormous district that I knew almost nothing about. I wanted to spend a couple of days in the northwestern region of district 1. I literally knew nothing about the northwest region of my district beyond the locations and amenities of the campgrounds at Medoc Mountain and Kerr Lake.

Also I wanted to do some campaigning in

Goldsboro. Goldsboro was my first stop on the way home from registering as a candidate, but I hadn't been back. In high school we'd travelled to Goldsboro for swim meets, and as a paramedic I've been through Goldsboro several times delivering patients to Chapel Hill or Durham. Goldsboro was the location of Seymour Johnson Air Force Base and I reckoned that I could meet some folks who shared my concern about being led by a person who didn't even know how to pronounce the word *corps* until after he became Commander in Chief of one. And maybe I could pose beneath the infamous Seymour Johnson / Morehead City road sign for a selfie to post on Facebook.

I knew that if I sent Kelli on vacation by herself she would still meet up with our friends and probably have an even better time without having to drag me along to all of the shows and excursions and whatnot. What purpose did I really serve on a cruise anyway, other than entertainment via the reliable expression of truncated refinement such as "ya gonna eat th' rest of that escargot"? The last week before an election is often the most important one; I could use the week off to finish the campaign strongly and finally let the Bertie and Craven County Republicans know that I was one of their candidates.

If I went on the cruise I would miss the First Congressional District Candidate Debate in Snow Hill on April 24th. I was looking forward to debating Jerry Grimes and John Carter just so I could finally be involved in discourse regarding the future of our nation that, as far as I could tell, was at a level of consequence unseen since the forefathers' decision to replace the Articles of

Confederation with the Constitution. I wanted the challenge. I wanted to see if I would remain calm or get flustered. I wanted to see if I could express myself when put on the spot. I wanted to tell everybody everything in this book, only in about ten minutes time and while somebody else got to pick the topics.

I was not looking forward to seeing the Woolard camp. After watching the New Bern Republicans praise Jesus every time he recited another party cliché I worried that if Good Ash were at the debate it would just turn out to be another pep rally for their golden boy.

I had other doubts about the debate. If there was one thing I'd learned about district 1 elections it was that nobody cared why you held your stance on an issue, only that your stance was the same as the national organization's. Being a politician is very much like being a minister, only a minister is blessed with the time to try to turn the congregation toward their way of seeing the big picture. Molding a congregation into being more Christ-like takes years of work. As a politician your only opportunity to do the right thing comes after lying for the six months that lead up to the election so that people will vote for you, followed by doing the right thing for your first eleven months in office while the people who voted for you aren't really paying attention, followed by your going back into campaign mode and continuing the lies so that you will get re-elected. And let's be honest, if a person wanted to take care of themselves they wouldn't be looking to the government for guidance in the first place, and that it why Democrats and Republicans are essentially the same thing.

Partisans of both sides are looking to the government for help with things that they should be doing themselves. Partisans don't want to know whether or not legislation will actually do what it was supposed to do, only that it has a good-sounding title like *No Child Left Behind* or *The Affordable Care Act*. They don't want to know if legislation is economically sustainable for a day, week, year, or decade. Currently they don't even seem to care if legislation is even constitutional. All that primary voters want to know is when you get to Congress if you will vote like Sean Hannity or Rachel Maddow. In essence, there is no point in having a debate because you don't have the time to change any voter's mind about an issue. A debate is more of a competition between candidates to see who can tell the most people what they want to hear. The things that the Republicans wanted to hear were that you demand lower taxes (even if you couldn't deliver them), that you were against pork-barrel spending (unless it was coming to them), that people would get their promised Social Security and Medicare benefits (even if the money is taken from their grandchildren), and that you would support a constitutional amendment banning gay marriage (as if that had anything to do with them). I am not much of a minister and consequently I am not much of a Republican. More relevant to the election however is that I am not much of a liar and thus I am not much of a politician.

The unfortunate difference between the primary election and the general election is that the results of the primaries are determined by the Republican and Democratic *partisans*-- the straight-ticket voters. It is not

300

until the general election that the regular voters voice their opinions about which candidate they dislike less. General elections are won by the person who spends the most money on advertising, and that is accomplished by the person who receives the most campaign contributions. In district 1, the Republican who receives the most campaign contributions is the one who promises to reunite church and state and who offers the most tax loopholes. The Democrat who receives the most campaign contributions is the one who promises the most entitlements and tax loopholes.

I knew that with the exception of maybe incumbent Butterfield and candidate Woolard, all of the primary candidates could draw a modicum of support from parties other than their own. There was even a handful of strangers who actually wanted me to win. But what was most important to me was that I had a wife who was going to be supportive of me long after I'd lost the primary to somebody who had cheerleaders. Kelli's mom had just been diagnosed with kidney cancer and we were so overwhelmed with that news that we were considering not going on the cruise at all. It just seemed wrong to go drinking and partying in the Caribbean when Kelli's mother, just two months out of early retirement, was sitting around waiting for the ravages of cancer treatment to start. After some thought we realized that Kelli's mother would not want us to postpone sucking the marrow out of life just because she was embarking on long and exhausting journey that she may not survive, particularly when there would be plenty of the worst part of the journey to share with her when we got back. Kelli and I decided to blow off the last week of the campaign and go on what might be our last cruise for a while.

We flew into Ft. Lauderdale on Saturday, April 24th and promptly hailed a cab. The cabbie was a Dominican man named Ivan who rested with his forearms on the steering wheel. He pointed an ear in our direction and said "where ya' goin". Ivan was our kind of driver- all business with none of the pesky cab-driver-slash-tour-guide chat about what Gloria Estefan video was shot behind some nondescript building-to-our-right. Since this was our third cruise we had learned that you only have to tell a cabbie the name of the ship you were going on and he would do the rest. "*Oasis of the Seas* at Port Everglade" we said in unison. Without a word the driver mashed the accelerator and we lurched out into traffic. Within five minutes we were inside the gates of the port, gazing upwards at the enormous *Oasis*. We met our friends at one of the bars on a lower deck of the ship and almost cried in the joy of seeing them again. We had champagne as we caught up with one another and for the first time in three months I emerged from the rabbit hole of politics and was swaddled in the light of reason, knowledge, and true compassion.

Once *Oasis* was underway and we had completed muster, we popped some more champagne, went up to the pool deck and watched as the American coast sank beneath the horizon. The water was a pure blue that I suspect is not appreciated by people who do not see life mostly in browns and yellows. Behind us was a large Carnival ship on a similar heading. We stayed on deck enjoying one another's company until the sky turned yellow (or pink or peach or orange or red or whatever you normal people see), then we went down to the Opus Dining Room for some grub and grog.

Formal dining on a cruise ship is perhaps the epitome of capitalism. The food is prepared to satisfy the diner rather than the government. The decor is hewn with the wealth of mastery that only arises after years of living in the poverty of apprenticeship. The breads and beverages are works of art that display the talent and individuality of those who create them and are crafted to please actual people rather than faceless numbers on a budget. The entrees are masterpieces which prove that splatter art is a nacho supreme served on a plastic plate. And Amit! Amit, our purveyor of beverages in the Opus Dining Room. In the East Amit means boundless courtesy. *Boundless courtesy* indeed: he whose name is the root for both the beloved-yet-overly-popular Buddha Amitabha as well as the efficacious yet lethal-at-high-doses antidepressant amitriptyline. Could there be a more perfect designation for the one who brings me ethanol in its full myriad of tastiness, or a more ironic one for someone who is a vegetarian, probably? Dear Amit, bringer of Fosters oil cans and vodka & cranberries, of bottles of bubbly and flutes for dispatching them. Praise thee Amit, fellow adventurer in ignoble flattery; maybe someday we will get shitfaced together.

The time we spent after Opus was a cheery blur of latched arms and fluid but clumsy feet. We found a bar that went up into the air and then came back down again, but it moved too swiftly for us to hop aboard. There was a merry-go-round and a dive pool. Salsa music filled our ears for a time and we felt ourselves swaying like sangria. As the Latin music faded we arrived at the Globe & Atlas Pub for a celebration of the one-millionth performance of *Sweet Caroline*, and it was good. We sang along. Then things started to become disconnected. There was a pint of something chocolaty and a croissant filled with the three P's: prosciutto, provolone and pesto. There was water too, but after the pint the water seemed too thin and flat to drink and it was hard to feel the cup against my lips. The last thing I remember was the sound of my voice shouting with a Scottish accent "*Free Bird!* Play us some bleedin' *Free Bird* for the love of . . .*" then the feeling of elbows against my sides, then darkness.

I dreamt I was at a show on *Oasis*. The curtain rose and we were bathed in blue light that emanated from the stage. Men in striped shirts and white pants were singing:

We sail the ocean blue,
And our saucy ship's a beauty;
We're middle class but true,
And we always pay our duty.
We love to be free
On the bright blue sea,
And we always pay our way;
When at anchor we ride
On the Cayman tide,
And we snorkel with the rays.

ENTER ZUCOTTI

Hail teabagger dependents– heroes of your nation!
Here is the start, at last, of all others' privation;
We'll take their pay – more than they can afford
If you welcome Little Zuccotti on board.

For I'm called Little Zuccotti – dear Little Zuccotti,
Though I could never tell why,
But still I'm called Zuccotti – poor little Zuccotti,
Sweet little Zuccotti I!

I've skins and tobaccy, I've needles and smacky,
I've chronic, and bullets, and knives;
I've got legislation so you can vacation--
just hand me control of your lives.

I've coffee and candy, no tea but I've brandy,
Sweet stogies and succulent weed;
I've con men and cronies, and Hollywood phonies,
And Clinton and Kerry and Reid.

Partake of your Zuccotti – dear Little Zuccotti;
Takers should never be shy;
So, take of your Zuccotti – poor Little Zuccotti;
Come, on your Zuccotti rely!

BOATSWAIN- Aye, Little Zuccotti – and well called – for you're the rosiest, the roundest, and the reddest beauty in all Pacific Heights.

ZUCCOTTI- Red, am I? And round – and rosy! Maybe, for I have dissembled well! But hark ye, my merry friend – hast ever thought that beneath a gay and frivolous exterior there may lurk a canker-worm which is slowly but surely

305

eating the heart out of the free world?

BOATSWAIN- No, my lass, I can't say I've ever thought that.

> ENTER JOHN MCLOO. HE PUSHES
> THROUGH SAILORS AND COMES DOWN

MCLOO-   *I* have thought it often. (All recoil from him.)

ZUCCOTTI- Yes, you look like it! What's the matter with the man? Isn't he well?

BOATSWAIN- Don't take no heed of him; that's only poor John McLoo.

MCLOO-   I say – it's a beast of a name, ain't it – John McLoo?

ZUCCOTTI- It's not a nice name.

MCLOO-   I'm ugly too, ain't I?

ZUCCOTTI- The concept of Botox obviously eludes you.

MCLOO-   And I'm three-sided too, ain't I?

ZUCCOTTI- You are acutely triangular.

MCLOO-   Ha! ha! That's it. I'm ugly, and they hate me for it; for you all hate me, don't you?

ALL-   We do!

MCLOO-   There!

BOATSWAIN- Well, Commander, we wouldn't go for to hurt any fellow creature's feelings, but you can't expect a chap with such a name as John McLoo to be a popular character – now can you?

MCLOO-　　No.

BOATSWAIN- It's asking too much, ain't it?

MCLOO-　　It is. From such a face and form as mine the noblest sentiments sound like the black utterances of a depraved imagination. It is human nature – I am resigned.

RECITATIVE

ZUCCOTTI- (looking down hatchway) But, tell me -- who's the man whose faltering feet with difficulty bear him on his course?

BOATSWAIN- That is the most average guy in all the fleet – Ralph Redbull!

ZUCCOTTI- Ha! That name! Remorse! Remorse!

MADRIGAL – RALPH

Our librettist:
Sir Gilbert was his name,
Would get the gist,
Of the Commander in Chief's game.
Sir Porter was the same.

ALL-　　*Sir Joseph Porter was the same.*

And Sullivan
The R. Kelly of his day,
Is unknown to men
Within the US of A
This is no "Have you had your sprinkle today"

ALL-　　*"Have you your sprinkle!"*

RECITATIVE – RALPH

I know the value of a catchy chorus,
But choruses yield little consummation,
When unfathomable debt lies here before us!
I love – and love, alas, above my station!

ZUCCOTTI- (aside) *He loves – and loves a lass above his station!*

ALL- (aside) *Yes, yes, the lass is much above his station!*

BALLAD – RALPH

A maiden fair to see,
A pearl of Democracy,
A bud of blushing beauty;
For whom proud nobles sigh,
And with each other vie
To rule the people's booty.

ALL- *To rule that booty.*

A suitor, lowly born,
With hopeless passion torn,
Average beyond denying,
Has dared for her to pine
At whose exalted shrine
A world of wealth is sighing.

ALL- *A world of wealth is sighing.*

Unlearned he in aught
Save that which love has taught
(For love had been his tutor);
Oh, pity, pity me –
To Washington DC,

I dare be a commuter!

ALL-   *The beltway is a nightmare!*

BOATSWAIN- Ah, my poor lad, you've climbed too high: our worthy Captain's child won't have nothin' to say to a poor chap like you. Will she, lads?

ALL-   No, no.

MCLOO-   No, no, captains' daughters don't marry foremast hands.

ALL-   (recoiling from him) Shame! shame!

BOATSWAIN- John McLoo, them sentiments o' yourn are a disgrace to our common nature.

RALPH-   It's like I'm in *The Twilight Zone*, that the daughter of a man who does less real work than Mayor McCheese may not love another who works as hard as Mr. Clean. For a person's a person no matter if he parks his Jaguar on Wall St. or his Pinto on Main St.

MCLOO-   Ah, it's a queer world!

RALPH-   Triangle Man, I have no desire to press hardly on you, but such a revolutionary sentiment is enough to make a Person Man shudder.

BOATSWAIN- My lads, our gallant Captain has come on deck; let us greet him as so brave an officer and so gallant a seaman deserves.

> ENTER CAPTAIN DELAWARE
>
> RECITATIVE – CAPT. and CREW

309

CAPTAIN- My gallant crew, good morning.

ALL- (saluting) Sir, good morning!

CAPTAIN- I hope you're all quite well.

ALL- (as before) Quite well; and you, sir?

CAPTAIN- I have Tricare and Blue Cross so apparently I'm awesome.

ALL (as before)-You do us proud, sir!

SONG – CAPTAIN

CAPTAIN- *I am the Captain of the Allegore;*

ALL- *And a right good captain, too!*

CAPTAIN- *You're very, very good,*
And be it understood,
I command a right good crew,

ALL- *We're very, very good,*
And be it understood,
He commands a right good crew.

CAPTAIN- *Though related to a peer,*
I can chip, putt, and steer,
Through any old par three;
I've not been compared to Quayle
For I learned from his great fail,
To never spell potato with an e!

ALL- *What, never?*

CAPTAIN- *No, never!*

ALL- *What, never?*

CAPTAIN- *Unless it's plural!*

ALL- *He spells potato with no e!*
  Then give three cheers, and one cheer more,
  For the hardy Captain of the Allegore!

CAPTAIN- *I do my best to satisfy you all –*

ALL- *We don't miss our Continent.*

CAPTAIN- *You're exceedingly polite,*
  And I think it only right
  To return the compliment.

ALL- *We're exceedingly polite,*
  And he thinks it only right
  To return the compliment.

CAPTAIN- *Bad language or abuse*
  I never, never use,
  Whatever the emergency;
  Though "back in chains" I may
  Occasionally say,
  I never use a BFD!

ALL- *What, never?*

CAPTAIN- *No, never!*

ALL- *What, never?*

CAPTAIN- *Hardly ever!*

ALL- *Hardly ever swears a BFD!*
  Then give three cheers, and one cheer more,
  For the well-bred Captain of the Allegore!

AFTER SONG EXIT ALL BUT CAPTAIN

ENTER LITTLE ZUCCOTTI

RECITATIVE – ZUCCOTTI and CAPTAIN

ZUCCOTTI- Sir, you are sad! The silent eloquence of yonder tear that trembles on your eyelash flows from a provenance far more heartfelt than any of your other secretions that I sell to your benefactors by the vial. Confide in me – fear not – I am the mother of all micromanagement.

CAPTAIN- Yes, Little Zuccotti, I'm sad and sorry – my daughter, America, the fairest flower that ever blossomed on ancestral timber, is sought in marriage by President Admiral Mugabe, our nation's first dictator, but for some reason she does not seem to tackle kindly to it.

ZUCCOTTI- (with emotion) Ah, poor President Admiral Mugabe! Ah, I know too well the anguish of a heart that loves but vainly! But see, here comes your most attractive daughter. I go – Farewell! (EXIT)

CAPTAIN- (looking after her) A plump and pleasing person! (EXIT)

ENTER AMERICA, TWINING SOME
FLOWERS WHICH SHE CARRIES IN A
SMALL BASKET

BALLAD – AMERICA

Sorry her lot who loves too well,
Worshipping those who sell hope vainly!
Sad are the hordes under the spell
Cast to make them behave most plainly;

312

Conceited are those who shake their head
And say that without them hope is dead!

Tragic the days when debt is made
With no equity for the fodder,
And the interest will still be paid
By all of our grandsons and daughters.
Corrupted are those who shake their head
And say that the state should tax the dead!

ENTER CAPTAIN

CAPTAIN- My child, I grieve to see that you are a prey to melancholy. You should look your best today, for President Admiral Mugabe will be here this afternoon to claim your promised hand.

AMERICA- Ah, father, your words cut me to the quick. I can defend – obey – even subsidize President Admiral Mugabe, for he is a legal citizen in the executive branch; but oh, I cannot love him! My heart is already given.

CAPTAIN- (Aside) It is then as I feared. (Aloud) Given? And to whom? Not to some gilded politician?

AMERICA- No, father – the object of my love is no politician. Oh, pity me, for he is but a humble sailor on board your own ship!

CAPTAIN- Impossible!

AMERICA- Yes, it is true – too true.

CAPTAIN- A common sailor? Oh, fie!

AMERICA- I blush for the weakness that allows me to

cherish such a passion. I hate myself when I think of the depth to which I have stooped in permitting myself to think tenderly of one so ignobly born, but I love him! I love him! I love him! (Weeps)

CAPTAIN- Come, my child, let us talk this over. In a matter of the heart I would not coerce my daughter – I attach but little value to rank or wealth – but the line must be drawn somewhere. A man in that station may be brave and worthy, but at every step he would commit solecisms that elites would never pardon.

AMERICA- Oh, I have thought of this night and day. But fear not, father. I have a heart, and therefore I love; but I am your daughter, and therefore I am proud. Though I carry my love with me to the tomb, he shall never, never know it.

CAPTAIN- You are my daughter after all! But see, President Admiral Mugabe's barge approaches, manned by twelve loyal Czars and accompanied by the admiring crowd of cronies, donors, and peeps that attend him wherever he goes. Retire, my daughter, to your cabin – take this likeness of him with you – it is an honor bestowed upon only those of the highest echelons of society - it may help to bring you to a more reasonable frame of mind.

AMERICA- A bobble head doll. My own thoughtful father!

EXIT AMERICA. CAPTAIN REMAINS AND ASCENDS THE POOP-DECK

BARCAROLLE – MUGABEE'S FEMALE

314

PEEPS (offstage)

Over the bright blue sea
Comes President Admiral Mugabe.
Wherever he may go
Pop-pop the corks of Moet go!
Cheer o'er the bright blue sea
For President Admiral Mugabe.

DURING THIS THE CREW HAVE ENTERED
ON TIPTOE, LISTENING ATTENTIVELY TO
THE SONG

CHORUS OF SAILORS

Mugabe's barge is seen,
And its crowd of queenly lasses,
We hope he'll find us clean,
And paid up on our taxes.
We sail, we sail the ocean blue,
And our saucy ship's a beauty.
We're hearty working men and true
And attentive to our duty.
We're fair and thoughtful men,
Whose fruits reflect our labors.
And if we're short on rent
We don't steal from our neighbors!

ENTER MUGABE'S ENTOURAGE. THEY
DANCE ROUND THE STAGE

PEEPS-   *Gaily hopping,*
            Never dropping,
            Flock the maidens to go shopping.

SAILORS-　　　*Flags and furs and gold cards waving!*
　　　　　　　They're not happy if they're saving!

PEEPS-　　　　*Sailors sprightly*
　　　　　　　Always rightly
　　　　　　　Welcome ladies so politely.

SAILORS-　　　*Their daily budget is tremendous,*
　　　　　　　One of them can far out-spend us!

CAPTAIN-　(from poop) *Now give three cheers, I'll lead the way!*

ALL-　　　*Hurrah! hurrah! hurray!*

ENTER MUGABE WITH COUSIN HILL

SONG – MUGABE

I am the monarch of the sea,
The ruler of the Bush Navee,
See me hide my sorrow for the debt it reaps!

COUSIN HILL- *And we are his cronies and his donors and his peeps!*

PEEPS-　　　*And we are his cronies and his donors and his peeps!*

MUGABE-　　*When at anchor here I ride,*
　　　　　　My bosom swells with pride,
　　　　　　And I wag my finger at Joe Wilson's tweets;

COUSIN HILL- *And so do his cronies, and his donors, and his peeps!*

ALL-　　　*And so do his cronies, and his donors, and his peeps!*

MUGABE-　　*But when answers are due,*
　　　　　　I like to guest star on "The View",

316

And bomb an Afghan village as it sleeps;

COUSIN HILL- *And so do his cronies, and his donors, and his peeps!*

ALL- *And so do his cronies, and his donors, and his peeps!*
His cronies and his donors,
Who may as well be his owners,
And his peeps!

SONG – MUGABE

When I was a boy I moved around
To wherever Marxists could be found.
I sought Alinsky, Wright and Ayers
And used their hatred as my stairs.
I hate armed forces but I love the irony
That now I am the ruler of the Bush Navee!

CHORUS-　*He hates armed forces, etc.*

On the Upper West Side I assumed the role
Of the Ivy League's most outcast soul.
I was the Kurt Cobain of New York State.
And I passed my tests without Bill Frate,
I was so disruptive of the community,
That now I am the ruler of the Bush Navee!

CHORUS-　*He was so disruptive, etc.*

Leather jackets and smokes made me so wise
A community I did organize.
With the poor folks saved I then struck the jaw
Of establishment by doing Harvard Law.
I hate that I'm elitist so skillfully

That now I am the ruler of the Bush Navee!

CHORUS-   *He hates that he's elitist, etc.*

I taught for a while then served a term
As Blagojevich's Senate worm.
I Twittered my deeds with the octothorpes,
And I polished my appearance like the Marine Corps.
I polished up my language so carefullee
That now I am the ruler of the Bush Navee!

CHORUS-   *He polished up his language, etc.*

I grew so rich that I had to laugh
When I moved onto Pennsylvania Ave.
I always voted at my donors' call,
And I never thought of thinking for myself at all.
I thought so little, they rewarded me
By making me the ruler of the Bush Navee!

CHORUS-   *He thought so little, etc.*

Now landsmen all, whoever you may be,
If you want to rise to the top of the tree,
If your soul isn't fettered to an office stool,
Be careful to be guided by this golden rule —
Stick close to your desks and never go to sea,
And you all may be rulers of the Bush Navee!

CHORUS-   *Stick close to your desks, etc.*

*   *   *

Hours later, Gilbert and Sullivan gave way to an aching head and shaky joints. As I lay on the bed-- face down, eyes closed-- I heard what sounded like Kelli getting dressed for spin class. One day I'm going to open my eyes and see why that's always such a noisy affair. Even half asleep I was aware of the bedding that was snuggling me like Jesus Himself had tucked me in. The sheets were crisp but not scratchy. The comforter simultaneously hugged without binding and the temperature within the covers was so perfect it was like floating. I listened to my beloved moving around inside the cabin. It sounded like a giraffe was donning biker shorts in a Sears dressing room. I tried to remember what I was dreaming about.

"Get up" said my giraffe. "We have 45 minutes before we have to be at the dock for our excursion."

Oh, right. I'd been conned into riding Waverunners. Ever since I worked for a place that rented Waverunners I'd silently vowed that I would never actually rent one myself-- although I have to admit that it *is* kinda fun. Of all the things we do on our cruises, more than anything I simply enjoy being with our friends. Well, that and the bedding. And the food. And the climate is nice too. And the booze. But I can take or leave the excursions. Usually I take them though, because if I didn't I'd be stuck not seeing my friends for most of the day.

"You up?" said Kelli.

"I'll exquisite day you buddy" I grunted into the pillow.

Suddenly the Captain's voice came over the intercom. "Good Morning" he started. I began to doze off. I imagined he was Captain Kirk.

"We are in orbit around Nassau in the Bahama system. Unfortunately, the . . . weather . . . is prohibiting us from enjoying the amenities of this relaxing and . . . hospitable port of call. Rather than spending the day in the rain we are going to head back out to sea and see if we can find some sunshine to enjoy. If you booked any excursions on Nassau your Sea Pass will be credited, or if you prefer, you may visit guest relations to put the value of the excursion toward something else."

This was good news, and it woke me back up a little bit. No excursions meant no Waverunners. Now I would get to hang out with the gang without having to hear RRRRRREEEEEEERRRRRRREEEEEEEERRRRRRRE EEEEEE for an hour or more. Rather, I would spend the day sittin' beside a pool full of strangers, drinking bevvies with crepe paper umbrellas on them and rating the believability of boob jobs as they cruised by.

I wondered how many of the Nassau residents would have to fish for dinner due to the rain. Cruise ships are to the Caribbean what the Hoover Dam was to the Nevada desert; but while I find the development of natural areas obscene, I have no problem with unloading my profit into the more impoverished regions of the earth where humanity has already left its big, stinky footprint. The elites of the world like to talk about the "invasion" of cruise ships into otherwise pristine environments and cultures. In reality, you can lose an entire cruise ship in the ocean and there would be so little environmental impact that it would take 73 years just to figure out where it sank, and when you did find it it would be an artificial reef. The cultures that

320

cruise ships invade are frequently host to a horrendous number of citizens on the brink of death from malnutrition. Perhaps there is no better case in point of this than one of Royal Caribbean's most frequented ports of call.

Labadee is a cove on the north coast of Haiti. The Haitian government has leased a portion of Labadee to Royal Caribbean International. Three months before our cruise, much of Haiti had been devastated by an earthquake. More than a handful of elites were fuming about how insensitive it was for a bunch of people enjoying the epitome of communal luxury on a cruise ship to show up and flaunt their wealth and excesses in the faces of people who were suffering from cholera, starvation, and traumatic amputations infected with gangrene. But blatant denial of the reality that the rest of us live in is not merely typical of the elitist mindset: it defines it. Being elites, they never suffer the burden of considering the consequences of their judgments. What would they have Royal Caribbean do: *stop* going to Labadee? The cruise line pays the Haitian government $6 for every guest who sets foot in Labadee, it employs over 300 people to provide the visitors with goods and services, and the shopkeepers of Labadee get to sell items for everybody's next yard sale for dollars on the *centime*. While the rest of Haiti is experiencing crippling poverty at a rate of over 80% and going hundreds of millions of dollars in debt just trying to keep people alive, Labadee is growing obscenely. Labadee-- which is to say Royal Caribbean International-- is constantly creating jobs and it is doing it without charity or government "stimulus". Why is this happening? Labadee is booming while the rest of Haiti flounders for the same reason that Marxist snobs hate cruise lines and mass tourism: because it is trickledown economics in its purest form. It is the systematic elimination of have-not-ism via the voluntarily exchange of wealth for goods and services with the haves. Somehow in our warped society the concept of donating money to an American nonprofit corporation and imagining that it is going to help a less fortunate person who may or may not exist in another part of the world is regarded as a generous, prosocial and altruistic act; whereas looking an actual Haitian in the eye and overtipping them for a flaming Dr. Pepper is considered a tragically proletarian waste of resources. But that's the problem with liberal elites: they project their own biases onto total strangers and call it empathy. Liberal elites are jealous of those who have more toys than they do because first and foremost they are materialistic, but also because they lack hope of ever changing social classes. This is the polar opposite of the impoverished people of the world who, when they gaze upon a cruise ship, envision themselves up there playing shuffleboard and overtipping for a Jäger bomb someday. Perhaps this is one more reason that I like going on cruises: because it is an escape from the hopeless un-reality of the American mass media version of poverty.

Rather than attempting to deconstruct the benefit that cruise lines bring to the ports that they visit, most critics focus instead on depicting cruise ships as being bad for the environment. Since the criticism of cruise ship passengers stems from stereotyping rather than intellect, the alleged evils of how another spends their vacation do not require foundations in reality. One of the most outstanding examples of 100% fabricated criticism of cruise lines is found in the film "documentary" *Turtle, the Incredible Journey*. Shore break, trade winds, and hurricanes be damned, the creators of *Turtle* actually accuse cruise ships of endangering loggerhead turtles by making the ocean bumpy with their wake. The irony of this is that the only thing that you are likely to see in the amazingly small wake of a cruise ship is dolphins playing in it. It begs the question of how much of the rest of *Turtle, the Incredible Journey* is completely fabricated BS.

So we spared Nassau from our disposable income and continued oozing through the Caribbean Sea, leaving in our wake a swath of impoverished locals and disoriented sea turtles. A couple of mornings later we woke up in port on St. Thomas, US Virgin Islands. From the port where *Oasis* was docked we could look across Long Bay and see the downtown area of Charlotte Amalie.

Charlotte Amalie is the capitol of St. Thomas. When the cruise ships aren't in port, Charlotte Amalie has a population of about 20,000, which is roughly 40% of the total population of St. Thomas. The inland portion of the island is green and hilly and speckled with flat, rectangular houses. The waterfront is rocky with smooth blue water. I suspect that it is merely a matter of time before the North Carolina Legislature attempts to add St. Thomas to the 12th congressional district.

The tourist area of Charlotte Amalie is filled with dozens of jewelry stores all right on top of one another.

The only things that disrupt the monotony of jewelry stores in Charlotte Amalie are kiosks full of T-shirts, post cards, and shot glasses. The overt touristyness of Charlotte Amalie makes the Outer Banks look tasteful by comparison.

I don't get away from my garden much so I don't know if jewelry stores in the continental US have giant posters of movie stars sporting watches, but every few feet in Charlotte Amalie another 4' by 5' print of some celebrity wearing a watch is on display for all to observe and throw up in their mouth a little bit. As stupid as this selling tactic seems, it must work or the jewelry stores wouldn't do it. What is up with that? Is there really a target demographic consisting of people who want to drop a couple thousand dollars on a watch simply because they saw a picture of Leonardo DiCaprio holding one? I mean the Kardashians seem that shallow, but how many Kardashians are there? Isn't one of the Kardashians married to Cornell West? He doesn't seem like the kind of guy who would buy a multi-thousand dollar watch just because Leonardo models it. No wonder the Tea Party struggles: the only celebrity it has is Ted Nugent and he ain't pretty.

I milled about smartly in Charlotte Amalie for a couple of hours. Well, I milled about looking for t-shirts for the kids anyway. It was hard to find anything for less than $30. It was as if somebody was trying to compensate for the bargain basement prices of the jewelry in Charlotte Amalie by grossly overcharging for t-shirts. I wasn't going to spend $30 on a child's t-shirt, and I didn't see many other people doing it either. I wondered if anybody in

Charlotte Amalie understood that if they lowered prices they would sell more stuff. Maybe the shop owners believed that people were going into the t-shirt shops, looking through the t-shirts, and then not buying anything because they weren't actually interested in buying anything to begin with. I guess it's possible: it's a big world. Or maybe the souvenir vendors weren't *greedy* enough to lower prices. Yeah, that's it. Maybe the shop owners were content to only sell a dozen t-shirts in a day, thereby leaving themselves with just enough money to buy a fifth of Cruzan rum after *Oasis* left port. Or maybe these were simply cruise ship prices. Maybe the people who wanted the Leonardo chronometer were the same people who found $30 worth of wit in a silkscreen that reads "St. Thomas It's More Fun Than Betty Ford". Then again, maybe souvenirs in St. Thomas were expensive because of the taxes. Maybe the evil shopkeepers of St. Thomas were exorbitantly taxed for their capitalist selfishness. Come to think of it I was offered some ganja on Dronnigans Gade at a rather affordable price and presumably that was not taxed. Coincidence? Hmmmm. Maybe weed is cheap in St. Thomas but t-shirts aren't because the latter is taxed and the former isn't.

All the contemplation of the yins & yangs of St. Thomas economics kept leading me to the same conclusion: that I should sharpen my savoir-faire by imbibing something with a culturally significant piece of fruit on the rim.

At around 1PM Vendors Plaza started to fill up with people. The streets became impassable to motor traffic, and as if to make sure that anybody who had a heart attack in Emancipation Gardens would never receive medical attention, a gigantic train of red trailers pulled up and stopped smack in the middle of the only road that provided definitive egress from the crowd. This was my kind of party. I love it when I'm trusted to be responsible for my own health and welfare. Suddenly I was liking St. Thomas a lot. No, seriously-- I find it oppressive when the government comes in and tells everybody how to party. "Keepin' it real while keepin' it safe" is for micromanaging elites, and danger is just part of the fun. Isn't a party about cuttin' loose and enjoying life? And isn't that enjoyment just a little more fulfilling if you, yourself are left in charge of your own safety? I bet if somebody got drunk in Charlotte Amalie and fell off the seawall and died that their family wouldn't sue the town for not providing their stupid loved one with a handrail, the bar for selling them alcohol, and God for making St. Thomas harbor beautiful. St. Thomas really *was* more fun than Betty Ford.

Suddenly I noticed that some of the shops were closing up. Nobody closes up shop smack in the middle of prime tourist hours. I guess the shop owners really *weren't* greedy enough to lower prices. I quickly dashed back to the bar to make sure I wasn't missing last call. Although the bar people assured me that they would remain open, I took responsibility of my own inebriation and slurped down a couple more culturally-significants before heading back out into the blazing St. Thomas sun. As I walked east I heard the distinct sound of steel drums playing. The music came pouring out of the narrow, whitewashed alleyways that wound slightly uphill and away from St. Thomas harbor. The music muted as I passed by the closed doors of the souvenir kiosks and through the cool air that spilled out of the jewelry shops, only to come back louder as I neared the next alleyway. Finally I reached the street named Fort Pladsen. Fort Pladsen left Veterans Dr. at a 90 degree angle and headed away from the harbor past the edge of Vendors Plaza and Emancipation Garden. Looking up Fort Pladsen I once again saw the train-line of red trailers that was blocking traffic. The trailers seemed to have grown. They were longer than I remembered-- and taller. The trailers were double-deckers filled both top and bottom with kids playing steel drums. The whole apparatus was bouncing as if it had some sort of hydraulic kit on the suspension and the music that I'd been hearing was rumbling in a lively rhythm to the bounce. The people around the trailers bounced too. It was loud fun, but the thing I was most impressed with was that the kids playing the steel drums were not reading music. They just played and played. These talented kids-- who looked to be between the ages of maybe eleven and eighteen-- had either already mastered the skill of jamming *en masse* with their peers located above, below, or behind them where they can't even see, or they had memorized hours of music. I admit that I was a little worried that all of the bouncing on the trailers might break an axle or collapse the top level down onto the bottom level, but that is just how I've come to look at the world as a paramedic. Eventually I learned that the band was the *Rising Stars Youth Steel Orchestra*. Printed boldly on the side of one of the trailers was a quote from the Rising Stars' founder, the Honorable Verne A. Hodge:

> "Nothing is so complicated that it cannot be simplified by hard work."

I'd never heard of the Honorable Verne A. Hodge, but I immediately liked him. We could do with a few more Verne Hodges back in the continental US. Can you imagine if a politician in the lower 48 suggested that people simplify their problems by working harder on them? He'd be thrown out of office in a week. Wasn't it President Carter who told everybody to "stop crying and start sweating"? See where it got him? In America the way we solve complicated problems is by crying for politicians to save us and to send the bill to our neighbors. The purpose of the American government is to allow the citizens to embrace their inner primate as government employees slowly become zookeepers. American citizens are incapable of choosing between what we have and what we want, and it is in our nature to exploit others. Rather than quoting Mr. Hodge or President Carter, Americans behave as Sigmund Freud theorized:

> "Most people do not really want freedom because freedom involves responsibility, and most people are frightened of responsibility."

One of the things I love most about the Caribbean is the prevalence of contrasts. By American standards almost all of the people in the Caribbean are poor, and yet if you find an unhappy person, nine times out of ten it is an American. The most beautiful places are uninhabited rather than fenced in and regulated by the government. And the

Caribbean people are so fearless and hardworking that if only they had the economic opportunities offered by American conservatism, well, then they would probably all be a bunch of whiny bitches like us too.

Whenever I'm in the Caribbean I think of a book I had to read in grad school called *The Mimic Men*. It is the tale of a self-absorbed, racist politician who seeks exile from an imaginary Caribbean island by going to London. Literarily it is a tragedy by way of aborted rebirth. Imagine *Crime and Punishment* only instead of murdering the Ivanovna sisters Roddy sticks an axe in his own frontal lobe and spends the rest of the book talking about breasts. Liberal arts people attempt to portray *The Mimic Men* as an indictment of Eurocentrism, but it doesn't stick. The book is a good portrayal not of the forces that perpetuate Eurocentrism, but of the shallowness of those who cannot slough off its system of Progressive values.

Why is it that the self-proclaimed open-minded people of the West always conflict themselves by hating the very Eurocentrism which makes them feel so superior in the first place? From the standpoint of liberty, Eurocentrism is clearly stupid-- which is why I prefer American Conservativism. I understand why Progressives dislike Eurocentrism, which makes it that much more confusing when so much liberal and Progressive ideology is rooted in Eurocentric garbage. *Race* was a fallacy invented by European Imperialists. *Social class* continues to be tracked by familial lineage in much of Europe. Can the alleged "importance in commentary" regarding either the demand for, or arguments against gay marriage be explained by anything other than a desperate adherence to the flamboyant prudishness of European Victorianism? Karl Marx was perhaps the quintessential Eurocentric thinker because he believed that his version of utopia was universally correct without once considering the existence of any of the demand sides of the economies of non-European cultures. The economic history of Europe is a continuous loop of peasants demanding redistribution of wealth from the aristocracy, followed by their being refused, followed by a revolution which ends when the revolutionaries fill the exact same positions of aristocracy with themselves and their friends. Does anybody ever wonder why liberals and Progressives are so convinced that wealth equals social class in America? Those who are hard-wired to believe in social class are so because they are inherently Eurocentric. Eurocentric Americans seamlessly integrate their unshakable affinity for material wealth with their belief in social class by imagining the former to be an indication of the latter. But none of this would be so bad if it were not for the ultimate Eurocentrism of Progressive dogma, which is the Naziesque belief that when it comes to implementing progress into law the ends justify the means. Progressive ideology is about progress and is therefore noble; whereas any dissenting thought is inferior because it is *not* progress and is therefore immoral. Eurocentrism dictates that the baseness of all that is not progress should, by hook or by crook, be brought up to code.

In order to maintain liberty, a government must recognize that social class will always exist within the human psyche. But social class should be just that: *social.*

Intelligent people should be more highly revered than educated people, and educated people should be superior to ignorant people. Those who follow the golden rule should be admired, while those who screw people over should be outcasts. But government-- if it is to be fair-- should be completely devoid of classifying people. In the eyes of fair government every law-abiding citizen should get equal rights, an equal number of votes, an equal quantity of government aid, an equal amount of government intrusion, and an equal level of taxation.

To be Eurocentric is to believe that class exists somewhere outside of the mind and therefore has a place in government. The Obamas characterize America as being "arrogant and downright mean" because they are projecting their Eurocentrism onto the rest of us. The Obamas have no idea what it means to be an American. In America we don't care if you're a king or a peasant because we judge you not by the color of your bandanna or the crest of your alma mater, but by the content of your character. To a real American it doesn't matter what the brainwashed goofballs call you back in the kingdom: everybody is equal to everybody else here in the good ol' US of A. The Obamas, and perhaps Progressives in general, think Americans are arrogant for *not* bowing down to people who imagine themselves to be superior to others. More specifically, Progressives think *you* are arrogant for not bowing down to the people whom *they* believe to be superior to you. But in the true America-- in America's founding principles-- nobody is so high or low that they deserve special treatment by the citizens in the form of gifts from the public treasury or by "separate but equal" rights. A fair government treats all its citizens the same. Society will always be biased: first because it is comprised of primates and second because some of those primates are too lazy to work smarter instead of harder. Government can be-- should be-- free of bias because it is an idea. Any idea that is free of discrimination will yield legislation that does not discriminate between citizens based upon the two-dimensional characteristics of race, social class, income, employment, and whatever happens behind closed doors between consenting adults.

The United States used to be an antithesis to Eurocentrism, but Progressives like Barry Obama are slowly making race, social class, and redistribution of wealth the American norm. Obama is the ultimate *Mimic Man*, and the only non-Eurocentric act that he has ever committed was switching his name to Barak so that he could win American elections. To see what the United States would be like without Obama's Eurocentric "values" of race, social class and Marxism I offer you *Oasis of the Seas*.

Oasis of the Seas is a big, stinking, capitalist monstrosity. When it is in operation, *Oasis* has a population density seven times greater than Manila. It is filled to bursting with people of all different cultures, colors, religions, nationalities and lifestyles; and we all get along with big, stupid grins on our faces. The sizes of our cabins reflect our incomes, and the extremes are enormous, but there is neither resentment nor superiority among us. Some eat pork, some don't. Some eat beef, some don't. Some eat meat, some don't; but there is no judgment. Passengers
332

from all over the world dress themselves in contemporary or traditional ethnic clothing as they see fit, and nobody stares or complains when somebody is different. Some wear diamonds while others wear lanyards with their room key on them, but the only redistribution of wealth that occurs is when somebody overtips a certain human being-- never the stereotype of a demographic. A cruise ship is about as close as an urban area can get to utopia. There are problems: *Oasis* is filled with primates after all. There are almost certainly unhappy workers on board, but they are not the ship's problem. There are days when I don't like my job either, but just as the workers on *Oasis* my job is the best I can do given my education and personality.

Royal Caribbean International is based in Miami. In order to employ more people however, not one Royal Caribbean ship is registered in the United States. All Royal Caribbean ships are registered in the Bahamas where the government and the people actually appreciate having jobs to take. The Bahaman Government likes having employed citizens so much that it actually invites corporations to come and provide jobs to its citizens by offering them lower tax rates. In Obama's America not only do the elites believe that it is better for the unemployed to remain unemployed than to be paid less than they demand, but they also feel that their opinion on this topic is so (Eurocentrically) superior that it should apply to people who subsist on far less than two dollars a day. Once again the Eurocentric attitude of believing that one's own idea of justice and economic policy is absolute due to the believer's social status is clung to by Progressives like a horny octopus to a bagpipe.

Our last night on board *Oasis* I slept in fits. As we crept toward the American coast the normally heavenly sheets spun tighter and tighter into a bulky and uncomfortable umbilicus that constricted my waist and bound my feet. The linens stuck to me as I dripped sweat and rolled back and forth in the pitch dark. Suddenly I sat up, out of breath. I saw our two boys sitting at the foot of the bed. They were staring, transfixed at the TV. No matter what I said to them they didn't hear me, they just kept staring at the glowing appliance. Nothing was visible except the TV and their little heads and torsos. On the screen was Barney the Big Purple Dinosaur. Barney was relentless in his insistence that everybody join him in song.

"I love you, you love me, we're a happy family" over and over and over. It was awful.

I tried to shout to my kids to turn it off but they didn't hear me. Nobody heard me. Suddenly I gained control of my limbs and I sat upright in bed. "Turn it off" I said. But my kids responded angrily. "Why do you hate Barney" they shouted at me. "You hate love! You hate sharing!" They spat the words at me. They hated me. "You don't want our family to be happy!"

"That isn't how it is" I cried. "You don't understand! I love you and your mom more than anybody on TV *possibly* could."

The boys were indignant. "You hate the *I love you* song so you hate *us!*" they shouted back. "You hate *everybody"* they shouted in unison. And then it came:

"You don't like Barry *because he's purple!"*

I woke up gasping for air. I put on my one shirt and one pair of shorts and left the cabin and walked up to the pool deck for some air. The railing was moist with condensation and the deck was so wet that it looked like it may have rained. The air was comfortably warm and there was a slight breeze coming from the forward motion of the ship. We had slowed significantly. In the darkness we crept toward the lights of American cities that twinkled on the horizon. Behind us the sky was turning tan or whatever color it is that muggles see when as the sun rises. The ship was much quieter now that it had slowed. I was alone on deck and I couldn't escape the horrible image of the people I cared about so much being corrupted by Barry the Dinosaur. Running my hand along the rail of the ship my fingers became soaked and I brushed them against my shorts. There in my lower pocket I felt the rectangular shape of my Motorola RAZR cell phone. I quickly unfolded it and switched it on for the first time in a week. Once it was ready to go I opened the photo gallery and looked at all of the wonderful pictures of my kids. They weren't hypnotized by Barney any more than I was. Barney was stupid! And there was the picture of them right after riding the Loch Ness Monster at Busch Gardens for the first time. And the one of Thomas and the fish he caught. And Josh as he rolled matzo balls. As I looked through my pictures the phone beeped repeatedly as new messages came flooding in. Eventually I decided that I'd better check to make sure nobody died or something. I received 22 phone messages from unknown numbers. After listening to six of them and not hearing anything but the bribery of people who wanted material things from me in exchange for their alleged support, I hung up and returned to the picture of the boys playing with our dog Pete on the beach. I love that picture. I smiled and took a deep breath of the salty air, held it for a moment, then walked back to our room. The day was May 3rd, 2010. Seventy-two hours later the primary election was over and life returned to relative normalcy.

Epilogue

After the primary I was able to relax and settle back in to being a decent person. I pushed the boys on the swings. I walked Petie on the beach. I took Kelli to lunch at the Nags Head Pier. All of my work as a candidate had imploded within a span of about 24 hours and it was a great relief to again be able to water my azaleas with one hand and flip the bird at cars with subwoofers turned to 11 with the other. There was just one thing left to do. I'd been given a check for $20 at the meeting of the Pitt County Republicans at Parker's Bar-b-que. It was my only campaign donation, and now that I was no longer a candidate I needed to return it to its rightful owner. I thought that mailing the check back with a letter saying *if I'd cashed this maybe I'd'a done better* would be a little impersonal, so I decided that I would return it in person. I figured the lady who wrote me the check would be disappointed with me for not using it on gas or something. I know she didn't give it to me so that I could reject her approval. What was I going to say-- "give it to a *conservative* Republican, I hear they *love* charity"? As always, I didn't care if I had somebody's approval; I just wanted to be able to explain my actions.

Maybe if my campaign donor had been home I wouldn't have had to write this book. I didn't want to just stick the $20 check in her door. Her neighborhood was nice, but nowhere in Greenville is *that* nice anymore. She had azaleas in her yard and there were still enough flowers on them to tell that most of them were pink. An azalea person. I wondered if she ever paused from her weed pulling to look up and direct an obscene gesture from within her flowered gloves toward some throbbing car as it oozed down her street. I reckoned not. Some people honor the First Amendment by showing restraint. I got back in the Matrix and drove down the street to the Kroger supermarket. They had a bunch of azaleas in front of the store that they were trying to get rid of while they still had flowers on them. In another week the flowers would be gone and Kroger would be stuck with a couple dozen small bushes that looked to the vast majority of Americans like every other shrub on the side of the road. I thought a purple azalea would look nice in my donor's yard, but it wasn't my place to push that on her. I purchased a small pink azalea and secured her check to the pot with a rubber band and a note. I left it on her doorstep.

I left Greenville and drove home down Hwy 11.

Glen Beck was on the radio talking as if the Constitution was the 28th book of the New Testament. The world had not changed at all. I'd run a weak campaign and lost. The popular people were out doing whatever it is that they do to stay that way, but for the first time in months I was getting to be myself again. In Bethel I turned east down Alt Hwy 64. The sky was a brilliantly clear blue and the tree farms shined with the pure green of new growth. The houses were sparse here, and one got the feeling that the hands inside them were busy. One hand in particular would have a diamond on it that was very much like the house itself: small, simple, and not purchased to sell for a profit but for building a family. I got tired of listening to Glen Beck and switched the radio over to a classic rock station called *The Shark*. For the past two months there had been little more than political ads on *The Shark*, but today they were back to selling used cars and pale, bland, predictable beer.

I hadn't been down Old Hwy. 64 since my dad was alive. Back in the 70's when we went on family trips to look at a garbage truck or something, we would travel down Hwy 64 through the crossroads town of Everetts. It was always as my sister and I were about to doze off when my dad would tell us to look out the window.

"Whoever sees the most yellow houses wins" he'd say.

Within a few minutes the first yellow house would appear. It had lap-board siding and single-paned windows. Multiple, skinny chimneys poked up through the metal roof, and sometimes there was a rocking chair under the big oak tree in the yard. Everybody in the car would see that first yellow house so it didn't really count, but it added to the excitement. Slowly, yellow houses would start popping up more frequently. Some would be almost in the road and others would be hidden behind trees in the distance. There would be several on one side of the road, and a kid had to be careful not to get caught up looking only out of one side of the car and miss the yellow houses going by on the other side of the road. Before too long the yellow houses would become more and more scarce, and after a while it became apparent that you'd passed them all. Dad would ask for a total, and Mom usually won.

I made it all the way to Williamston without seeing a single one of the yellow houses of Everetts. They must have all fallen prey to progress. As Old Hwy. 64 returned back to the broad, four lanes of US Hwy. 17 I pulled over into the gravel. I stepped out and removed the campaign magnets from the doors of the Matrix and tossed them through the back hatch. I got back into the driver's seat and looked around. The road before me was smooth and empty with nothing in sight but open sky and low fields of patchy spring wildflowers. Thank you Alice Walker. I had my elbow out the window. The sun was bright and the air had the freshness of the first warm days of spring. As I pulled out onto the road that had run through my entire life, the commercials on the radio went off and Carlos Santana came on. It was one of my favorite songs and I churned through the gears until I reached cruising speed. I turned the radio all the way up and listened to Santana sing *I'm*

Winning as the hum of the amps joined the hum of the tires. There wasn't a single person in sight to give me the finger. I sped back toward Kelli and the boys and Petie and the ocean and sweet anonymity.

Index

Back cover images (from top) courtesy of:

Roberts, E. (Photographer). (2009).
Henry Does Not Like the "Cone of Shame"
[Digital Image]. Retrieved from http://www.flickr.com/

Jack-Jack T. (Photographer). (2012).
Bobby
[Digital Image]. Retrieved from http://www.flickr.com/

Trophygeek. (Photographer). (2012).
Cone Technology Doesn't Fix the Dog's Shame
[Digital Image]. Retrieved from http://www.flickr.com/

Bjork, P. (Photographer). (2014).
A Cone-Shaped Hell
[Digital Image]. Retrieved from http://www.flickr.com/

Pets Adviser. (Photographer). (2011).
Dog Martini Costume for Halloween
[Digital Image]. Retrieved from http://www.flickr.com/
for more costumes please visit http://www.petsadviser.com

Dente, M. (Photographer). (2006).
Gaucho
[Digital Image]. Retrieved from http://www.flickr.com/

Schappell, D. (Photographer). (2002).
Darcy with Head Cone After Surgery
[Digital Image]. Retrieved from http://www.flickr.com/